Fruitful

LIVE A LIFE OF ABUNDANT HARVEST

ANGELA P. JOHNSON

WARRIOR RAISER, LLC
COLUMBUS, OHIO

Published by Warrior Raiser, LLC® ·
Copyright© 2022 Angela P. Johnson

ISBN: 979-8-9857862-0-0

Subject Heading: FRUITFUL / WOMEN / BIBLE STUDY

To order additional copies of this resource, email info@warriorraiser.com or order online at www.warriorraiser.com.

Editorial Team

Allison Myers
Content Editor

Jessica Ordonez
Copy Editor

Steven Petrosino
Original Art pp 31,100, 109, 195

Canva®
Cover/Interior Art &Design

Matthew Constance
Production Editor
Constance Creative®

Jill Sisson
Production Co-Editor

Elizabeth Rivas
Marketing Consultant

WARRIOR RAISER®

To Derrick:

My best friend, the voice of reason, and my constant support.
You encouraged me to stay the course, write the words, and finish the work.
Your confidence in me means more than you'll ever know.
You are a gift to me, my Love.

Acknowledgments

There are so many people I need to thank for this project. Embarking on a self-publishing journey with no formal literary training was often an overwhelming task. At multiple points throughout the writing of this study, I had to talk through concepts, ask questions, and seek prayer and counsel from the amazing people God has placed in my life. Without my tribe, *Fruitful* would never have come to fruition. (Yes, the pun is intended.)

Elliott, Elias, and Eleanor, you three are the most extraordinary fruit of my life. Being your mommy has given me a depth of understanding of the Father's heart, and I am forever grateful for the lessons you teach me every single day. Keep seeking Jesus. You will always find Him. Abide in Him, and He will abide in you!

Lynn Petrosino, my mother, a.k.a. the Silver Fox, you have always been my number one fan. You cheerfully took the kids on days so I could work, sacrificing your time so I could fulfill a dream and calling. Thank you for teaching me what peacemaking truly looks like. You are an amazing mother, Mimi, and most importantly, a beautiful example of living for Jesus.

Steve Petrosino, my father a.k.a. the Mensa Genius, thank you for sharing your insight into the viticulture world and using your artistic talent to add some imagery to this study. It helps to have a sommelier and clinical scientist as a father who is also passionate about biblical truth. I love discussing theory and biblical concepts with you. You bring a depth of knowledge to the content, and I am eternally grateful I have your DNA.

Erica Fouss, Julie Savageau, Alisha Long, Lisa Alvarez, Cass Hunter, Angela Garnes, and the Original Beechwold Bible Study Ladies, you encouraged me to begin, and you have been the best cheerleaders along this journey. I have coveted each of your prayers, and I could not have done this without you, my warrior mammas.

Angela Buck, Jess Hammond, Jenny Ratliff, and Kerry Smith, thank you for talking through ideas over coffee or lunch. You planted seeds of encouragement and spurred me to action. You four are deep wells that bring forth living water. I am blessed to call you friends.

My Potter's House and Adventure Church Bible Study Ladies, thank you for participating in the infant stages of this study. Your feedback and experience helped get this project over the finish line. With fresh eyes, you offered critical input, and I'm forever grateful to each of you.

Melissa Spoelstra, I am thankful for your generosity of time, knowledge, resources, and, most importantly, spirit. In a world replete with selfish endeavors, you graciously make room at the table for the newbies. My friend and mentor, it is a delight and pleasure to serve Jesus alongside you.

Table of Contents

About the Author

Angela and her husband, Derrick, have three beautiful children, Elliott, Elias, and Eleanor (Nora). They also have a seven-pound cavapoo named Koki.

Angela holds a master's in public health along with two bachelor's degrees, and she is a registered nurse. She left full-time nursing to pursue full-time vocational ministry and is now on staff at her church, overseeing life groups and assisting with women's ministry.

Angela has a passion for teaching and sharing The Word of God through the written and spoken word. She's known to her family as "The Storyteller" and loves when people connect her teachings with understanding and experiencing Jesus for themselves. You can read more of her work at www.warriorraiser.com or join her on the Warrior Raiser podcast as she brings biblical teaching and discipleship resources to challenge and equip women who are hungry to deepen their relationship with Jesus.

When she's not writing or speaking, Angela enjoys singing, worshiping, leading Bible study, crafting, playing outside with her kiddos, shopping, going out to dinner with her husband (without the kiddos), and spending time with friends and family.

A Letter From the Author

Do you ever wonder what you should be doing with your life? Have you ever asked yourself what your calling is? Do you even, at times, believe you've wasted years being unproductive for the Kingdom of Heaven? Have you ever caught yourself saying you're "just a [fill in the blank]"? Or do you just need reassurance that what you are doing with your time, gifts, and energy is what you're actually called to do?

For many years I answered "yes" to each of these questions.

This Bible study was birthed out of a deep conviction from the Holy Spirit to dig in and truly discover what the Lord has called me to—and that is you, Dear Friend. You see, I'd repeatedly found myself in conversations with others who felt stagnant and unproductive. I'd hear friends share that they felt each day was some version of the same thing, feeling that life was passing them by and they weren't fully participating. Heart-to-heart discussions had common themes like anxiety and indecision. I'd hear others echo my own thoughts of fear, hesitant to move ahead with a dream because they didn't want to fail or didn't know what to do or how to move forward.

I pray this study helps you discover your passion—what makes your heart stir inside. I pray that by the end of our time, you would understand what fuels you and that the presence of God would move you forward so your life can be used mightily for the Kingdom of Heaven.

My question to you, Dear Friend, is this: Are you ready?

This Bible study is for those who want to truly discover their life's ministry, no matter where they are in their relationship with God. It's an in-depth study into the biblical truths about WHO we are called to be and WHAT we are commanded to do. Our Creator calls us to be PEOPLE WHO BEAR MUCH FRUIT.

The expectation is that you experience a new revelation like never before and gain a new understanding of who God is and who you are to Him. The requirements are to just show up, every day that you can, for as long as you can. Remember that God doesn't want us to check the proverbial box of spending time with Him. He wants us to spend time with Him because we want to get to know Him and have a desire to understand His ways. Thus, the journey of seeking the Lord begins with prioritizing Him and working to give Him first place—over your spouse, your children, your career, yourself, *everything*. While each day won't be the perfect "hour of coffee, worship music, and Bible study," if you put in the time, He will show up.

Our textbook is the Bible; however, you will see that I reference a variety of versions. This is done to present an all-encompassing view of The Word. You can use your favorite version, but access to online sources may be helpful. (I like blueletterbible.org and biblehub. com.)

The outline is simple. There are seven sessions with six weeks of study, typically five days per week. Of course, some days are longer than others, so take the days and weeks at your own pace, genuinely seeking to grasp the content rather than simply trying to stay on track.

Each week offers an opportunity for interaction with biblical text, journaling, prayer, video teaching, and group discussion. Daily facts called "Dig Deeper" and a week's end, practical application called "Be Fruitful" help to solidify learning. You can use this section personally or collaboratively with friends and family, so be creative in how you express your discoveries!

Dear Friend, it is now time to "Study to shew thyself approved unto God, a workman that needeth not to be ashamed, rightly dividing the word of truth" (2 Tim 2:15, KJV). Our subject is bearing fruit, so let's study it, divide it, and understand it so that we might show ourselves approved. I am excited to have you join me as we journey through discovering our specific fruit and how we plant, produce, protect, prune, and eventually harvest it.

So, let's begin this fruit-bearing journey together!

Grace & Peace,

Angela

Introduction

JESUS THE STORYTELLER

When Jesus lived on Earth, He taught the concepts of Heaven and of God using parables. He used these lessons to make significant comparisons as His earthly stories had heavenly meanings. Knowing that Jesus lived in an agrarian society, where most people would have had experience living on farms or working with food crops and livestock, He often used symbolic narratives of ordinary, agricultural life. His audiences would have included shepherds, grape growers, wheat farmers, laborers in fruit orchards, and families raising livestock, as just a few examples.

Matthew 13:34 speaks of Jesus' storytelling when it says, "Jesus always used stories and illustrations like these when speaking to the crowds. In fact, He never spoke to them without using such parables" (NLT). Jesus Himself noted His propensity for storytelling when He quoted the Prophet Isaiah by saying, "I will speak to you in parables. I will explain mysteries hidden since the creation of the world" (Matthew 13:35, NLT).

His own disciples were curious as to why Jesus spoke to His audiences in parables, and He explained, "You have been permitted to understand the secrets of the Kingdom of Heaven, but others have not. To those who are open to my teaching, more understanding will be given, and they will have an abundance of knowledge" (Matthew 13:11-12, NLT). To put it another way, to those whose hearts were hardened towards God, the true meaning of these instructional lessons was hidden.

Ultimately, Jesus used parables to hide (or conceal) the meaning from those who choose to reject the Gospel message while, simultaneously, His stories clarify (or give a fuller sense of understanding) to those who choose to believe.

JOHN 15 — The Foundation of Our Seven-week Study

Before diving into the foundation of our study (John 15), it's important to look at the verses that precede it. The precursor is the last meal—The Last Supper—that Jesus had with His disciples before His crucifixion. During this meal, Jesus tells the men who have been His closest followers for the past three years, "Dear children, how brief are these moments before I must go away and leave you!" (John 13:33, NLT). He continues, "I don't have much more time to talk to you because the ruler of this world approaches. He has no power over me, but I will do what the Father requires of me, so that the world will know that I love the Father. Come, let's be going" (John 14:30-31, NLT).

Knowing that Jesus had just revealed His remaining time with them would be brief, His disciples would likely be hanging on His every word. They proceed to get up from the table and eventually cross the Kidron Valley before entering a grove of olive trees—the place where Judas Iscariot would betray Jesus with a single kiss (John 18). So, what happens in between getting up from the table and the kiss of betrayal?

John 15 happens.

Scholars think Jesus and His disciples probably found their way through a vineyard on their way to the grove of olive trees. Perhaps Jesus stopped for a profoundly teachable moment in this vineyard and began with, "I am the true vine, and my Father is the vinedresser..." (John 15:1, ESV).

Before we begin our study on bearing fruit, let's take a moment to read through John 15 and hear what Jesus Himself has to say about the matter.

John 15:1-17

ESV

1 I am the true vine, and my Father is the vinedresser.

2 Every branch in me that does not bear fruit he takes away, and every branch that does bear fruit he prunes, that it may bear more fruit.

3 Already you are clean because of the word that I have spoken to you.

4 Abide in me, and I in you. As the branch cannot bear fruit by itself, unless it abides in the vine, neither can you, unless you abide in me.

5 I am the vine; you are the branches. Whoever abides in me and I in him, he it is that bears much fruit, for apart from me you can do nothing.

6 If anyone does not abide in me he is thrown away like a branch and withers; and the branches are gathered, thrown into the fire, and burned.

7 If you abide in me, and my words abide in you, ask whatever you wish, and it will be done for you.

8 By this my Father is glorified, that you bear much fruit and so prove to be my disciples.

9 As the Father has loved me, so have I loved you. Abide in my love.

10 If you keep my commandments, you will abide in my love, just as I have kept my Father's commandments and abide in his love.

11 These things I have spoken to you, that my joy may be in you, and that your joy may be full.

12 "This is my commandment, that you love one another as I have loved you.

13 Greater love has no one than this, that someone lay down his life for his friends.

14 You are my friends if you do what I command you.

15 No longer do I call you servants, for the servant does not know what his master is doing; but I have called you friends, for all that I have heard from my Father I have made known to you.

16 You did not choose me, but I chose you and appointed you that you should go and bear fruit and that your fruit should abide, so that whatever you ask the Father in my name, he may give it to you.

17 These things I command you, so that you will love one another.

Session 1
CREATION TO REVELATION

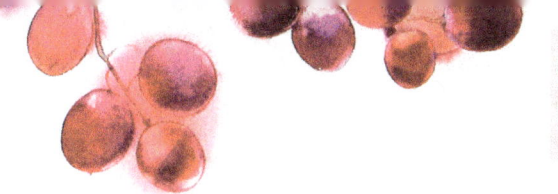

Session 1
VIDEO TEACHING

KEY VERSE

"Yes, I am the vine; you are the branches. Those who remain in me, and I in them, will produce much fruit. For apart from me you can do nothing" (John 15:5, NLT).

THE BIG IDEA

Fruit has been a part of our story from beginning to end. From Creation to Revelation and so many times in between, we read lessons tied to our obedience and our fruitfulness.

Genesis 2:15, says,

"The Lord God took the man and put him in the Garden of Eden to

_____and _____"(ESV).[1,2]

Adam's role was to be a _____ but also a _____ of the sacred space God had given him.

In John 15, Jesus instructed us to _____ and to _____.

Discuss

What drew you to this study?

What do you hope to gain from this study?

Finish this sentence: "I am here because_____."

What comes to mind when you think about being fruitful or bearing fruit?

How do you think understanding spiritual fruit helps us focus on what we should be doing with our lives?

Session 2
WHAT IS FRUIT?

Session 2

VIDEO TEACHING

KEY VERSE

"When you produce much fruit, you are my true disciples. This brings great glory to my Father" (John 15:8, NLT).

BIG IDEA

Each of us is called to bear much fruit. However, our fruit will be as unique as we are.

No_____ bears fruit for itself.

No matter what type, color, or variety of fruit we bear, it's _____ for God.

Fruitfulness looks _____ for each and every one of us.

Our _____ is a result of our _____.

Video sessions available at warriorraiser.com/fruitful   #FruitfulBibleStudy
  Answers: *fruit; all; different; fruitfulness/faithfulness*

16   FRUITFUL

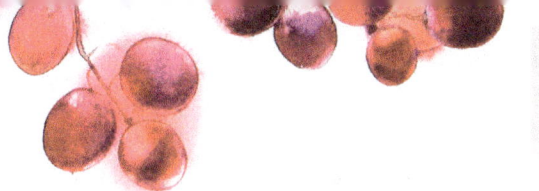

Discuss

What stood out to you most from the imaginative journey to the Mediterranean vineyard?

Think back through the questions asked and discuss your answers:

- *Do you know what your fruit is?*

- *Do you know what it's not?*

- *Do you know the best environment for you to produce it in?*

- *Do you know what influencing factors inhibit or enhance your fruitfulness?*

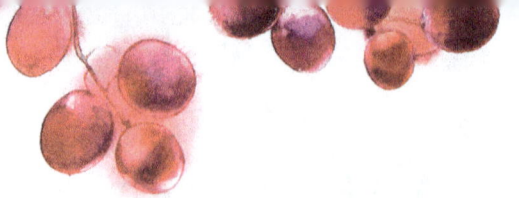

Day 1:
DEFINING FRUIT

I come from a robust family tree of scientists and medical professionals. My grandfather, grandmother, and father were/are all professionals in the health sciences. In addition, I have a health background and am married to a dashingly handsome physician. So I understand and appreciate the importance of learning the basics to better grasp the world around us.

On the first lecture day of any class, the instructor usually explains the root of what you're studying. For example, botany is defined as "the scientific study of plants," and a plant is defined as "a living thing that usually produces seeds and typically has a stem, leaves, roots, and sometimes flowers."[1,2]

As we unwrap what it means to "bear fruit" and to "live a life that produces a harvest," we've got to understand the basic principle of what we are working toward—bearing fruit. This means we'll need to break that down and define and understand what "fruit" is and what it means "to bear."

So, as Sister Maria (a.k.a. Julie Andrews) sang in *The Sound of Music*, "Let's start at the very beginning, a very good place to start."

UNDERSTANDING THE SIX BIBLICAL DEFINITIONS OF FRUIT

In Greek, the word for fruit is *karpos*, and *Vine's Expository Dictionary of New Testament Words* presents six definitions of fruit:[3]

1. "The fruit of the trees, vines, of the fields."
2. "The fruit of one's loins, i.e., his progeny, his posterity."
3. "Advantage, profit, utility."
4. "Praises, which are presented to God as a thank offering."
5. "To gather fruit (i.e., a reaped harvest) into life eternal (as into a granary) is used in figurative discourse of those who by their labors have fitted souls to obtain eternal life."
6. "That which originates or comes from something, an effect, result."

For the rest of Day 1, we are going to examine each of these six definitions of biblical fruit and discover that there are many ways for believers to bear fruit.

Definition #1. "The FRUIT of the trees, vines, of the fields."

Let's start with the most obvious one—FRUIT from plants.

Look up the following verses and write the portion relating to fruit:

Genesis 1:11

Genesis 1:29

Before the creation of mankind, God created fruit. However, once Adam and Eve were formed (Genesis 1:27), God gave them one small but vital restriction.

In Genesis 2:16-17, what is God's warning?

God never said, "Don't climb up that hill over there on the east side of the garden, or you will surely die." Nor did He tell them, "Do not drink from the stream on the south side of the garden, or you'll surely die." Instead, the warning was about FRUIT!

Why do you think God chose fruit in the garden as the tool for obedience?

The tree—and eating its fruit—represented a choice. The fact that the Tree of Knowledge of Good and Evil was in the middle of the garden (Genesis 2:9) meant Adam and Eve were faced with a continual choice to obey God, making willing love possible. It's not that God planted "temptation" and "wickedness," but rather that He planted "a choice" in their midst. Because of His love, He gave us the endless choice to *willingly* obey rather than *forcing* us to obey.

Definition #2. "The FRUIT of one's loins, i.e., his progeny, his posterity."

Our children (whether biological or adopted) are the FRUIT of the womb.

In the following verses, <u>UNDERLINE</u> the portions that relate to the fruit of the womb:

"And God blessed them, and God said unto them, Be fruitful, and multiply, and replenish the earth, and subdue it..." (Genesis 1:28a, KJV).

The Message Bible says it this way: "And God wanted good to come to them, saying, 'Give birth to many. Grow in number. Fill the earth and rule over it...'"

We must raise our children (the fruit of our womb) in the ways and knowledge of Christ (Proverbs 22:6). After my husband and I decided I'd stay home to raise our children, I struggled with feeling like I was "just a stay-at-home mom." I had lost my identity. In early 2013, I began attending a Bible study with a group of women whom I didn't know well. As we introduced ourselves, a woman named Lisa stated that she was a stay-at-home mom, but, more than that, she was "raising warriors." Her statement had a profound impact on me. She was raising warriors, which meant I am raising warriors. We, who are blessed to be raising children, are warrior raisers.

What's even more profound is they are not ours. Our children belong to God. We see this concept in 1 Samuel 1:27-28, where Hannah says, "I prayed for this child, and the Lord has granted me what I asked of him. So now I give him to the Lord. For his whole life he will be given over to the Lord..." (NIV). Other versions say that Hannah "lent" him to the Lord. In Hebrew, the word for lent is *sha'al*, which means she "borrowed" him from the Lord.[4]

Our babies are our responsibility to train up—to raise as warriors for the Kingdom of God—but they ultimately belong to our Heavenly Father. Rest in the truth that your children are the Lord's, and He loves them exponentially more than you do. Even more, you never parent alone; He comes alongside you every step of your parenting journey. And, as Genesis 1:28 says, God wants good to come to you through your children.

If you are a parent or grandparent, or would like to become either one, know this: The most precious thing that God will ever entrust (or lend) to you are your children. They are a gift. They are His, and they are His reward. Therefore, your children are the most significant responsibility and potential for your legacy and impact on this world.

Dig Deeper
The mandrake (or dudaim) was interpreted as "sexual love" and was called "the love apple of the ancients." Believed to aid in fertility, it also has an uncanny resemblance to the womb.[5] Read about a race to conception between two sisters and their battle over mandrakes in Genesis 30:14-22.

©Morphart /Adobe Stock

Definition #3. "Advantage, profit, utility."

What in the world does that definition mean? It means our financial gifts are FRUIT.

Turn to Romans 15:26-27. What type of contribution did the believers give to Paul's ministry?

In verse 28, some versions define their contributions as "bounty" or "fruit."

Now read Philippians 4:10-20. Write the words from the passage that relate to our financial fruit (specifically vv 15-19):

In these verses, Paul thanked the Philippians for their financial support of his ministry and said, "Not that I seek the gift, but I seek the fruit that increases to your credit" (Philippians 4:17, ESV). In other words, where we focus our financial efforts produces fruit.

Turn to 1 Timothy 6:10. What is the root of all evil?

Be careful not to read this verse too fast. Money is not the root of all evil, but rather the *love* of money is. That's why Paul gladly thanked the Philippians for their financial investment in his ministry. Having money (or even wealth) is not bad. However, you don't need to have an excessive amount of wealth to make an impact. The story of the widow's two mites in Luke 21:1-4 is a perfect example of a loving act of the poor outweighing the bounty of the rich. Compared to those who gave only a tiny portion of their surplus, she gave everything she had, which was only two mites (equivalent to a halfpenny), and Jesus said she gave more than all the rest.

As the Scriptures teach, God doesn't need "our" money, which is why her two mites were more valuable than the others; that's how Heavenly economics works! In fact, what we choose to do with our money and how we feel about it reveals the nature of our hearts. As Matthew 6:21 says, "Where your treasure is, there your heart will be also" (NIV).

In the end, what's most important in our giving is not whether or what we give, but rather *why* we give. Financially investing in the Kingdom of Heaven is a reflection of our heart's motivation. Do we invest or give to check the proverbial "good Christian" box? Do we give tithes and offerings because we don't want others to look sideways at us at church? Or do we give out of an overflow of obedience to the Father? Do we use what we've been entrusted with to produce fruit for the Lord? Do we sow into ministries and missions, and give to the poor, widows, and orphans out of obligation or willful obedience?

Proverbs 3:9 says, "Honor the Lord with your wealth and with the firstfruits of all your produce" (ESV).

UNDERLINE what we do by giving God the firstfruits (the best) of what we have.

Leviticus 27:30 says, "A tithe [one-tenth of all we earn] of everything from the land, whether grain from the soil or fruit from the trees, belongs to the LORD; it is holy to the LORD" (NIV).

UNDERLINE to whom the tithe belongs.

Fill in the blank based on Leviticus 27:30.

A tithe is_____to the LORD.

Definition #4. "Praises, which are presented to God as a thank offering."

Giving praise and expressing gratitude to God is the FRUIT of our lips. In other words, our lips bear fruit when we offer thankful acknowledgment to the Lord.

Using the NIV translation, fill in the blanks for the following Scriptures:

Psalm 34:1:
"I will_____the LORD at all times; his_____will always be on my lips."

Hebrews 13:15:
"Through Jesus, therefore, let us continually offer to God a sacrifice of praise—the_____ of lips that openly profess his name."

Psalm 150:6:
"Let_____that has breath_____the LORD._____the LORD."

I love how the entire book of Psalms ends with an instruction to praise God, and no one is exempt.

Praise (the fruit of our lips) is our acknowledgment of God's power, authority, wisdom, and worthiness. The one receiving such praise is not required to give a response because praise is unidirectional; it's a one-way street. We praise God. He does not praise us. And just as God does not need our money, God does not need our praises. If He doesn't get it from us, He says in Luke 19:40, "I tell you, if these [people] keep silent, the stones will cry out [in praise]!" (AMP).

It's important to remember that we're instructed to praise Him for our own benefit. In his book, *Exploring Worship: A Practical Guide to Praise & Worship*, Bob Sorge writes:

> *God has commanded us to praise, not because of what it does for him but because of the changes it brings in us. It places us in proper relationship to God and is a necessary step for us in the process of self-abasement. God receives ample praise from his other multitudinous creations—he will manage quite well if you or I refuse to praise him.*[6]

Turn now to John 4:23. Whom is God seeking?

Dig Deeper

Ringing rocks, a.k.a. *lithophonic rocks*, are rocks that resonate like a bell when struck. Ringing rocks are used to make lithophones—musical instruments made from rocks which, when struck, produce musical notes.[7]

Praise (and worship) is a matter of the heart expressed from a surrendered life. That's why God is seeking true worshippers—not empty worship.

Offering the fruit of our lips also sets and establishes the atmosphere, which is why Psalm 100:4 instructs us to "Enter His gates with thanksgiving, and into His courts with praise" (KJV). It's why we begin church services with praise and worship. We *sing* The Word to prepare our hearts and minds to *receive* The Word. However, this should be more than a once-a-week activity—it should be a daily pursuit. And remember: Praise is more than singing; it is the adoration we give our gracious Father.

If you can, take time right now to offer God the fruit of your lips.

Definition #5. "*To gather FRUIT (i.e. a reaped harvest) into life eternal.*"

Leading others to Christ is the FRUIT of our witness. Those who come to Christ through our witness and testimony are fruit that we bear.

Using the NIV, in Romans 1:8-17, Paul writes that he has longed to go to Rome to spread the Gospel because it has the power of God to bring salvation.

What does verse 13b say he hopes to obtain?

In 1 Corinthians 16:15-16, Paul speaks of the household of Stephanas and refers to them as the first what?

The "fruit of our witness" can sometimes be intimidating to those of us who feel like we don't have the spiritual gift of evangelism (Ephesians 4:11-12, 2 Timothy 4:5). But remember that even though we may not have this specific gifting, we're ALL called to evangelize (or to produce eternal fruit).

The Greek word for evangelist is *euaggelistēs*, which means "a bringer of good tidings." That can be you, and that can be me. In fact, it *should* be you and me—we should all seek to be "heralds of salvation through Christ."[8]

Turn to Acts 1:8 and answer the following questions:

What do we receive when the Holy Spirit comes upon us?

What do we become?

Where are we told to go?

This verse signifies the importance of being a witness and not just saying you're a witness. I liken this to a nurse or physician who sits across from a patient, listing all the risk factors associated with smoking while simultaneously taking deep, long drags from a lit cigarette and blowing the exhaled smoke directly into the patient's face. What's the likelihood the patient would see that healthcare provider as credible? Would the patient take the advice and follow the medical professional's health recommendations? Probably not. Like the nurse or doctor, we have to walk the walk and not simply talk the talk.

Ultimately, Jesus' last commandment in Acts 1:8 must be our first priority. I pray God directs our steps to the ends of the earth and makes all of the crooked paths straight along the way (Proverbs 3:6, Isaiah 42:16). I pray He reveals where He wants us and whom He wants us to bear witness to—with both words and silent actions.

Definition #6. "That which originates or comes from something, an effect, result."

ANY work, act, or deed done through our relationship with Jesus produces fruit, which is the FRUIT of our good works.

Titus 3:14 puts it this way: "And let our people learn to devote themselves to good works, so as to help cases of urgent need, and not be unfruitful" (ESV). In other words, when we're doing good works for the Lord, we're producing fruit.

Look up Ephesians 2:10. What does this verse mean to you?

Let's end our day with John 15:8, which says, "My true disciples produce much fruit. This brings great glory to my Father" (NLT). Here, Jesus gives us even more insight into the purpose of our spiritual fruit. We prove our love and adoration for God by the good fruit of our lives, and through this fruit, He is glorified.

Thank you for digging through all six examples of spiritual fruit. I hope you have a better understanding of ALL the ways fruit is defined in the Scriptures and have been encouraged that there is more than one way to produce fruit for the Lord. As we move forward in this study, we'll explore how our fruit is planted, produced, protected, pruned, and ultimately harvested!

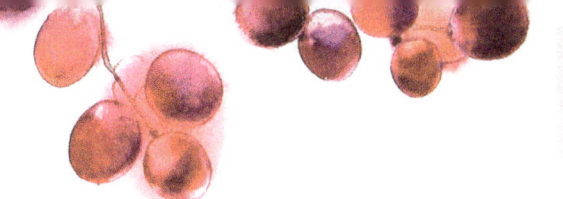

Day 2:
INTERNAL FRUIT

During my freshman year in high school, I had an English teacher I absolutely adored. Mrs. Snedaker made learning fun. I made every effort to do well and follow her instructions because I wanted to understand the content, but I also wanted to please her.

When it comes to our relationship with our Heavenly Father, we should have a yearning to do good—not out of fear or obligation but from a true heart's desire to keep and obey His teachings in order to please Him. Obedience isn't a requirement of our salvation, but it's a quality of it; it becomes a natural byproduct of a human heart that beats in tandem with the heart of the Heavenly Father.

In John 8:31-32, Jesus told the people who had faith in Him, "If you keep on obeying what I have said, you truly are my disciples. You will know the truth, and the truth will set you free" (CEV).

UNDERLINE what stands out most to you in the verse quoted above.

Read John 14:15, 14:21-23, and 15:10. Summarize the message these verses convey:

LIFE IN THE SPIRIT: The Source of Our Internal Fruit

During Day 1, we examined the many biblical definitions of fruit. Today we'll study the internal fruit of believers, which begins with the Holy Spirit.

Read the following two verses about the Holy Spirit:

Romans 8:5 says, "Those who are dominated by the sinful nature think about sinful things, but those who are controlled by the Holy Spirit think about things that please the Spirit" (NLT).

In Galatians 5:16, Paul said we have to choose to walk and live in the Spirit: "But I say, walk and live [habitually] in the [Holy] Spirit [responsive to and controlled and guided by the Spirit]; then you will certainly not gratify the cravings and desires of the flesh (of human nature without God)" (AMP).

What do you think it means to walk *and* live life in the Spirit?

Paul writes in Galatians 5:22 that when the Holy Spirit controls our lives, He produces fruit in us. Fill in the chart and list the nine kinds of internal fruit found in Galatians.

1. _____   6. _____

2. _____   7. _____

3. _____   8. _____

4. _____   9. _____
   (long-suffering)   (temperance)

5. _____

Note that the fruit of the Holy Spirit is the qualities we see in Jesus Himself. We should also notice how the verse doesn't refer to "fruits" in the plural. These are not things that we can choose, like picking apples from a tree. The Holy Spirit, living within us, wants to produce this collective fruit in our lives—ALL of it.

Galatians 5:25 continues its discussion of the Holy Spirit by saying, "Since we are living by the Spirit, let us follow the Spirit's leading in every part of our lives" (NLT). How amazing is it that the Holy Spirit desires to lead us in our lives! How is the Spirit interested in shaping our lives? The answer is found in Romans 8:28-29: "And we know that God causes everything to work together for the good of those who love God and are called according to his purpose for them. For God knew his people in advance, and he chose them to become like his Son..." (NLT).

As the Scriptures reveal, God has called you to a purpose, and that purpose is to make you like Jesus.

He wants you to think and act like Jesus. As believers in Christ, we have the Holy Spirit living inside of us to help us do just that. When we allow the Holy Spirit to lead us, He becomes involved in every decision we make—from how we prioritize our day to how we treat a less-than-kind server to how we handle the life-altering moves across the country. It's constant work, but we need to surrender ALL areas—even the seemingly mundane parts of our lives.

Can you recall a time when you followed the Holy Spirit's leading, recognizing you couldn't do it on your own? If yes, what was the end result?

Turn to Philippians 1:9-11 and answer the following questions:

What did Paul pray the believers in Philippi would grow in?

What did he pray they'd always be filled with?

What does verse 11 mean?

We are constantly challenged to grow in the knowledge of God and urged to develop our faith so we might be fruitful, bringing glory and praise to God.

SELF EXAMINATION AND THE BELIEVER

Turn to 2 Peter 1:5-11 and read.

What qualities do *you* need to make more of an effort to develop? (vv 5-6)

Peter wants us to understand that we, as Christians, are already fully equipped to lead the life God has called us to lead. However, we must do our part. Unlike eternal salvation, this requires effort (v 10). If we want our lives to produce fruit, then we have to follow the instructions and "make every effort to respond to God's promises..." (1 Peter 1:5, NLT).

Read Matthew 7:15-23. What do these verses mean to you?

Dig Deeper

"A wolf in sheep's clothing" is an idiom derived from Matthew 7:15 that means one's basic nature eventually shows through one's disguise.

©vladischern /Adobe Stock

The world accuses the Church of hypocrisy, and I firmly believe those charges are valid. The Church has always attracted certain people who know the language of Christianity but are all surface with no depth. These individuals may have had a superficial, spiritual experience and profess to have a belief in Jesus, but their lives don't reflect the will of God. They may produce "good" works, but those works can still be "dead" works. They may be active in ministry, but their fruit is not God-honoring.

If we want to distinguish true from false actions, we need to ask ourselves this: Does this action help me grow in love, grow in joy, grow in peace, grow in patience, grow in kindness, grow in goodness, grow in gentleness, grow in faithfulness, and grow in self-control? This is a call to examine our motivations to determine whether we are genuine in our faith.

Sadly, some profess to know Christ but don't have the root of the Gospel within them. How terrible it would be to end up on Judgment Day and hear Christ say, "I never knew you. Depart from me" (Matthew 7:23). This is why, even though it's never easy, it's always a good idea to self-examine. Being in ministry, I've had to honestly ask myself: *Am I doing this in the name of Jesus, or is it, in reality, for myself? Am I doing this to get an "attagirl," or am I doing it for God to receive glory? Is there too much of Angela* [insert your name if you need to] *and too little of Jesus?*

In addition, I frequently have to ask the Lord to help me with my judgment and criticism of others. As I grow closer to Him, these areas become glaringly obvious, and I know I can't let these thoughts fester. As true believers, people who want to bear good fruit, the evidence of our faith is having genuine remorse and true sorrow for our wrong thoughts or actions. True Christians want to seek sincere repentance so our lives won't hurt our testimony or ruin our witness for others.

Read Psalm 139:23-24.

Now pray and ask the Lord to bring to light anything in your life that hinders you from Him—anything that offends Him—and then WRITE your prayer below.

Remember that if you ask Him, He will lead you, so be ready!

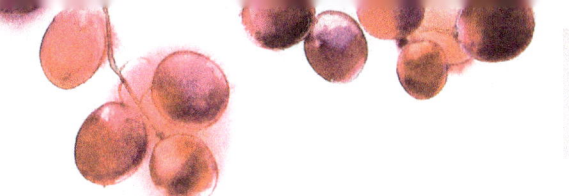

Day 3:
EXTERNAL FRUIT

One summer, my family and I planted a garden in our backyard. In the excitement of getting the infant plants into the ground, I threw out most of the plastic tags and labels that had come with each one. I told myself it'd be fine and I'd remember what each plant was. As they began to grow, there were some that I could differentiate easily. However, when it came to my peppers, I couldn't recall which were yellow and which were red. While I couldn't initially determine which was which, I was confident that as they matured, they'd eventually grow fruit to indicate what they were. I never doubted they'd produce fruit because that's what plants do. However, much to my chagrin, one of my pepper plants never fruited. Luckily, the other squeezed out one pitiful yellow pepper and, by default, I was able to determine that the red pepper plant was a complete dud.

Throughout today's study, we will uncover the reality that we all can bear outward, or external, fruit. Whether we produce a bountiful harvest or never even pop out one measly little pepper, we've all been created to produce good fruit.

In the following pages, we'll work from the framework that we produce this good fruit when we have pure motives and allow God to work "through something we do, an effect we have, or the result of our action" (the sixth definition of fruit).

Fruit is ANY ACTION of ANY BELIEVER that PLEASES GOD.

Do you remember learning about conditional statements in school? Maybe you more commonly refer to them as "If-Then" statements. We use them all the time in parenting. For example, "Elliott, *if* you clean your room, *then* you can watch TV." Most of us understand the conditions and their resultant outcomes. The Bible is full of conditional statements too, and the first chapter of Colossians opens with one.

In Colossians 1:9-10, Paul begins with thanksgiving and prayer for the Christians in Colossae. He acknowledges that, since hearing the truth of the Good News (the Gospel of Jesus Christ), lives everywhere have been changed. Paul tells them he has prayed and asked God to fill them with the knowledge of His will through all the wisdom and understanding that the Spirit gives (v 9). The next words are key: "So that [some translations say then] you may live a life worthy of the Lord and please him in every way: bearing fruit in every good work, growing in the knowledge of God" (NIV).

Using the previous verse, can you <u>UNDERLINE</u> the conditional statement?

Now read John 15:16. Explain what Jesus said in this verse.

At this point, I hope you've grasped the concept that, as a believer, the principle of bearing fruit is NOT a choice. We have been APPOINTED and COMMANDED to GO and BEAR FRUIT!

But don't worry. If God commands us to do something, He'll also equip us for that specific calling.

Read Hebrews 13:20-21. Summarize what these verses mean to you.

DISCOVERING HOW MUCH FRUIT TO BEAR

Please understand that EVERY believer bears some amount of fruit at ALL times. However, some might wonder how much fruit we should be bearing. Let's go back to the beginning of John 15 and analyze the amount of fruit that every Christian bears throughout his or her life.

Look closely at the following verses and UNDERLINE the four AMOUNTS of fruit that Jesus mentions *(I've given you the first one)*.

> "Every branch in me that <u>does not bear fruit</u> he takes away, and every branch that does bear fruit he prunes, that it may bear more fruit." (v 2)

> "I am the vine; you are the branches. Whoever abides in me and I in him, he it is that bears much fruit, for apart from me you can do nothing." (v 5)

As these verses reveal, we can bear *no* fruit, bear *some* fruit, bear *more* fruit, or bear *much* fruit. What should be our aim as believers? Take a look at John 15:8 for the answer.

John 15:8 says, "This is to my Father's glory, that you bear much fruit, showing yourselves to be my disciples."

 **CIRCLE what AMOUNT of fruit brings God glory.**

FRUIT-BEARING LESSONS FROM THE LIFE OF GIDEON

I want to end the day with the story of Gideon. If you've never heard it or read it before, you can find it in Judges chapters 6-8. I'll summarize the high points here:

Because the Israelites sinned against God, they'd been under siege from their enemies, the

Midianites, and were in the midst of a famine. The Israelites were driven from their land and compelled to hide in mountainside caves. If any Israelite could grow grain, he'd bury it in pits in the ground or empty winepresses so that the Midianites couldn't find it. Enter Gideon. One day, Gideon was separating wheat in a hidden winepress when an angel of the Lord appeared to him. The angel said, "The Lord is with you, mighty warrior. Go out boldly, and save your people from the power of the Midianites."

Gideon responded, "O, Lord, how can I save Israel? Mine is a poor family in my tribe, and I am the least in my family."

And the Lord said to him, "Surely I will be with you, and I will help you drive out the Midianites."

Gideon then said to God, "If you are truly going to use me to rescue Israel as you promised, prove it to me." Through three different signs, God demonstrated that He would fulfill His promise to Gideon and that the Israelites would be victorious.

Like Gideon, I went through a particularly isolated period of my life. I'd just had my second son, Elias, and I felt lonely and disconnected. One Sunday, during the benediction prayer, I felt the Lord speak to my spirit and say, "Angela, if you want friends, do something about it."

Dig Deeper

The winepress (*gath* in Hebrew) is where the grapes were pressed. This was normally a limestone basin cut into the rock. Usually they were square but sometimes round. Grapes would be carried in baskets and laid on the floor of the winepress, and the men usually did the pressing.[10]

It's been eight years since I had that revelatory moment. At the time, I attended another church's monthly Mothers of Preschoolers (MOPS) group and led a small discussion group. So, when the Lord essentially told me to get out from "my winepress" and "be bold," I felt a stirring to launch my own MOPS charter. My response to Him was a Gideon-like response: *Lord, how can I start a group that brings mothers together? I don't even have any friends. If you want me to do this, you're going to have to bring women to me.*

Do you remember the part about God empowering us? Well, I've learned first-hand that He equips those He's called, but we are ultimately responsible to use what we've been given by God to bear fruit for Him.

As I write this, the ministry I birthed is growing and thriving. When you are barren and your life isn't producing fruit—let alone *much* fruit—the Holy Spirit can speak to you and provide guidance.

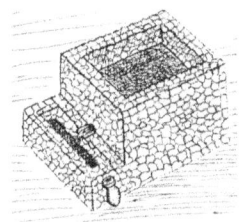

He has chosen you, will meet you right where you are, and bids you step out and be bold, you mighty warrior! He wants each of us to bear MUCH fruit, and He will empower us with the tools, resources, or even the other people necessary to complete the task.

Okay, it's time for more self-reflection. CIRCLE the AMOUNT of fruit you believe your life is bearing today.

- I have *none*.
- I believe I am bearing *some* fruit.
- Lately, I've been bearing *more* fruit.
- I know my life is bearing *much* fruit!

Have you been stuck in complacency or on a plateau? If yes, why?

Have you thought, "I just don't have time"? If so, what hinders you?

Is there anything you feel the Lord is calling you to do?
(Maybe start a Bible study group, foster a child, switch careers, go back to school, reach out to that parent at the bus stop, or start a business. Whatever it is, remember that if He's called you to it, He will equip you through it!)

If you're still thinking, "I just don't know what my fruit is," then join me in prayer to close our day:

Heavenly Father, I know You have chosen and empowered me to bring You glory with the fruit of my life. I honestly don't know what that looks like or have any idea of my true calling, but I know I have an earnest desire to seek after You, know You, and understand Your ways. I trust You to reveal Your perfect will for my life because I long to bring You glory. In Jesus' name, I pray. Amen.

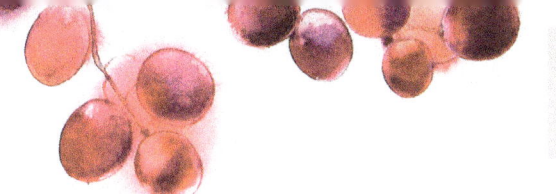

Day 4:
THAT'S NOT MY FRUIT

I have three young children, and in our home, we have endless loads of laundry and prolific toys, craft supplies, wrestling matches, random pieces of things that "must belong to something," and oodles of books. Amidst those books, there is one, in particular, that's been passed down from my oldest son, Elliott, to my middle son, Elias, and now to my youngest, Eleanor (Nora). The book is *That's Not My Dinosaur.* Yes, poor Nora has had to endure the bequeathing of many boy items in her short life.

Each child has loved flipping through the touchy-feely pages of a little white mouse's adventure to find his unique dinosaur. It's a tale that's had them exploring the 3D surface of a dinosaur on every page until they reach the final one, building up to the moment when they finally find the right one and say, "That's my dinosaur!"

The plot is simple, but I think the *That's Not My Dinosaur* adventure applies to adult audiences as well. Sometimes, when we don't know what we want to do, we have to try some "dinosaurs" before we finally find the right one. Although you may not yet know your specific fruit, today's study will help you rule some out and give you the confidence to say, "That's not my fruit."

We each have a specific calling given to us by God. As Paul writes in 2 Corinthians 10:13, "We, however, will not boast beyond measure but according to the measure of the area of ministry that God has assigned to us…" (CSB). Paul's words were a response to critics who believed he was not as spiritually sound as other, seemingly superior apostles. He exposed their faulty evaluation in that they measured him against (or compared him to) others in order to gauge his effectiveness.

When we use others as the barometer for our Christlikeness, the assessment will always be inaccurate. First of all, we already have THE standard to whom we should compare ourselves—Jesus. Beyond that, Paul understood what God had assigned him to do, and it would never be or look the same as anyone else's assignment. We're all given a unique sphere of influence and an individual capacity to change the world around us for the Kingdom of God.

UNDERSTANDING YOUR METRON

In 2 Corinthians 10:13, Paul uses the word "measure" when referring to his ministry, and the Greek translation for measure is *metron.*[11] Let's examine two definitions of metron in order to deepen our understanding of what Paul had to say.

Definition #1. An instrument for measuring; the rule or standard of judgment

UNDERLINE what the word *metron* is referring to in the following verses:

"Do not judge, or you too will be judged. For in the same way you judge others, you will be judged, and with the measure you use, it will be measured to you" (Matthew 7:1-2, NIV).

"'Consider carefully what you hear,' he continued. 'With the measure you use, it will be measured to you—and even more'" (Mark 4:24, NIV).

Definition #2. A determined extent, portion measured off, measure or limit

UNDERLINE what the word *metron* is referring to in the following verses:

"Because of the privilege and authority God has given me, I give each of you this warning: Don't think you are better than you really are. Be honest in your evaluation of yourselves, measuring yourselves by the faith God has given us" (Romans 12:3, NLT).

"But to each one of us grace was given according to the measure of Christ's gift" (Ephesians 4:7, NKJV).

"From him the whole body grows, fitted and held together through every supporting ligament. As each one does its part, the body grows in love" (Ephesians 4:16, NET).

In other words, your metron is your portion measured off—a specific and set boundary. It's the revelation that God has designated a particular gift and sphere of authority, anointing, and influence for YOU.

Each of us can be fruitful, and that happens best when we're operating within our metron, where our identity, style, passions, and motivation can flourish. When we function within the "determined extent" or given portion God has "measured off" for us, we can produce "much fruit" and, ultimately, a bountiful harvest.

While we *can* operate outside of our metron, it's when we are within its boundaries that we'll find the most grace, favor, and freedom to thrive. The Lord's boundaries aren't meant to stifle or limit us; rather, they are for our protection and our good.

When we purchased our home, what most attracted us to the property was the back yard; it is open without homes behind us. There are acres of fields and trees, a myriad of wildlife, and when I sit at my kitchen table, my view is uninhibited.

The land behind our home is sanctioned, run-off land because it belongs to the neighboring water reclamation facility. However, before purchasing our house, I'd never seen our soon-to-be neighbors.

The first time I walked over the hill at the far end of our property, I was overwhelmed by the enormity of what I saw. At the bottom of the hill stood a 15-foot-high fence enclosing four enormous water tanks behind the reclamation plant. This fence is not visible from our backyard, but it is a necessary boundary for the facility, community, and wildlife surrounding the property. The occasional duck floats on the surface of the tanks, but those tanks have a specific purpose—they are responsible for separating sludge from scum. They are necessary and essential, but I don't want my curious children anywhere near them.

Thus, the boundary is for their protection. If my children or any wildlife found their way into one of those reclamation vats, they could die. The boundary not only promotes the neighborhood's safety but also protects the extensive mechanical equipment that sits *inside* the fence. If something were to happen to those tanks, the water in our community would be negatively impacted with potentially detrimental effects.

In the same way, the fences (or metrons) in our lives aren't intended to limit us but to protect and help us.

DETERMINING YOUR METRON

Your metron is determined by the sphere of authority God has assigned to you. Let's read about the very first example of this found in the Bible.

Turn to Genesis 1:26-28.

What were God's instructions?

What was Adam given dominion over?

Turn to Genesis 2:15.

What was the territory (or metron) that Adam was given?

What were his primary responsibilities?

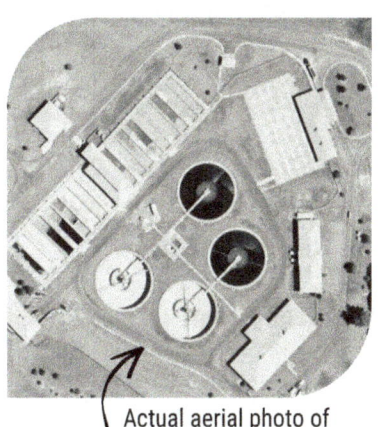

Actual aerial photo of my neighbors

God gave Adam dominion and a designated territory, which required cultivation and protection. Like Adam, our responsibility is to *tend* to and *keep* our specified area—our ministry assignment. Functioning beyond our sphere of authority is never wise and almost always causes unrest. We know how the story in the Garden ended. Adam let his guard down, failed to protect his territory, and ultimately did not pass the test of obedience set before him.

If we go back to the first passage of the day (2 Corinthians 10:13), Paul said that he wouldn't "boast" about things done outside of his authority. Why? Because he knew he could only boast about what had happened within the boundary of *his* God-given assignment.

Why do you think Paul was careful to stay within his territory?

Paul understood that going beyond your territory means entering into someone else's area for which you're not responsible. God isn't accountable for finishing something He didn't begin. If you're outside your metron, you're outside the authority given to you.

Let me explain this another way. I played collegiate basketball and was a student-athlete in the truest sense, meaning my athletic endeavors complemented my academic studies. Time on the court was secondary to time spent in the books, but the basketball court was its own classroom, full of life lessons I've held fast to throughout my adulthood. My coach often said, "Defense creates offense." This means that when you're guarding your designated opponent —when you're in the right spot, covering your area or zone—you can protect the basket. And, if you're on guard enough, you might make a defensive move that leads to the opponent making an error (a turnover), which could result in a scored basket on the other end of the court. Every so often, I'd get out of my zone, and the player I was supposed to be guarding would beat me. If I stepped out of my designated territory, I would miss an opportunity or allow the opponent to score.

So defend your territory, but also be ready to go on the offensive and move forward within the boundary of your metron.

Turn to Hebrews 9:14. Write it here:

Some translations use the term "dead works." What do you think that means?

Anything we do through our own ambition and motivation—even if it's giving to a good cause, raising money for a charity, or volunteering for those who are hurting and hungry—is "but filthy rags" if God's not in it. That's a tough one to swallow.

THE DANGERS OF WORKING WITHOUT THE LORD

There are so many examples of "made-made" works getting in the way of the Lord's promises in the Bible. In Genesis 15, we see a reminder of the Lord's covenant with the octogenarian, Abram, and His promise to give him descendants numbering the earth like stars in the sky.

Turn to Genesis 16 to read what happened after the Lord made the covenant with Abram.

What was Abram and Sarai's man-made work?

Why was this a "dead work"?

Abram and Sarai were tired of waiting and felt that they needed to help the situation along to fulfill the Lord's promise. They stepped out of their "zone" and took things into their own hands. They used their energy to bring about something that only God could fulfill (Galatians 5:23).

Now turn to Romans 7:18. Rewrite this verse in your own words:

At times, we can get caught up in an area in which we were never intended to be. Let's examine three key reasons why we can find ourselves participating in dead works outside of our metron.

Dig Deeper

The Middle East conflict we know today (the Arab-Israeli conflict) was birthed from Sarai's dead work.[12]

Fill in the chart below:

	List your key takeaways from the following verses:	Personal Reflection Write answers to the following questions:
OBLIGATION **2 Corinthians 9:7**		Was there a time when you committed to a task or assignment out of *obligation* but knew it wasn't your calling or metron?
OVERBURDENED **Exodus 18:13-27**		Have you ever felt *overburdened* by something you were doing, maybe in your job, ministry, or even something you volunteered to do?
OUR PRIDE **John 12:43** **Matthew 6:1**		Can you recall a time when you did something simply to be recognized? Have you held on to something because you felt you'd lose your identity if you let it go? Or did you hold on because you didn't think anyone else could do it better?

Dead works are sneaky because they appear as good works externally but actually come from our flesh. If we're not seeking God first in every area, we might find ourselves committed, overburdened, or white-knuckling something we were never meant to do.

Remember, a need is *not always* a calling.

There are a lot of needs out there, but you're not called to answer them all. It's okay to say "No" to good things so you can say "Yes" to the best things God has for you. It's never selfish to be a good steward of the calling and metron we've been given. Sometimes, when we say "No" we give space for *someone else* to say "Yes."

As we end this day, answer the following questions:

Has God laid anything on your heart that you believe to be your metron—your measured-out and designated territory/ministry assignment/sphere of influence?

Has the Lord placed you in a physical place, position, or group of people where you have a physical presence and spiritual stewardship?

Do you currently have anything in your life (ministry, work, etc.) that you feel is a "dead work"?

If you're still struggling to find your designated place in the Kingdom of God, that's okay. We'll work through specific things we can do throughout our time tomorrow to understand the fruit God has given us to bear. If we ask Him, He'll reveal His will for our life, and sometimes that means letting go of "good things" that aren't "God's things" for you.

I hope that you now have a new understanding of what your spiritual fruit IS NOT, and by the end of tomorrow's study, I pray that you will have a revelation of what it IS so you can bear MUCH of it!

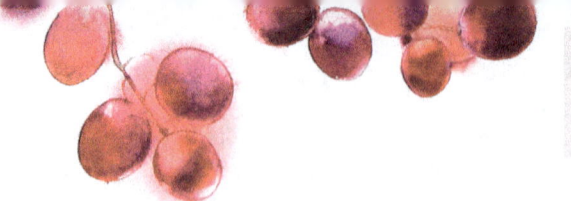

Day 5:
MY SPECIFIC FRUIT

I remember a song my mother used to sing to me by Sandi Patty called "Masterpiece" circa 1989. As a mother, I now sing this same tender ballad to my three children. This song is so precious because of the constant reminders that we are God's beautiful workmanship and divinely designed to be the masterpiece He created us to be.[13]

When God formed you and fashioned you in your mother's womb (Psalm 139), He did so with intentionality and purpose. The God of the universe has created YOU for a specific purpose, and a significant part of that purpose is work—YOUR fruit. Through today's study, we'll work to discover what God has created you to do, what He's calling you to be, and how He's gifted you for it all.

Okay, so let's start with Scripture to give us a framework.

Turn to Ephesians 2:10 and write the three main points of the verse here:

1.

2.

3.

As Ephesians reveals, your unique design (your abilities, gifts, and desires) was fashioned by God to equip you to fulfill your unique purpose and calling. Whether you're 18 or 98, your life has purpose. As long as there is breath in your lungs, your life has purpose.

On February 21, 2018, Billy Graham, the man known as "America's Pastor," died at the age of 99. In 2013, during the week of his 95th birthday, he delivered his final message through more than 480 television stations across the United States and Canada.[14] Even at 95, his life still had purpose—God wasn't finished with him yet.

Before we can figure out what our specific role in our small slice of life should look like, we need to truly grasp the concept that we matter to a big God. In Psalm 139:13-18, we read about the Creator of the Universe making us, knowing us, and thinking about us.

The Scriptures say:

> *You made all the delicate, inner parts of my body and knit me together in my mother's womb. Thank you for making me so wonderfully complex! Your workmanship is marvelous—and how well I know it. You watched me as I was being formed in utter seclusion, as I was woven together in the dark of the womb. You saw me before I was born. Every day of my life was recorded in your book. Every moment was laid out before a single day has passed. How precious are your thoughts about me, O God! They are innumerable! I can't even count them; they outnumber the grains of sand! And when I wake up in the morning, you are still with me! (NLT)*

Now turn to Matthew 10:29-30. Write your summary of these verses here:

Dear Friend, God has precious and innumerable thoughts about you. You are valued and loved by an infinite God!

Turn to Ephesians 3:16-21. Write down everything that speaks to you most:

Pause here and just let those verses soak in.

In Psalms, the term *Selah* is used occasionally. It means "to praise" or "to pause and reflect upon what has just been said." One definition says it's a "pause to breathe and reflect on the important words just uttered."[15] I don't know about you, but when I read that the God of Heaven and Earth intricately formed me, that I was not a mistake, and that He thinks precious and innumerable thoughts about me, that moves me. I am constantly in awe of His unconditional love, His loving me despite myself and without my having to do anything for Him. That's the amazing thing about the Father's affection for us—it's not earned or deserved—it's given freely. *Selah*.

Through this love—a love that He gave first (1 John 4:10)—we have the choice to love Him deliberately in return. One way we demonstrate our love is through obedience to do what He has commanded, such as bearing much fruit. As we obey, we use our God-given gifts and talents to accomplish what He's asked.

UNDERSTANDING OUR CALLING

Now, look up Ephesians 4:1. What does it say to do?

What do you think about the concept of a "calling?"

So often I considered a "calling" only for people in vocational ministry, but regardless of *who* we are or *what* our background is, if we are in Christ, we have a calling. YOU have a calling! And the truth about a calling is that it's yours and yours alone. Even more, your calling uses your specific desires and gifts.

I'm sure some of you are thinking, "Okay, that's great, but how do I truly know what my specific calling is?"

We've come to the point in our study where we will work through how we identify the calling the Lord has on our lives and how we discover God's perfect will for us. It all begins with Step #1.

Step #1. Seek the Lord

Read Matthew 6:33 and write what it means to you:

Now turn to James 1:5-7. What is required of us to gain wisdom?

God doesn't hide His will for our lives close to His chest like a skillful poker player. He'll always reveal His desires for us if we seek Him first and ask by faith for wisdom to know our calling. Just remember, you have to expect Him to answer!

If you haven't been looking to Him first or seeking His will, or you simply haven't asked Him yet, take some time now and write a prayer to the Lord here:

Step #2. Seek Honest, Wise Council

Turn to Proverbs 22:17-18. What is your takeaway after reading it?

Fill in the blanks of the following verses.

Proverbs 11:14 (ESV) says:
"Where there is_____, a people falls, but in an_____of counselors there is safety."

Proverbs 15:22 (ESV) says:
"Without counsel plans _____, but with many advisers they _____."

Proverbs 19:20 (ESV) says:
"_____to advice and_____instruction, that you may gain wisdom in the future."

Consult with mature, godly friends or family members. Ask them what they see as your gifts and abilities, and how you should move forward. Those who have traveled farther down the road can provide valuable insight. I've heard it said this way: You have to have people who KNOW you to NO you. Godly counsel can also offer a distinct perspective and help you sort through emotions, telling you what you NEED to hear and not what you WANT to hear. Just remember to maintain a posture of humility by being open to listening to the opinions of others, even if you don't fully agree with what they have to say.

Who are three people who would give honest feedback concerning your strengths, gifts, passions, and abilities?

1.

2.

3.

If you don't have Godly counsel currently, then list potential people to reach out to in the future.

In this next section, I want you to answer as many questions as you can and be truly honest. Don't be falsely humble and don't get caught up in what you *think* is important or what you *should* be doing. This is an exercise in self-discovery, so be true to yourself.

1. What do you ENJOY doing?

2. What do you DISLIKE doing?

3. What do you do WELL, and what are your STRENGTHS?

4. If money weren't an issue, what would you do with your TIME?

5. What are you PASSIONATE about?

6. If you could spend an ENTIRE DAY doing or talking about ONE thing, what would it be?

7. Do you have a DREAM or DESIRE to do something that you haven't yet?

8. What SEGMENT of the population are you drawn to help?

9. Your life experience has rendered you an expert at something. What's your EXPERTISE?

10. Lastly, what do you HAVE? What have you ALREADY been given?

Let me explain this last one. In 2 Kings 4, a widow cried out to the prophet Elisha for help, fearing creditors would enslave her two sons as payment for their debts. Elisha said to her, "Tell me, what do you have in the house?" The woman responded, "Nothing at all, except a jar of oil" (v 2). Through her obedience, God supernaturally multiplied the oil, giving her a surplus to sell and repay her creditors. She experienced an incredible breakthrough by using what she already had.

So, what do you ALREADY have?

If you look at your answers, I hope, you'll see common threads that run through the questions. Your responses will have some outliers (the random bits that are a part of who you are but are not necessarily related to your life's purpose). For example, unless you're called to work with animals, loving your dog is probably not related to your calling.

Disregard the outliers and look for repeated themes. Put those themes together, and at their intersection, you'll likely have a picture of *your specific calling*. (You'll probably find that your calling has been your heart's desire for a very long time.)

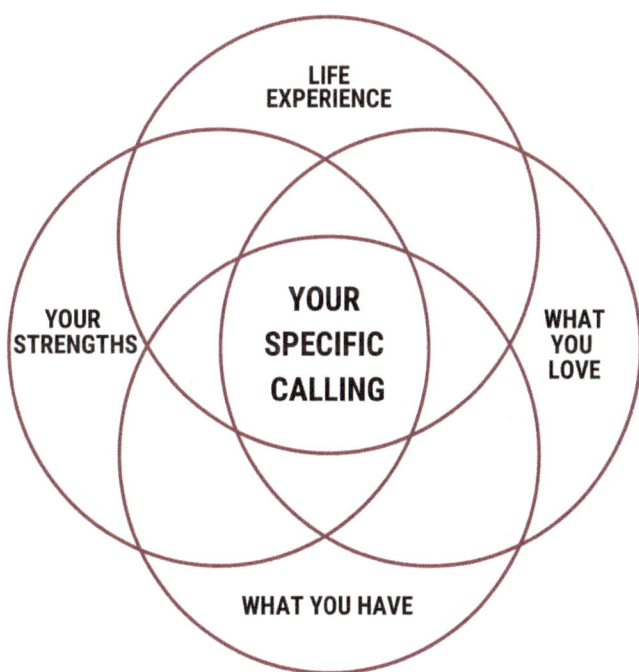

In their book, *A Case for Calling*, Drs. Thomas Addington and Stephen Graves define calling as "God's personal invitation for me to work on his agenda, using the talents I've been given in ways that are eternally significant."[16] I want to remind you that your calling is yours alone. Your calling is based on your unique desires, strengths, and passions and can be achieved with what you already have.

Let's take some time to discuss the spiritual gifts that are also related to our calling. Look up the following Scriptures that list the various spiritual gifts, and write those spiritual gifts in the chart below. (I've completed 1 Corinthians 12:1-11 for you.)

The Spiritual Gifts

Romans 12:4-8	1 Corinthians 12:1-1	1 Corinthians 12:28	Ephesians 4:7-13
1.	1. Wisdom	1.	1.
2.	2. Word of Knowledge	2.	2.
3.	3. Faith	3.	3.
4.	4. Healing	4.	4.
5.	5. Working of Miracles	5.	5.
6.	6. Prophecy	6.	
7.	7. Discernment	7.	
	8. Speaking in Tongues	8.	
	9. Interpretation of Tongues		

Now that you've read and studied these passages, CIRCLE the specific gift/gifts from the chart that you believe the Holy Spirit has given you.

The Word of God says that we've been given these spiritual gifts as a means of helping the entire body—the body of Christ. God desires us to be equipped to do His work and build up the body of Christ so "that the whole body is fitted together perfectly. As each part does its own special work, it helps the other parts grow, so that the whole body is healthy and growing and full of love" (Ephesians 4:16, NLT).

In other words, we have to DO our part.

Whether we are the eyes, the hands, or the big toe of the body, it's our responsibility to find our specific calling and use the spiritual gifts we've been given to help the body become *healthy, growing, and full of love.* This is our divine design and our eternal significance. As Theodore Roosevelt once wrote, "Do what you can, with what you've got, where you are."[17]

If you don't know what your spiritual gifts are just yet, that's okay. Begin by praying and seeking the Lord, but know there are practical resources available to gain deeper insight into your specific gifts. (For more information on these gifts, please see this week's "Be Fruitful.")

This leads us to our final step.

Step #4. Start Moving and Maintain!

Let's assume you've got clear direction on your calling and gifts, and you've sought wise counsel. Now it's time to start moving!

Match the Scripture with our instruction and the Lord's promises to help us:

	Be DOERS, not just hearers of The Word…and you will be blessed.
Proverbs 3:5-6	TRUST in the Lord…and He will make your path straight.
Isaiah 42:16	Make sure you devote yourself to (MAINTAIN) your calling… because it is excellent and benefits everyone.
Mark 16:15,20	
	He will lead us, guide us, illuminate our path, smooth out the road before us, and never forsake us.
Ephesians 2:10	
Titus 3:8	You are God's MASTERPIECE created to do good things that He has planned for us.
James 1:22,25	
	Let the whole world know who Jesus is…and He'll work with you and confirm you.

In the end, we must be willing to move out of our "comfort zones" in order to fulfill our divine purpose. One of my favorite biblical examples of this is when Abram (later to be renamed Abraham) was commissioned for ministry. In Genesis 12:1, God gave him the directive: "Leave your country, your relatives, and your father's house, and go to the land that I will show you" (NLT). Because Abram had NO idea where he was going, he had to rely upon God entirely. He had to trust God to fulfill His promises. Like Abram, you may have been called to do something, but the steps to get there may be unclear.

Remember, Dear Friend, God has intentionally designed, prepared, and commanded you to use your calling and gifts for your *specific* fruit. As long as we're willing to obey Him and be doers of The Word and not just hearers, He will guide us, protect us, and make our paths straight one step at a time.

As we end the week, I want to remind you that it is never too late to discover your specific calling. God loves you enough to have created you with precision and purpose, so it's time to fulfill His perfect will for your life and be the masterpiece that He's created you to be!

WHAT IS FRUIT?
from generation to generation...

BE *fruitful*

Here are this week's ways to DIVE DEEPER by yourself, with friends, or with family. You may not get to everything, but it's a way to reinforce the learning and share what you've personally discovered throughout the week with others!

DISCUSS

This week we discussed what fruit is and what it is not. We learned that we each have specific fruit, both internal and external.

Using the prompts below, start a discussion to solidify the learning!

- What's your favorite fruit and why?
- If you couldn't see, how would you describe your favorite fruit?
- What do you want to be when you grow up? What do you love to do?
- What unique talents or gifts God has given you? What special skills or gifts do you see in others?
- Of the fruit of the Spirit, which type do you struggle with most and why?
- What are you doing to use your gifts and talents? Why are boundaries good?

DESIGN

Using the prompts below, start creating your own masterpieces!

- Paint a portrait of fruit
- Modeling clay time! Sculpt your favorite fruit!
- Draw a picture of your favorite fruit.
- Write a sentence about your favorite fruit.
- Find a Fruit of the Spirit coloring page online and make a work of art.
- Check out Pinterest for all the fantastic fruit craft ideas!
- See what Etsy designers are doing with fruit— maybe purchase something or be inspired to create it yourself.

DISCOVER

- Visit your local grocery store and explore the fruit section, looking for new-to-you fruit. Touch and feel the textures. What do you notice? How do they smell? Take it home and try it!
- Visit a local fruit farm for pumpkins, berries, apples, pears, something local to your region!
- Go to a garden center and use your senses to explore the vegetation. Take a new plant home and care for it!
- Go on a nature walk and see the fruit growing around you. See how creative our God truly is!
- Find virtual fruit farms online if you don't have anything nearby.
- Visit: https://www.freeshapetest.com for a free assessment of your spiritual gifts.

FOR THE KIDS

- Listen to "The Fruit of the Spirit" songs by visiting:
  - www.youtube.com/watch?v=Rezg4jYFoj0
- Watch "Superbook -Elijah & the Widow" by visiting YouTube or other online resources.

DIG IN

READ

- Go to your local library and find books on fruit.
- For children, here are a few my kids have loved:
  - *Eating the Alphabet: Fruits & Vegetables from A to Z* by Lois Ehlert
  - *Fruit Bowl* by Mark Hoffman

REVIEW

- Parables—Discuss why Jesus used them.
- *Karpos*: Greek word for fruit.
  - Discuss the different ways we produce fruit.
- *Metron*: A set boundary

WHAT IS FRUIT?
from harvest to table...

Whether you're cooking for one or having a potluck, enjoy the process of artfully putting the ingredients together to make a delicious masterpiece. Be encouraged to consider the elements of your week-long study that apply to the recipe you are preparing.

DELICIOUS DELIGHTS

FRUIT SALAD MEDLEY

Serves 6

INGREDIENTS

- 1 cup fresh strawberries, cut
- 1 cup fresh blueberries
- 1 cup fresh grapes, cut in half
- ¼ cup unsulfured dried cranberries
- ¼ cup currants or golden raisins
- 3 apples (2 gala, 1 Granny Smith), diced
- 2 small pears, diced
- 2 oranges, peeled and cut
- ¼ cup chopped, pitted dates
- ¼ cup unsulfured dried cherries
- ½ cup chopped pecans, lightly toasted
- 2 tsp orange zest

INSTRUCTIONS

- In a large bowl, combine everything.

APPLE PIE FRUIT SMOOTHIE

Serves 2

INGREDIENTS

- 2 medium apples
- 2 Medjool dates or 2 regular dates, pitted
- ¼ cup walnuts or almonds
- ¼ cup raisins
- 1 tsp cinnamon
- ¼ tsp vanilla
- 2 Tbsp ground flax seeds
- 1 cup soy, hemp, or almond milk
- ½ cup ice optional, for frozen smoothie

INSTRUCTIONS

- Blend all ingredients in a high-powered blender until smooth and creamy.

Session 3
HOW IS IT PLANTED?

Session 3

VIDEO TEACHING

KEY VERSE

"Do not despise these small beginnings, for the Lord rejoices to see the work begin, to see the plumb line in Zerubbabel's hand" (Zechariah 4:10, NLT).

THE BIG IDEA

The seed is the small beginning.

OBSCURITY means:

- **The state of being _____ , inconspicuous, or unimportant.**

- **The quality of being difficult to _____ .**

- **A thing that is _____ or difficult to know.**

- **Synonyms include:**
  - **Insignificance, _____ , lack of fame/honor/recognition, ingloriousness,_____ , mystery, and oblivion.**

The phrase, "God's Workers" is translated in Greek as *sunergos* and it means:
"To _____ together, to be a partner in _____."

_____

_____

_____

_____

_____

Video sessions available at warriorraiser.com/fruitful   #FruitfulBibleStudy
Answers: *unknown; understand; unclear; anonymity; limbo; work/labor*

52   FRUITFUL

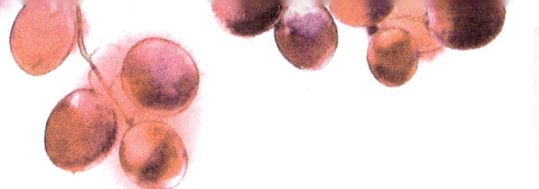

Discuss

Have you ever felt like you've been hidden in obscurity for a while? If so, describe.

What comes to mind when you consider those "Heroes of the Bible" who had to wait a long time for their God-given promises to be fulfilled?

How does it make you feel knowing that the Lord didn't wait for Zerubbabel to finish the temple to rejoice?

As you consider your "partnership" with God to fulfill your calling, as Psalm 37:3 says, are you "trusting God *and* doing good"? Are you "cultivating faithfulness"?

When you consider your "small beginnings," what comes to mind first?

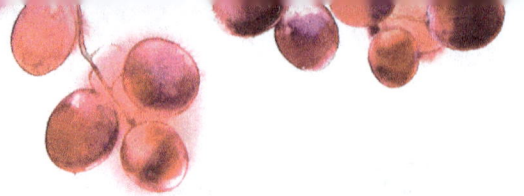

Day 1:
THE SODBUSTER

I love plants. As a young girl, I developed a deep appreciation for all things green from both my mother and her mother, my Nonny. Everything touched by either of these creative Italian women seemed to flourish, making gardening appear effortless.

Growing up in Ohio, you quickly develop a fondness for the changing seasons. (If you don't, you move south.) Some of my favorite things about the onset of spring were the frequent trips to the local garden center with my mother. With my younger brother in tow, we'd go in and out of rows of plants, and she'd take us up and down each colorful, life-filled aisle. We'd read the names of all the plants and determine whether they were annuals or perennials and what type of environment they'd need to thrive. It was my own personal botany lesson.

Some years, my mom would let me pick from the array of seed packets, and we'd grow produce, starting from dormancy. The anticipation of the garden and summer harvest was exhilarating. I loved the potential of the tiny seedlings—a fresh start to the season.

Over time, I've come to find that the garden parallels many of life's lessons. In John 15, when Jesus took the disciples through a garden—a vineyard—He gave His final life lesson before His crucifixion.

Jesus compared life in the Spirit to the simplicity of a grapevine. Through this analogy—this parable—we've learned that our life's calling is to bear fruit, and this week, we'll study the process of how our fruit is developed. In order for a seed to mature to produce fruit, it needs a method (either passive or active), a tool, or a person for the process to be completed.

This brings me to today's title: The Sodbuster.

A sodbuster is "a farmer who works the soil."[1]

THE SODBUSTER'S COMMITMENT

Farming has been said to be a way of life, a lifelong commitment. It's not a typical job where you can give your two weeks' notice and quit because you don't like the benefits package. A farmer is committed to their land, and most often, multiple generations are devoted to farming specific land. They are invested. They focus on one field at a time and never haphazardly spread seed hoping it will miraculously yield a harvest. In other words, there is purpose to their methods.

Write Proverbs 21:5 here:

Commitment to your calling—your fruit—takes time, and proper planning prepares the way for prosperity!

Did you know research states that 80% of New Year's resolutions fail by mid-February?[2] Because our culture has no "stick-to-it-iveness," no perseverance, we don't keep our word. We work, using our human effort, to do something only God can empower us to do. We grow weary of the task, get bored, or something seemingly more interesting comes along, and so we quit.

Look up 1 Corinthians 15:58 in the ESV and fill in the blanks:

"Be_____ , _____ , always abounding in the work of the Lord, knowing that your_____ is not in vain."

Read Colossians 3:23. WHO are we commanded to work for?

Read Ecclesiastes 9:10. HOW are we commanded to work?

Read 1 Corinthians 10:31. WHY are we commanded to work?

I don't know about you, but I want to be a woman of my word. I want to fulfill the promises I make to myself, to others, and to the Lord. When I commit to something, I want to stick to it. We have to remind ourselves when we are in the trenches—wanting to give up while we deal with difficult people or challenging situations—that this is all part of the fruit-bearing process.

Did you know God values commitment? Just do a simple search, and you'll find His Word filled with countless promises to provide and deliver. We see this in Isaiah 55:11: "It is the same with my word. I send it out, and it always produces fruit. It will accomplish all I want it to, and it will prosper everywhere I send it" (NLT).

<u>UNDERLINE</u> the last part of the above Scripture.

What this means is that if God said it, then He is faithful and willing to complete it. His word will prosper and achieve His intended purpose. If we are made in His image and His likeness (Genesis 1:27), then we should value our word and our promises just the same. God places an extreme priority on being people of our word.

Growing up, the concept of "staying true to your word" was highly valued in my home. If I tried to skirt out of a commitment without just cause, my mother would often say, "Swear to your hurt and change not." As a teenager, hearing this phrase would almost always elicit an eye roll from yours truly. I never really understood the historical importance of the phrase—or even what it meant—until I became an adult. So, if your mother didn't routinely tout this phrase, let me explain its origin.

Look up Psalm 15:4. Write it here:

What do you think David meant by the last part of that verse (4b)?

David knew the Israelites would understand the gravity of his words. This Scripture was a direct reference to a story they knew well: the story of Jephthah, which was a benchmark for keeping commitments even when it hurts. It's a lesson in staying true to our promises even if it takes great effort, is uncomfortable or is boring, or if we get a seemingly better offer.

Let's dissect this lesson a bit to fully understand the weight of David's words.

Turn to Judges 11, and answer the following questions:

    Who was Jephthah? (v 1)

    Who were the Israelites warring against? (v 4)

    What did Jephthah become? (v 11)

    What was Jephthah's vow to the Lord? (vv 30-31)

    Did Jephthah ever consult the Lord on how to advance? (vv 29-31)

What was the outcome of their war? (vv 32-33)

Who came out to greet Jephthah? (v 34)

What was Jephthah's response? (v 35)

Who else, besides Jephthah, was directly affected by his vow? (v 39)
(Note: Don't overthink this one)

What did Jephthah ultimately do? (v 39)

Dig Deeper

Some scholars believe that this was not a physical sacrifice of Jephthah's daughter's body but of her future. There is some speculation that she was given in permanent servitude to the temple and never married or bore children.[3]

Many times we begin with good intentions, and then something comes along and we waiver; we become weary in our well-doing. Our schedules change, our circumstances fluctuate, and we lose sight of what we've committed to and what we've promised.

Thus, the lesson of Jephthah's vow is two-fold. First, always consult the Lord *before* committing to something. I'm confident Jephthah would tell us today that we should go to God before we make a decision (Matthew 6:33; Proverbs 3:5-6). Seek Him first, acknowledge Him, pray, and ask for discernment. Second, if you commit to something, then stay the course; swear to your own hurt and change not.

In the end, just as the farmer is committed to his land, crop, and harvest, we have to be committed to producing our fruit. This takes preparation, sacrifice, mental fortitude, and a commitment to our word.

THE SODBUSTER'S COMPLEXITIES

Farming is demanding, dirty, and exhausting work, and it is not without risk. While much effort goes into farming land, the outcome is still very much dependent on outside influences. In other words, there are no guarantees with farming. The farmer times the planting of the seeds and is faithful in laying the foundation for a successful crop, but the complexity of the environment (weather, pests, soil conditions, etc.) can always affect the outcome of the harvest.

Write Ecclesiastes 11:4 here:

Some of you know you're being drawn, pulled, or called to something. Maybe you've known it for a while, or perhaps last week's study time helped reveal a dream that you know the Lord had placed in your spirit. Perhaps you're scared to take the first step. Maybe you don't know where to begin, and all the "what ifs" are so overwhelming that you're hesitant to even start. But, as Ecclesiastes 11:4 says, if we wait for our definition of perfect timing, fruit will never be produced.

Today, I want to challenge you to consider what, or who, God is calling you to. Here is a bit of encouragement from Hebrews 13:21: "May he equip you with all you need for doing his will. May he produce in you, through the power of Jesus Christ, every good thing that is pleasing to him. All glory to him forever and ever! Amen" (NLT). See! The Lord equips those He's called!

I also pray that you remember He has chosen you and will meet you right where you are, and you're never alone. If we ask, He'll empower us with tools, resources, or even the people necessary to complete the task! While we may never have a clear vision to see all that we've been asked to do, and even though the path may seem uncertain, God is always faithful. He will shed just enough light for us to see our very next step. So, take that first step...then take the next...one step at a time.

Write Psalm 119:105 here:

As you steward and nurture your calling, remember that The Word is alive, and it will always light the way for you.

When we seek the fragments of light in God's truth, He illuminates our path one step at a time. All we have to do is trust Him. Though the complexities of our environment can affect the outcome of our harvest, Proverbs 3:5-6 assures us that if we trust Him with our whole heart, lean into Him, and seek His will, then He will direct our paths.

THE SODBUSTER'S CULTIVATION

The pain of farming's complexities is momentarily forgotten once the harvest is ready. When all the preparation and labor have produced a bountiful crop, farmers rejoice. But, before any of that happens, they have to continuously cultivate their land. They have to prune, weed, irrigate, protect, fertilize, and care for their crops. Farmers have an unwavering commitment to the harvest and know every ounce of personal investment has the capacity to reap a great reward.

Write Ecclesiastes 11:6 here:

Again, we see the idea that diligence produces plenty! The cultivation of ANYTHING worthwhile takes time, effort, and resolve.

Now let's look at some biblical history and the sodbuster's importance.

ADAM: THE FIRST SODBUSTER

During Session 2, we discussed Adam's metron within the Garden of Eden and his instructions to "tend and care for it" (Gen. 2:15). Then, after Adam disobeyed, God confronted him.

Turn to Genesis 3:17-23.

What is Adam's punishment for *his* sin?

After the banishment from Eden, what did God send Adam out to do?

From that moment, farming became one of the only means of survival for the entire human race.

JESUS: THE ULTIMATE SODBUSTER

Turn to Matthew 13:24-29.

What's this parable about?

In Matthew 13:37, WHO is the farmer?

How do you see Jesus as our spiritual farmer?

Dig Deeper

At his birth, Noah's father believed Noah would bring relief from the painful toil of working the soil (Genesis 3:17-19; 5:29). After the flood, Noah was given the command to "be fruitful and multiply" (Genesis 9:7), becoming the second sodbuster and planting the first vineyard (Genesis 9:20).

Praise the Lord, we have the perfect example—for everything—in Jesus. Through Him, we have an example of the greatest seed sower there ever was, and Jesus used these agricultural parables to reveal the mysteries hidden since the creation of the world (Psalm 78: 1-4). He equated the ministry of His kingdom with farming so that people yesterday, today, and forever would have one more way to understand the truth of Jesus Christ. I'm grateful we have so many illustrations to understand Him. It is evidence that He is a relatable, Heavenly Father, and He is a personal Savior who personalizes His message for each of us.

Like earthly farmers, Jesus, The Ultimate Sodbuster, has an unwavering commitment to the harvest. In fact, He was so committed that He willingly laid down His life, being crucified on the cross, in order to reap a harvest of great reward—His church. We, too, have the ability to be committed to own our harvest, and OUR FRUIT is a great reward, which brings us to our final example.

YOU & ME: THE GOSPEL SODBUSTERS

Turn to Mark 4:3, and write it here:

In Mark 4:14, *who* is the Farmer?

Now turn to Mark 16:15. What does Jesus command us to do?

We are ALL commanded to spread the truth of the Gospel until Christ returns.

We are ALL called to sow the seed. Help us, Lord, to be faithful sodbusters.

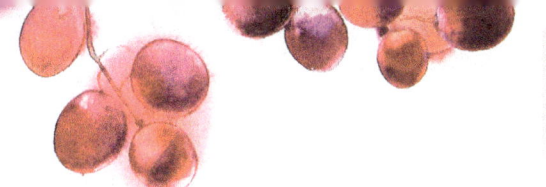

Day 2:
THE SEED

Have you ever heard something and, from the moment it went through your ears and traveled to your brain, you had a perfect understanding of what you'd just absorbed? This is called an epiphany.

I can recall a few of the epiphanies I've had, such as the time my friend Amy told me to turn my pop can tab around so it could hold my straw. Then there was the time, at age 12, when I learned Elvis Presley's song lyrics weren't, in fact, "Return Jacinda" but rather, "Return to Sender." I know, I know, these are crazy, mind-blowing revelations, right?

Then there was the time I heard the saying, "Though you can easily count the seeds in an apple, it's impossible to count the apples in a seed."

I remember thinking, how simple the phrase was, yet how profound the idea—a small, single seed can yield exponential dividends. And just like the physical seed, both you and I can also yield exponential dividends, which are our eternal treasures stored in Heaven (Matthew 6:19-20).

In yesterday's study time, we unwrapped the complexities of the sodbuster—the one who carries the seed. Today, we'll discuss the seed itself and how something so small has so much potential and promise.

As we dissect the intricacies of the seed, I'd like to begin with two main principles: the promise and the presence.

THE PROMISE & THE PRESENCE

Principle #1. The Promise

When you first think about—or look at—a seed, what things come to mind?

Zechariah 4:10 says, "Do not despise these small beginnings, for the LORD rejoices to see the work begin, to see the plumb line in Zerubbabel's hand" (NLT).

According to the above verse, <u>HIGHLIGHT</u> what we are told NOT to despise.

> **Dig Deeper**
> Mondegreen (mon·de·green) is a misunderstood or misinterpreted word or phrase resulting from mishearing the lyrics of a song. Example: "We built this city on sausage rolls" vs. "We built this city on rock and roll."[4]

That's exactly where we all begin: small.

When I was pregnant with my first son, Elliott, I remember wanting some sort of measurement standard to conceptualize his growth. I found a website that sent me weekly updates on his intrauterine growth status. Most women don't realize they're pregnant until the first few weeks have passed, but by the end of the fourth week, the life inside is about the size of a poppy seed. By the fifth week of gestation, the baby is no bigger than the size of an apple seed. Even secluded in the womb, deep in obscurity, we are a seed. We have a heartbeat. We are a promise.

We've been hashing out the revelation of your calling (your fruit) through the pages of this study. Some of you have huge visions and dreams for your life, while others are still hoping the Lord reveals those to you. I don't want us to lose sight of the simple moments right where we are, moments that have lasting, ripple effects for the Kingdom.

Before you become discouraged with this topic, I want to challenge you to scour your memory and think back to dreams or goals that have actually come to fruition. Consider those meaningful experiences that have become indelible tick marks on the timeline of your life. I suspect more than one of your hallmark moments has had a small, humble beginning.

Maybe you had an uncomfortable first visit to a church's singles group that eventually led to meeting the person you are married to now. Perhaps you made the scary decision to leave your job and start out on your own, and now you're flourishing. It could be that you made that difficult step into your first AA meeting, and now here you are, sober and free. Maybe you can look back on a simple request for forgiveness, which led to a reconciled relationship.

Dig Deeper

A plumb line is a measurement tool. It's a cord with a weight attached to one end that helps builders determine the exact vertical point.[5]

Whatever your story, answer the following:

What is a dream or goal (big or small) that's ALREADY come to fruition?	What were the FIRST small steps you took to achieve this outcome (your small beginning)?

When we examine the path that led to personal achievement, we often realize it began with a modest step forward, which in time reaped a greater harvest greater than we could've imagined.

In retrospect, we can look back on those beginnings with amazement and gratitude, and we realize the powerful significance of that moment—a seemingly trivial beginning—that we didn't value at the time. With hindsight, we could cringe at the thought of not taking the initial step that opened such important doors for us.

Unfortunately, the benefit of the small beginning is often lost on us when we embark on a new endeavor. All the energy it will seemingly take to pursue our dream seems daunting, and we become overwhelmed with its unattainability. It feels like there is little to nothing we can do to move forward. But by looking at our situation through the lens of faith, we see that in the middle of little and nothing, God always directs us to do *something*.

Let's look at a few examples in Scripture where we see how God exemplifies "the small beginning."

Using the following references, write the small beginnings for each.
(I provided the first one and have filled in all the outcomes for you.)

Biblical Example:	The Small Beginning	The Outcome
***Example:* Jochebed** Exodus 6:20 Exodus 2:1-3	*Gave birth to Moses, kept him hidden for months, then bravely laid him in a reed basket and placed him along the edge of the Nile River.*	*Moses' life was saved. He became the adopted Prince of Egypt, ultimately, delivering the Israelites from Egypt.*
Abigail 1 Samuel 25:1-4		*David recognized Abigail's divine intervention to keep him from sinning through revenge. David trusted the Lord to defend him. Abigail later became one of David's wives.*
Rahab Joshua 2:1-24		*Jericho was defeated and the Israelites entered the Promised Land. Rahab is in Jesus' lineage, remembered as a hallmark of faith requiring action. (Joshua 6:17-25; Matthew 1:1-5; James 2:25)*

Now I want to challenge you to think about the latter part of today's verse. Zechariah 4:10. The Lord rejoices to see what?

We are the ones who have to take the first steps for the work to begin. Remember the list of biblical examples you just completed? Every one of those people had to do something; they had to do *their* part!

Turn to 1 Corinthians 3:9. What does it say we are?

Read 2 Corinthians 6:1 and write it here:

Whether your translation says, "partners," "co-workers," or "workers together," it represents the Greek word, *synergeō (soon-erg-eh'-o)*. It means to be a fellow worker, to cooperate, to be knit together, to work together, or to be a partner in labor.[6]

WE have to do OUR part.

Remember that a small beginning is often the very step needed to open yourself up to the provision of Christ. Pray earnestly and ask the Lord if your dream aligns with His best intentions for your life. Take an honest inventory of what you can do to start moving toward your goal. Don't look with contempt on, or despise, the small beginning. Think of it as the launching point for a journey of faith.

James 1:5 has been one of my life verses, and I have repeated its promise back to the Lord in my prayers many times. The Scripture says, "If you need wisdom, ask our generous God, and he will give it to you. He will not rebuke you for asking" (NLT).

After reading this Scripture, what does it mean to you?

Turn to Hebrews 4:16 and paraphrase it here:

These Scriptures give us permission to boldly come before the Creator of the Universe and ask Him to share His desire for our lives. When we ask Him, He'll never resent us. When we're living in the center of His will for our lives, we're safe, we're equipped, and we're prepared to move forward in the work He's called us to do.

Now let's move on to the next principle that the seed represents.

Principle #2. The Presence

Even though we begin our work with a small beginning, the Scriptures are clear that we are never alone in the process. Philippians 1:6 says, "And I am certain that God, who began the good work within you, will continue his work until it is finally finished on the day when Christ Jesus returns" (NLT) Zechariah 4:6 also has this to say: "'Not by might nor by power, but by my Spirit,' says the LORD Almighty" (NIV).

God—who called us, remains with us, and gives us His promise—tells us again and again that we never do this life alone. It's that partnership again!

Read John 14:16-17. *Who* does Jesus promise will come in His place?

God has given us His Holy Spirit to be with us, all the days of our life. Regardless of your Bible version, this is translated from the Greek *paraklētos* (par-ak'-lay-tos). Synonyms for the Holy Spirit include Counselor, Comforter, Encourager, Helper, Intercessor, and Advocate. This means the Holy Spirit is an ever-present (Psalm 139:7) and all-knowing (2 Corinthians 2:10) resource for any, and every, situation of our lives.[7]

Read the following verse and <u>UNDERLINE</u> what Jesus says the Holy Spirit will do?

> "But when the Father sends the Advocate as my representative—that is, the Holy Spirit—he will teach you everything and will remind you of everything I have told you" (John 14:26, NLT).

Jesus spoke again of the Holy Spirit in John 20:22 when He suddenly appeared to the disciples following His resurrection and said, "Peace be with you. As the Father has sent me, so I am sending you." Then Jesus breathed on them and said, "Receive the Holy Spirit" (NLT).

Although Jesus doesn't physically breathe on us today, from the moment of our salvation, we also receive the Holy Spirit.

Turn to 1 John 2:27. Once you have received the Holy Spirit, what does this verse say you now have?

There are two meanings of the word "anointing." Let's dive in and see what this word truly means, especially since we're given access, as followers of Christ, to receive it!

The word <u>anointing</u> in Scripture is either *physical* or *spiritual*.

UNDERSTANDING PHYSICAL ANOINTING

The Hebrew word *mashach* (maw·shakh') means "to pour, sprinkle, or smear the consecrated oil for preparation and sanctification, or to be set apart for a holy, godly purpose." For example, oil was involved in the anointing of prophets, priests, and kings for their inauguration. It was also a mark of respect sometimes paid by a host to his guests. In addition, oil was used physically and symbolically for cleansing, protecting, soothing, and healing.[8]

Here are some biblical examples of how physical oil was used:

- For **beautification** or as a cosmetic agent (Esther 2:12)
- For **healing** (James 5:14)
- As **fuel** (Exodus 27:20)
- As a **protective barrier** (Psalm 23:5)
- For the **consecration of a king**, such as the anointing of David to be the future king of Israel (1 Samuel 16:13)

Now turn to Mark 14:8. What did Mary of Bethany do for Jesus?

These are a few examples of the ways in which the oil could be used. In antiquity, oil most commonly came from olives. Today, if you ask the average person what olive oil is used for, they'll likely answer, "for cooking." A simple biblical search reveals that olive oil was used in food, yes, but also for lamp oil, healing ointments, and cleansing soaps. Olive oil provided sustenance, light, healing, and cleansing properties.

While there are many illustrations of how oil was used throughout the Bible, I want to point our attention back to *the seed*. We've talked about the *promise* of what the seed represents, but, as we near the culmination of today's study, I want to shed light on where this oil—this anointing oil—comes from.

In order to produce oil, the entire olive—flesh and seed combined—must be crushed and pressed. This is necessary because the crushing and pressing tears the flesh to facilitate the release of the oil. And, because we've referenced vineyards throughout this study, I'd also like to point out that grapeseed oil comes directly from the seed of the grape and is also acquired through the crushing and pressing of the seed itself. For both types of fruit (the olive and the grape) crushing and pressing releases the oil.

Now that we've covered the physical anointing, let's turn our attention to the spiritual anointing.

UNDERSTANDING SPIRITUAL ANOINTING

The Greek word *charisma* (khä'-rē-smä) means favor freely given or a gift of grace.[9]

This anointing is a proper noun, and it is the spiritual gift, the endowment of supernatural power given to us by the Holy Spirit. This anointing is the free gift we receive with salvation. It is the gift of God's grace made available to us through the death and resurrection of Jesus Christ, and this anointing represents the supernatural presence of the Holy Spirit.

Let's unpack what else the Bible teaches about the spiritual anointing of the Holy Spirit.

<u>UNDERLINE</u> what Peter says we'll receive in the following verse:

> "Peter replied, 'Repent and be baptized, every one of you, in the name of Jesus Christ for the forgiveness of your sins. And you will receive the gift of the Holy Spirit'" (Acts 2:38, NIV).

1 Corinthians 2:12 says, "And we have received God's Spirit (not the world's spirit), so we can know the wonderful things God has freely given us" (NLT).

How would you explain this verse to a child?

Turn to 1 John 2:20.

> **As true believers in Christ, who are we anointed by?**

> **What does the Holy Spirit do for us?**

As the Scriptures reveal, all believers are anointed by the indwelling of the Holy Spirit, meaning we have the Holy Spirit within us. Some of us walk more closely in the Spirit, but there is not a true believer who does not have the Holy Spirit.

To go further, the Bible reveals in Romans 8:8-11 that if you don't have the Holy Spirit, then you do not belong to Christ. Ultimately, as believers, God anoints us with the Holy Spirit, and as long as we receive it, this "charisma" remains forever with us—counseling, comforting, encouraging, helping, interceding, and advocating for us.

As we finish today's lesson, let's examine Jesus' final life lesson before His crucifixion. Along the journey with the disciples, Jesus and His followers made their way to an olive grove called Gethsemane at the foot of the Mount of Olives (Mark 14:26), across the Kidron Valley (John 18).

Turn to Mark 14:32-34 (NLT).

Where are they? (v 32)

What does Jesus say in verse 34?

Now examine the two verses below and CIRCLE the word (or concept) that is repeated.

"But he was pierced for our transgressions; he was crushed for our iniquities; upon him was the chastisement that brought us peace, and with his wounds we are healed" (Isaiah 53:5, ESV).

"Yet it was the will of the LORD to crush him; he has put him to grief; when his soul makes an offering for guilt, he shall see his offspring; he shall prolong his days; the will of the LORD shall prosper in his hand" (Isaiah 53:10, ESV).

For the forgiveness of our sins and the releasing of the *spiritual* anointing, Jesus' flesh had to be crushed.

Remember how we learned that the entire olive had to be crushed and pressed to release its oil? Well, it was no coincidence that Jesus, the Messiah, spent His last evening in an olive grove in preparation for this necessary process. Even more, the Scripture names the *exact* garden, which is important because we often find purpose and revelation in the use of the specific name. When we discover the etymology or origin of a word and the development of its meaning, we gain profound understanding.

Using this concept, let's look at some important words that appear in the verses and piece together a complete story.

1. **Gethsemane** in Hebrew means "press of oil"; the corresponding Aramaic word is mesah, which means "anointing oil."[10]

2. **Kidron** in Hebrew means "mournful, dark, dusky place."[11]

3. **"Messiah"** in Greek is *Christos* and means "the anointed one."[12]

Jesus Christ (*the anointed one*) made His way through a mournful, dark, and dusky place to offer His flesh to be pressed and crushed with grief to the point of death to pay the price for our sin. Jesus knew He had to fulfill His earthly mission in order for the Holy Spirit to come and abide with—and in—us. The messianic significance of this act is that He became the Mishchah (*the physical anointing*) so we could have His Charisma (*the spiritual anointing*)!

Thus, the Messiah, the seed of the Gospel, was crushed to the point of death to bring undeserved grace and favor, the gift of the Holy Spirit, and, ultimately, eternal life. *Selah.*

Let's end today in prayer.

Lord, help us remember our small beginnings and our dreams that have already been fulfilled. Remind us of our Heavenly calling: to work together with Your Spirit, carrying Your seed wherever we go. Let our lives help others know Your goodness. We never want to take for granted the sacrifice that was made on the cross. Without Your crushing and piercing, we wouldn't be able to live in freedom from our sin. Without Your crushing and piercing, we wouldn't have Your anointing within us today. Thank You for leaving Your Holy Spirit to counsel, comfort, encourage, help, intercede, and advocate for us. We love You. In Jesus' name we pray. Amen.

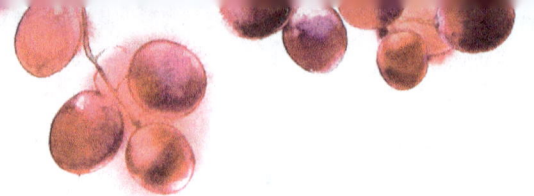

Day 3:
THE SOIL

Since the beginning of human existence, soil has had significance. As Genesis 2:7 says, "And the Lord God formed a man's body from the dust of the ground and breathed into it the breath of life. And the man became a living person" (NLT).

Whether you've thought about it or not, soil is essential to life as we know it. It's so important that there is, in fact, an official World Soil Day. It's true! Mark your calendar for December 5th and throw dirt a party! All jokes aside, the life-giving ground beneath our feet is vital to our survival because without soil we wouldn't be able to provide food, fuel, animal feed, medicine, and raw materials for clothing, household goods, and other essentials.

What's more, the water absorption and filtration properties of soil play a role in reducing pollution, and soil also provides both the foundation and base materials for buildings, roads, and other infrastructure. When discussing soil as a medium for plant growth and support, anyone who's done even a little gardening recognizes how the quality of the soil can change the outcome of the harvest.

Clearly, soil is an underrated player in our daily lives.

FINDING ITS WAY TO THE SOIL: A SEED'S JOURNEY

One does not need to be a brilliant botanist to know that plants come from seeds, but first a seed has to get into the soil before it can become a plant. While you probably know most of the ways this happens, there are a few bizarre methods for seeds to find their way into the soil.

Here's a summary of some of the unique ways:

- **Weight (gravity):** When fruit has ripened, its heaviness causes it to fall to the ground. Examples include apple, pear, orange, and coconut.

- **Whip it (to launch or throw):** This is also called *ballistic dispersal*, and, as the name suggests, some plants explosively eject their seed into the air! The sandbox tree—commonly called "the dynamite tree" due to the sound of its fruit exploding—uses this method, and the explosions are powerful enough to launch the seed over 320 feet! Examples include impatiens, mistletoe, squirting cucumber, geranium, and peas.

- **Wind:** This is when a simple breeze or a gust of wind takes the seed and parachutes it to a new destination. Think of summers in the yard making wishes with dandelions, which is also an adult's nightmare if you're trying to keep your yard weed-free! Examples include dandelion, maple, and tumbleweed.

- **Water:** Here, floating fruits use the force of the current for their propagation. Examples include water lily, palm tree, and mangrove tree.

- **Waste it:** Animals or birds eat the fruit and excrete the undigested seeds as waste, transplanting them to a new location. Examples include blackberry, raspberry, blueberry, and cherry.

- **Wear it:** Some plants hitch a ride on the hair, fur, or wool of animals as well as our clothes and hair. Examples include burs, barley, stick-tights, and krameria.

- **Willfully immerse it:** This is when seeds are purposefully planted (immersed) in the ground, either by animals or humans. Examples include squirrels burying nuts and humans farming crops.

The lesson here is that to bring forth a harvest, we have to willfully immerse—or plant—the seed first.

THE FOUR BIBLICAL SOILS

Today, you'll be referencing two main passages as we examine what the Bible has to say about soil: Mark 4:1-9 and Matthew 13:1-23. I encourage you to put a bookmark in each section as we work through the material.

Now turn to Mark 4:1-9. What are the four types of soil listed (or where did the seed fall)?

1.

2.

3.

4.

Turn to Mark 4:14. How does this Scripture reiterate what we learned yesterday?

What does Matthew 13:19 say the seed is?

THE FIRST SOIL

Look up Mark 4:15 and Matthew 13:19.

How did Jesus explain this type of soil?

What happens to the seed?

Mark 4 begins with the sower going out to sow. In antiquity, they plowed rows in their fields with the help of an animal or by hand. The sowers walked up and down these rows, carrying a seed bag over their shoulder, showering seeds onto the pathway. Imaginably, these paths were dry and beaten down, compacted by the feet of those who'd walked on them. Because of this, they'd become as hard as pavement, so the seed falling on this footpath may as well have been falling on concrete (and we know how well concrete produces vegetation).

Why did Jesus use birds as an analogy for Satan?

Birds are a very familiar problem to any farmer—past, present, and future. That's why scarecrows, nettings, visual repellants, and a sundry of plastic decoys are available. Jesus knew His audience would understand this and that birds follow the seed. In fact, they fly behind, waiting to swoop down and pluck up any accessible seed. Not surprisingly, there is no chance for the seed to take root in this type of soil because Satan (i.e., the birds) comes INSTANTLY to steal The Word, ruining any future hope of the Gospel message growing.

Unfortunately, some people are so hardened to the Word of God that they reject it outright. They do not hear it with faith because they have none and, ultimately, never begin the journey of discipleship. For most of you in this study, the Gospel message has already taken root in your heart, but that doesn't mean we're free from "the evil one [who] comes and snatches the seed away from [our] hearts" (Matthew 13:19, NLT).

Turn to 1 Peter 5:8. Write the verse and the command Peter gives:

Now turn to Job 1:7-8. The Lord asks Satan, "Where have you come from?" How does Satan answer, and what does he say he's been doing?

We have a REAL and PRESENT enemy: Satan. He's *constantly* on the alert, roaming the earth with the sole purpose of finding victims to destroy. He wants to destroy your happiness, peace of mind, dreams, relationships, and future. He wants to destroy YOU! And, if you ever get close to hearing or receiving The Word, he'll do his best to snatch it up before it gets rooted in your spirit.

For years, my husband, Derrick, and I would fight on our way *to* church and then get into some sort of silly argument over where to get lunch (or something else equally stupid) on our way *back* from church! We started to call these our "Sunday Fights" because we came to expect them.

One cold Sunday in November, in the middle of an epic "Sunday Fight," filled with anger, I made Derrick abruptly stop our van so I could get out and walk home three blocks—in a dress and heels, freezing in the late fall Ohio air.

I'm embarrassed to even share that with you now because, when I got home, all three of my small children had been in the back of our van sobbing because they thought Mommy had left them. I really let the devil win that day. Once things had cooled, I was instantly assaulted with two of the enemy's hallmark tactics: regret and shame. I was besieged with thoughts of, *I'm a total Christian failure, total wife failure, and total mom failure.* Strife, a lack of peace, and thoughts of condemnation and shame are evidence that Satan and his demonic forces are at work.

Though Derrick and I can now joke about my angry walk home (over something neither of us can even remember), we know there is a *very real* and *very present* adversary. He's a patient enemy who's studied us with diligence and knows the precise ammunition to launch at us. Though you may never have walked home angry in a dress and heels, I know most of you have experienced some sort of opposition because we ALL have the same enemy, and his schemes are not unique or original.

You should NEVER be surprised that anywhere seed is sown—when you've been hearing or studying The Word, or when you're on your way to or from an amazing church service, retreat, ministry luncheon, or even participating in *this* Bible study—you'll INSTANTLY be a target for the birds.

Remember, 1 Peter 5:8 begins with, "Be careful! Watch out for attacks..." (NLT). Other versions say, "Be on the alert!" (NASB). In other words, we have to be on guard and ready for the attacks when the devil tries to use his tired antics on you. However, Ephesians 6:11 gives us hope when it says, "You will be able to stand firm against all strategies and tricks of the devil" (NLT).

THE SECOND SOIL

Now, look up Mark 4:16 and Matthew 13:20.

> **How did Jesus explain *this* type of soil?**

> **What happens to the seed?**

I live just outside of Columbus, the capital of Ohio. While it may not be New York City, Columbus is teeming with art, music, theater, museums, culture, and the pride and joy of our city: The Ohio State Buckeyes. It's a nice place to live, work, and raise a family. Every summer, the city puts on an annual Independence Day celebration called "Red, White & Boom!" It is the Midwest's largest fireworks display, with the entire downtown becoming a hoard of people and cars. This event is the largest single-day event in Columbus, with around 500,000 people working to stake claims on the downtown riverfront. It's as though they are marking their territory in the California Gold Rush. People can get nasty, and it can be brutal amidst the bustle of live music and the classic array of food, artists, and vendors. The event culminates at night, yet the extravagant fireworks display, set to music from one of our local radio stations, lasts for only 26 minutes—not even half an hour![13]

You're probably wondering why on earth I'm talking about "Red, White, & Boom!" and how fireworks have anything to do with the rocky soil Jesus taught about in these verses. You see, the rocky soil is just like all the excitement and thrill of the fireworks—the joy and splendor of the extravagant display—only to be left with ash and soot after the pop and fizzle of the bright lights has ended 26 minutes later.

We just read that the second scattering of seeds falls on rocky ground and sprouts up quickly, only to be withered away by the sun. This soil illustrates a shallow-hearted person who seems receptive and responds immediately—and even receives it with JOY—but only superficially.

This rocky soil is representative of someone who appears to respond enthusiastically to Christ, only to renounce Him once persecution heats up. Unlike the previous example, these individuals profess a belief of some kind in God's Word; however, their faith is shallow and inauthentic.

In this soil, The Word is unable to take deep root because the environment of their hearts is shallow and their <u>faith is fickle.</u> The Scripture says *each* person who responds positively to The Word of God *will* face affliction or persecution (Matthew 13:31). But without a firm foundation, they'll be unable to withstand the hostile elements—persecution and suffering—and their shallow spiritual roots will wither away and die. This is why outward fervor is not always a sure sign of true conversion; no matter how enthusiastic the response may seem to be in the beginning, without deep roots, a person will "fall away," leaving behind ash and soot of the once-dazzling, 26-minute fireworks display.

Turn to Jeremiah 17:7-8. How does the tree mentioned in these verses compare to the seed grown in rocky soil?

In speaking of true salvation, Charles Spurgeon wrote the following:

> *To get up a whirl of excitement, and to have people influenced by that excitement, so that they think full surely that they are converted, has been done a great many times; but the bubble has, by-and-by, vanished. The balloon has been filled until it has burst. God save us from that. We want sure work, lasting work, a work of divine grace in the heart. If you are not converted, pray do not pretend that you are. If you have not known what it is to be brought down to see your own nothingness, and then to be built up by the power of the Spirit upon Christ as the only foundation, oh, remember that whatever is built upon the quicksand will fall with a crash in the hour of trial. Do not be satisfied with anything short of a deep foundation, cut in the solid rock of the work of Jesus Christ.*[14]

A bursting balloon or a fizzling firework just won't do; we should never be satisfied with <u>anything short of a deep foundation</u>, firmly rooted in Jesus Christ.

How does Ezekiel 36:26-27 relate to this rocky soil study?

Turn to Ephesians 3:17-19. Summarize what these verses mean to you.

Now, look up Mark 4:18 and Matthew 13:22.

How did Jesus explain *this* type of soil?

What happens to the seed?

This third type of soil, the kind situated "among the thorns," represents a heart too enthralled or too preoccupied with worldly matters. Jesus revealed about this soil that "the worries of the world, and the deceitfulness of riches, and the desires for other things enter in and choke the word, and it becomes unfruitful" (Mark 4:19, NASB).

Though seed does grow in this soil, what does Scripture say about its growth?

This is not a hard-hearted unbeliever or a shallow person with no foundation of faith. Rather, this soil is well plowed with enough depth to promote growth. However, the outside influences of the world consume the good seed and choke it out. Ultimately, the problem is not with the soil but with the competition for the soil. If the competitors—the thorns and weeds—were removed, the seed would grow and multiply.

Match the appropriate Scripture reference with the outcome:

Luke 16:13	The temptation and snare of wealth plunges us into ruin and destruction.
1 Timothy 6:9-10	If you love the world, God is not in you.
James 1:8	A double-minded man is unstable in all his ways.
James 4:4	No man can serve two masters.
1 John 2:15	A friend of the world is an enemy to God.

Here is what Mark 4:19 has to say about this kind of soil: "Then the cares and anxieties of the world and distractions of the age, and the pleasure and delight and false glamour and deceitfulness of riches, and the craving and passionate desire for other things creep in and choke and suffocate the Word, and it becomes fruitless" (AMP).

This third soil is a lesson in priorities. There will always be people and things that compete for our time, money, and attention. What do you love more? Whom do you love most?

I don't want us to miss this point; not all of the thorns and weeds that invade our lives are inherently evil. Neither material wealth nor pleasure is wicked. When properly prioritized, wealth and pleasure should be received with thanksgiving as gracious gifts from the hand of God, and there are many "good" things with which we can fill our time: our family, friends, employment, altruism, etc. However, even these "good" things can distract from—and compete with—the most important thing: God.

When you think of physical weeds, why are some more difficult to get rid of than others?

In Mark 4:19 (see above), CIRCLE all the things that creep in, choke, and suffocate the Word.

Take an honest inventory of anything that may be distracting you right now. Self-examination is difficult, and it takes courage to do it well.

What are your weeds and thorns? What are the cares and anxieties of the world—of your world—that try to creep in and suffocate The Word, attempting to make you fruitless?

List the priorities you need to re-evaluate.

Why are some of your weeds more difficult to get rid of than others?

If we're not careful, even if we begin as good soil, the thorns can move in, distracting us with worldly cares and concerns that leave us fruitless and barren.

In her book *Uninvited*, Lysa TerKeurst writes this of God:

> *He is the great answer to our every desire...He may very well give us good gifts. He may entrust to us relationships and success and blessings of all kinds. After all, He loves to give good gifts to those He loves. But He will not honor the chase of these things.*[15]

Unless we decide to make God our ultimate priority—to seek Him first and to make His Kingdom and His righteousness the most important thing in our lives (Matthew 6:33)—we will forever be pursuing empty alternatives that will eventually choke Him out.

THE FOURTH SOIL

Now turn to Mark 4:20 and Matthew 13:23.

How did Jesus explain this type of soil?

What do you think makes soil "good"?

What makes soil "fertile"?

Good soil means the soil has the right nutrients, pH balance, texture, and filtration. Sometimes when the seed falls on good soil and a root takes hold, a beautiful plant grows and produces fruit. Jesus uses this good soil to illustrate someone who has heard and received The Word of God and allows it to take root and grow within his or her life.

This person represents true salvation that bears good fruit.

At the end of Mark 4:20 and Matthew 13:23, what three amounts did the harvest produce?

1.

2.

3.

The seeds that fall on fertile, rich soil produce a crop that varies in its yield. Do you recall the answers you gave on Day 3 of Session 2, regarding the amount of fruit that every believer produces? SOME fruit, MORE fruit, and MUCH fruit.

Each soil received seed, but not all produced quality fruit. When it came to the good soil, Jesus said it produced a crop yielding thirty, sixty, or one hundred times what was sown. Everyone can receive seed—The Word of God. Everyone also has potential for harvest—living a fruitful life. However, the ones who produce *much* fruit will be the ones most yielded to the cultivation process.

Jesus used this parable of the four soils to teach how important the state of our heart is to our receiving the Gospel and how our choices and actions ultimately prove our salvation. Our response to The Word determines the depth of our relationship with the Lord. Seed in good soil will produce good fruit, and the evidence of our salvation is revealed by the type of fruit we bear.

Let's pray to end the day:

Father, create in me a soft, fertile, and open heart that is readily yielded to Your Word and Your commands. Help me recognize any weeds that have been competing for Your place in my life. Help me to know exactly how to get rid of them so that I may be fruitful for You. In Jesus' name I pray. Amen.

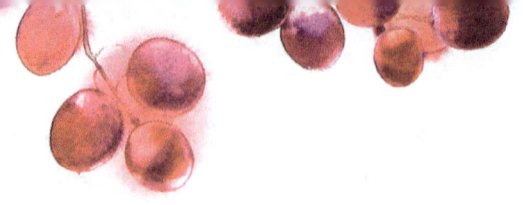

Day 4:
THE SEASON

In late 1965, the song "Turn! Turn! Turn!" became an international hit for The Byrds. Though the sequence of the words was rearranged for the song, Peter Seeger's lyrics were taken, almost verbatim, from Ecclesiastes 3:1-8. If you're not already singing the tune in your head, here is the scripture Seeger used to craft his famous chorus:

> *To everything*
> *There is a season*
> *And a time to every purpose, under heaven*[16]
> *(Ecclesiastes 3:1, NKJV)*

The changing of seasons provides us with undeniable evidence of God's creative handiwork. The beauty of His creation is displayed with the turning of every season. When you are able to stop and soak up the majesty of the landscape, it is truly a wonder to behold.

The circadian rhythm of the world around us follows the "tick-tock" of the clock. The atmosphere changes, and nature steps in line and follows suit.

As King Solomon wrote, there is a time (or a season) for everything:

> *To everything there is a season, A time for every purpose under heaven: A time [a]to be born, And a time to die; A time to plant, And a time to pluck what is planted; A time to kill, And a time to heal; A time to break down, And a time to build up; A time to weep, And a time to laugh; A time to mourn, And a time to dance; A time to cast away stones, And a time to gather stones; A time to embrace, And a time to refrain from embracing; A time to gain, And a time to lose; A time to keep, And a time to throw away; A time to tear, And a time to sew; A time to keep silence, And a time to speak; A time to love, And a time to hate; A time of war, And a time of peace. (Ecclesiastes 3:1-8, NKJV).*

When I read those poetic words, something in my spirit is stirred. It's a reminder that change is inevitable. There is a time to plant and a time to uproot. Nothing stays the same forever.

Write Ecclesiastes 3:11 in your own words here:

A TIME TO PLANT

Genesis 8:22 says, "As long as the earth endures, seedtime and harvest, cold and heat, summer and winter, day and night will never cease" (NIV).

According to Genesis 8:22, what cycles never cease? List them here:

1.

2.

3.

4.

In the beginning, God instituted seasons of change—of sowing and reaping. He repeated the lesson throughout the Bible to indicate the importance of the message. What we plant, where we plant, and when we plant matters.

Let's dive in and look at <u>what</u> we're planting.

We've already talked about the seed as the essence of the Gospel (the promise and the presence), but I want to bring balance to our lesson today and look at the other side of the coin. If we *aren't* sowing the Gospel message, the truth about who God is, then what, exactly, *are* we sowing?

Turn to Galatians 6:7-10 and fill in the following answers:

1. **You will ALWAYS_____ _____ _____ _____!**

2. **If you sow to please your FLESH, you will harvest _____.**

3. **If you sow to please the SPIRIT, you will reap _____.**

Now turn to Job 4:8. Rewrite the verse in your own words:

Whether we're planting seeds of the Spirit or planting seeds that satisfy only our flesh, we are *always* planting seeds.

I once heard a speaker reference Genesis 8:22 and say that "seedtime and harvest" could be interpreted as "seed, time, and harvest." In other words, when we plant something, it always takes time for the harvest to mature—whether it is good or bad fruit.

Occasionally, we have the opportunity to see immediate results from what we've planted, but more often than not, it takes many seasons to see the full outcome of our choices. Sometimes we don't even see the results in our lifetime. Generations may pass before there is a complete return of all of our sowing—good or bad.

By now, we have an understanding that whatever is planted will grow. If we plant grape seeds, we're not going to get cantaloupe; we'll get grapes. As a reminder, on Day 2 of Session 2, we read about the differences in good and bad fruit (Matthew 7:15-23), but now let's take another look.

Read Luke 6:43-45:

A good person produces what?

A bad person produces what?

What you say comes from where?

Dig Deeper

A Generation is all of the people born and living at around the same time (approximately 20-30 years), and it includes the time when children are born, grow up, become adults, and have their own children.
Baby Boomers: 1946-1964
Gen X: 1965-1980
Gen Y: 1981-1996
Gen Z: 1997-2015[17]

Though we may profess with our mouths that Jesus is Lord, do our actions look like His? It's important that we be aware of the fruit we are producing, whether with our actions or our words. In addition, Philippians 2:12-13 says we are to "work out your own salvation with fear and trembling, for it is God who works in you, both to will and to work for his good pleasure" (NIV).

What does "work out your own salvation" mean?

Charles Spurgeon once said this about true faith and the fruit we bear:

> *The children of God are a holy people, washed, purged, sanctified, and made zealous for good works; and he who talks about faith, and has no works to prove that his faith is a living faith, lies to himself and lies before God. It is faith that saves us, not works, but the faith that saves us always produces works: it renews the heart, changes the character, influences the motives, and is the means in the hand of God of making the man a new creature in Christ Jesus.*[18]

UNDERLINE ALL the things Spurgeon said faith produces in us.

Our fruit should be evidence of a life lived for the Lord, and the faith that saves us should always produce these good works. Thus, though we are justified through the death of Christ (and this justification was imputed—or given freely—to us), we are still called to work out our salvation. This is known as *sanctification*, and it always follows justification. As Spurgeon said, "Remember that you are perfect in Christ Jesus and accepted in the Beloved, but, at the same time, give glory to the Holy Spirit, and remember that you are not yet perfect in holiness, but that the Spirit's work is to be carried on and will be carried on all the days of your life."[19]

To put it another way, after receiving the free gift of God's salvation, we do our part to work out our salvation and always bear good, abundant fruit until we are called home to Heaven.

Now turn to the following verses and fill in the blanks. (I used the NIV.)

Ephesians 4:30
"And do not_____the_____ _____of God, with whom you were sealed for the day of redemption."

1 John 1:9
"If we_____ our sins, he is faithful and just and will_____us our sins and_____us from all unrighteousness."

Ask the Lord to reveal anything you need to confess that is grieving the Holy Spirit. If there is anything you felt convicted about, take some time now to repent. God is faithful and just. He will forgive us and purify us, so we can continue to live a life without any hindrance.

Psalm 119:59-60
"I have _____ my ways and have _____ my steps to your statutes. I will hasten and not delay to _____ your commands."

Once you've examined your heart and motivations and sought forgiveness on anything that hinders your relationship with God, turn your focus back to living a life that pleases our Father.

CONTINUE SOWING IN THE SPIRIT

Though we began talking about sowing seeds of the Spirit, we also have to look at the dangers of sowing in our flesh, as this will be our constant battle in life—the flesh. We war against what we know we should do and against our carnal selves. However, this perpetual battle doesn't make us any less valuable to the Lord. Even the apostle Paul wrote about what he knew he should do and the constant struggle of what his flesh continued to do (Romans 7:14-25).

This is evidence of our humanity—our sin nature and the fact that we will work out our salvation until the day we die.

Ultimately, what we plant (the seeds of the Spirit or of the flesh), where we plant it (the soil), and when we plant it (the season) matter.

PHYSICAL AND SPIRITUAL SEASONS

You may live in an area where you don't experience drastic climate changes, but we can all understand that the seasons we experience physically parallel the seasons we experience spiritually. Reflecting on the seasons helps us make sense of where we are in our fruit-bearing process.

Ecclesiastes 3:11 says that God has made everything <u>beautiful</u> and <u>appropriate</u> <u>in</u> <u>its</u> <u>time</u>. That means that no matter what season you may be going through, God is ultimately in control. Realizing that truth helps us endure because, no matter what season we're in, seasons are NORMAL, seasons are NOT FOREVER, and seasons WILL CHANGE.

And remember, <u>God's timing is perfect</u>.

In order for us to fully experience His peace throughout the seasons of life, we have to discern, accept, and come to appreciate this fact. Reconciling ourselves to God's timing is essential to avoiding feelings of despair, frustration, and outright rebellion. Submission to the sovereign plan of our Heavenly Father will help those of us who want to "help" Him hurry things along or move ahead of His guidance. As we read earlier, *to everything, turn, turn, turn, there is a season, turn, turn, turn, a time for every purpose under Heaven.* As Christ's followers, we *will* journey through specific seasons in our lives.

As we end this day, I am going to take you through each season, and I want you to ask where you find yourself today.

Dig Deeper

Dormancy comes from the Latin word *dormire*, which means "to sleep."[20]

WINTER

In nature, winter, while beautiful in its own way, is a long, dreary, and seemingly lifeless season. For certain plants, when temperatures markedly decrease, photosynthesis is inhibited and plants enter a time of dormancy so cold weather, ice, and snow do not harm them.

When their leaves have fallen off and the plants turn brown and appear dead, the nutrients of the plant are actually being stored internally. In winter, most plants are pruned so that all the stored energy is directed where it needs to go; then, in the springtime, the plant becomes healthy, vibrant, and has the optimal chance for growth and development. Thus, during the winter months, plants are alive but are not actively growing. This is a period when growth, development, and physical activity are temporarily stopped.

Spiritually, this season can be difficult. Those "winters" in our lives can make us feel like God is being silent. We may feel stagnant and unable to see any progress. Life feels dark, cloudy, and cold. From the outside, we might even feel that we appear spiritually dead yet are still enduring some of the pruning process.

During this season, it's difficult but necessary to allow God to make changes in us. It's a time for storing up energy, strengthening, and maturing our spirit. This season can be a time of rest, introspection, and examining our hearts and motivations. During times of dormancy, we have to realize that God is still working in us because He desires to transform us, making us more like Him. We just have to let Him do His work.

Read Psalm 23:2-3. What does it say the Lord does for us?

Turn to Psalm 37:7. Write what two things we are told to do:

1.

2.

Philippians 1:6 says, "And I am sure that God, who began the good work within you will
_____."

Sometimes the Lord has to make us lie down and enter a season of rest, and we have to do our part just to be still and wait patiently because, ultimately, His promises are guaranteed. He will finish all that He began.

SPRING

In nature, spring is a time of cleansing and restoration from the difficult days of winter. After a time of depression and barrenness, spring brings new life. It is a time of transition and new growth. Refreshing rains come, along with scattered thunderstorms and even more pruning.

This is the season when most flowering plants bloom, and this powerful act of nature symbolizes the revival of life—the ground physically springs forth! The earth begins its annual tilt toward the sun, and the daylight hours increase in length.

In a spiritual sense, this season can bring a time of joy and refreshment after dormancy and hardship. Isn't it fitting that Jesus' own resurrection occurred in the spring?[21] It is the ultimate example of life renewed! While this season brings new and exciting experiences, it is not without the pruning of our flesh—a necessary, but unpleasant, time when God shapes and molds us to look more like Him.

Write Song of Solomon 2:11-12 here:

Dig Deeper

Following Passover, Jesus' body rested in the tomb on the Sabbath and rose from the dead on the Feast of Firstfruits (the Sunday after Passover—see Leviticus 23:9-14).

Ezekiel 34:26 says, "I will make them and the places surrounding my hill a blessing. I will send down showers in season; there will be showers of _____" (NIV).

Look up Psalm 104:30. What does the Lord do to the earth?

SUMMER

Regardless of where you live, summer is the warmest, and often the driest, season of the year. Of the four seasons, summer has the longest days and shortest nights. It's the time of greatest plant growth and maturity. Because of this, there's a need for more water than usual to sustain plant life.

In a spiritual sense, you may see abundant fruit in this season. Maybe your ministry is flourishing, you're truly enjoying life, and you're seeing growth and maturity in all the work in which you've invested. But you must not forget, that although the summer sun radiates life, it can also burn. You've got to protect yourself from drying and burning out. You've got to stay hydrated, and the way to do that is to stay watered by The Word of the Lord. This can be a time of needing more spiritual food than usual to stay replenished. If you protect yourself well during this season, you may come out stronger than ever before.

Read Psalm 63:1-5. As David cries out to God, where does he find himself, and what does he do?

AUTUMN

Maybe it's because I was born in the fall, but I always have a profound appreciation for the splendor of this season. Pumpkins, sweater weather, hayrides, Thanksgiving, and all the glorious scents bring me immense joy.

In this season, the sheer beauty of the leaves changing color is a reminder that the vegetation has lived its full life, and what doesn't fall away must be cut away and pruned again. The cooler weather provides a much-needed reprieve from the harshness of summer's heat, and we witness the cycle continuing as the earth prepares for winter. Leaves fall from trees, and we know that another time of transition is approaching. Fall is also marked as a time of harvest, a gathering of the fruit of the season, and we mustn't forget that either.

Spiritually, this season is a time of change too, a beautiful and inevitable one. It's the time for more correction and shaping from God as He prepares us for the long winter. We may have to let go of anything hindering our relationship with God and let it fall away from us. In this, we recognize the impermanence of all things. But in God's graciousness, we're able to celebrate the harvest before we settle into the still and solace of the cold months ahead. Our pace slows, we rest, and we spend time discerning where we've been and where we're headed.

In the end, the cycle of seasons in nature is the perfect metaphor for the cycle of our Christian walk. The only thing constant is change, and that's what working out our salvation looks like: Seasons of Change.

I don't know about you, but I'm grateful that I'm not where I once was. While I still await much more growth and maturity, I'm thankful I'm not where I began. This is sanctification and what walking with Jesus looks like—changing how we think and act in order to be more like Him. Through every season of life, we grow and learn, and little by little, we are able to produce a rich and overflowing harvest. Then, after each harvest, we'll turn to another season and begin again.

As we close today, what season are YOU in and why?

Remember, Dear Friend, our God is forever faithful no matter your season.

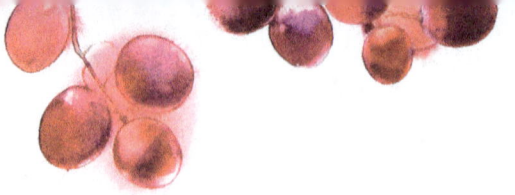

Day 5:
THE SURROUNDINGS

Can I be honest with you? I had the perfect outline of what I wanted to write for this day, and then the Lord took me on a journey—and it wasn't a particularly joy-filled one.

It started with my four-year-old daughter, Nora.

It was a Sunday morning, and I was helping my mother work with the preschoolers at our church for the upcoming Christmas program. During this time, I had the unique opportunity to witness my Nora truly experience rejection—a rejection that brought her to tears. Now granted, it was a four-year-old's rejection, but even at that young age, we still feel the sting of not belonging or being unwanted.

As we worked through our montage of Christmas songs, Nora was holding hands with one of her little girlfriends when another girl came into the mix. The child who'd been holding Nora's hand abruptly cast her hand aside, pushed her out of the way, and said she couldn't stand there anymore. Then this child went on to hold the new girl's hand. Nora stood alone as big tears streamed down from her dark, chocolatey-brown eyes and poured out over her tiny face.

She struggled to find a spot where no one would see her crying and quickly tried to wipe her face with the back of her arm. I could see her lip quivering as she looked to me for comfort and reassurance. Thankfully, Mimi (my mother) immediately stepped in, gently moved Nora, and swiftly (but gently) told the other girl, "Nora didn't want to hold your hand anyway." Then, Mimi turned to Nora and said, "Here, you can hold *her* hand," and the outstretched hand of a smiling, five-year-old Amelia helped to soften the blow of Nora's hurt heart. It definitely helps when your grandmother is in charge, but on that day, my mother won major Mimi points! Still, in those brief moments, my heart truly hurt for my baby because rejection at *any* age stings, whether you're four, forty, or eighty-four.

In the end, Nora didn't need to subject herself to holding the hand of someone who was waiting for a better offer, and she didn't need the fickle friendship of someone who was not truly interested in investing in her. I know these lessons will continue to resurface in her life, and I pray God gives me the grace to explain to all three of my children that who you surround yourself with matters.

Though the trials of childhood and adolescence are seemingly simple and insignificant, to that child, in that moment, they are monumental, and the sting of the rejection is very real.

I think the reason I hurt so much for Nora was that I could relate. I'd also been feeling disconnected from friends I had once considered close. As we discussed in yesterday's study time, I personally had the sense that I was entering into a new season of life with so many things: friends, family, ministry, and more.

My role in local ministry was shifting, and I was transitioning into a quiet place of preparation. Pieces of me and some of the fruit I'd produced had been harvested, but other things had fallen off like withered, dry leaves in autumn because they'd served their purpose for that season of my life, and they were finished. I hunkered down, being made ready for a seemingly long winter season. And if I'm completely honest, it was different, it was difficult, and it was, at times, uncomfortable.

Has there ever been a time in your life when you felt the sting of rejection from a one-sided friendship? If so, can you briefly describe what happened and how it made you feel?

During this time of transition, I truly had to adjust my perspective on more than one occasion and check the motivation of my heart. I had to pray and ask the Lord to help me with my pride. I had to purpose in my spirit not to take offense and work to give others the benefit of the doubt so that bitterness and resentment would not creep in and take hold.

During this season, I read something profound in Lysa TerKeurst's book *Uninvited*. She wrote, "There is something wonderfully sacred that happens when a girl chooses to realize that being set aside is actually God's call for her to be set apart."[22] This was a complete "ah-ha moment," and I knew I was in the midst of all the uncertainty for a reason. I was going through something—a specific season—for a divine, beautiful, and appropriate purpose.

Dear Friend, something happens when we're *set apart*. We have the opportunity to see our surroundings for <u>what</u> they truly are and for <u>who</u> they include.

Has there ever been a time—past or present—when you have felt set apart or set aside?

Can you look at the situation with the wisdom of hindsight to see why God may have allowed it to happen?

Sometimes we go through those painful situations because the Lord knows we need to be set apart for something different or even something greater. If we stay, we will never grow or thrive, and the process of bearing our fruit will be hindered.

SET APART IN THE SCRIPTURES

Now I want to turn your attention to some biblical examples of this.

The entire book of Nehemiah is a compilation of Nehemiah's memoirs, and it reads like a story. It begins with an introduction to Nehemiah. He was a Jew born in exile, living as a servant (a cupbearer) to the king of Persia, King Artaxerxes. He was likely living in the lap of luxury in the King's palace when he found out the people of Jerusalem were in great trouble and distress. The walls of their city had been torn down, and their gates had been burned down as well. As a result, Nehemiah felt a deep call in his spirit to rebuild the walls and, subsequently, gained divine favor from the King to go on a reconnaissance mission that eventually ended in rebuilding and restoring the wall. In a nutshell, King Nebuchadnezzar had destroyed Jerusalem 152 years before Nehemiah's time, but once Nehemiah had his dream and began walking out his calling, the walls were finished in just 52 days (Nehemiah 6:15)!

I've just given the "CliffsNotes" version of the story, so I encourage you to take the time to read the entire book. Still, for the purposes of our study time, turn with me now to Nehemiah 4:1-4.

What was Nehemiah experiencing?

The lesson here is that not everyone is for you.

There are people whom you should NEVER allow permission to speak into your life. Even Nehemiah had those who opposed what he was doing—his calling. Maybe you have some "friends" or influencers whom you've allowed access into your life who are not in your corner. Perhaps you need to change your surroundings and enlist the support of people who are FOR you, not against you.

But maybe you don't know how to do this. Some of these "friends" have likely been a part of your life for so long that you're unsure how to establish a new boundary with them. Let's look to see how Nehemiah handled this.

Turn to Nehemiah 4:4 (NLT). What are the first three words of this verse?

1.   2.   3.

Now read Nehemiah 4:9. What two things did they do?

1.   2.

First, they prayed. But they didn't stop at praying. Then, they set a guard over the wall.

Sometimes you have to guard your heart to protect yourself. The very same concept is true when we consider the fruit-bearing process. We have to consider environmental factors because our surroundings have both a direct and indirect impact on the fruit we bear. We will discuss this in more detail later in the study, but sometimes you have to do specific things to protect yourself and your fruit. Who and what we surround ourselves with will affect the outcome of our harvest.

Maybe you can relate to this. I've had to continuously learn the lesson that it is vital to my physical, mental, emotional, and spiritual well-being to surround myself with people who have a healthy influence on my life. Though people may not be purposefully against you, when you summarize the effect they have upon you, it is negative. Therefore, you recognize certain things about their influence that spur you to create better boundaries (or set a guard over yourself) when it comes to your relationship with them.

Turn to Proverbs 4:23. Write it here:

EXAMINING OUR SURROUNDINGS

Now I'm going to have you work through an exercise related to YOUR SURROUNDINGS.

I want you to think about who is in your circle of influence. Then complete the diagram below. Fill in the names of those who comprise your intimate and close relationships, those who are your acquaintances, and those who are other social influencers (outside of your circle).

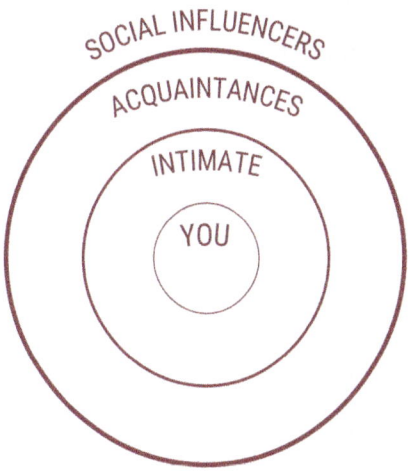

SOCIAL INFLUENCERS
ACQUAINTANCES
INTIMATE
YOU

My guess is that you don't have too many names written in your inner circle.

Go ahead and take some time to specifically think through the names/relationships in your "Intimate and Close Relationships" circle and answer the following questions about them:

1. **Are they takers or givers?** (Are you overcome with dread or joy when you see their name on your phone?)

2. **Is there reciprocity in your relationship(s)?**

3. **Do they challenge you to grow in your relationship with the Lord?**

4. **Do they challenge and encourage you to find and fulfill your calling?**

5. **Do you pray together?**

6. **Do you feel "filled up" or "drained" when you are together?**

7. **Would you go to this person in a crisis or difficult time?**

8. **Would they give you godly counsel?**

9. **Have they come to you in a crisis or difficult time? If so, how frequently?**

If, after completing this list, you feel confident that you have a tribe of people who are for you and have your best interests at heart, then consider yourself blessed. Conversely, if you've completed this list, feel a bit dejected, and aren't quite sure what to do next, let's look to the perfect model that Jesus gave us during His time here on earth.

Jesus definitely surrounded Himself with specific people during specific times, and they were people whom He sought out and chose purposefully. He did not select His closest companions haphazardly.

Turn to the following verses and FILL IN the chart:

	Setting/Situation	Individuals with Jesus
Luke 6:12-16		
Luke 8:1-3		
Matthew 17:1		
Mark 14:32-34		
John 19:26-27		

Jesus purposefully selected specific disciples for certain moments in His life, even to the point of entrusting the care of His own mother to John ("the disciple whom he loved") from the cross as he hung there dying.

Our surroundings matter. They impact us. They affect the soil, the seed, and, ultimately, the fruit we bear.

If, at the end of this day, you're still feeling at a loss for a lack of nourishing connections, I encourage you to ask the Lord for help. Ask Him to bring godly people into your life. He will help you enlist the support of those who will challenge you to grow in your faith, be there for you when you need them, pray with you and for you, and speak the truth in love.

Remember, God knows our desire to be known and loved.

Dig Deeper

Allelopathic plants can chemically impede the growth of competing plants. Certain plants just don't like each other and should never be planted together.[23]

He made us for companionship, but there is also personal accountability in a prayer like this. There's a famous quotation by Ralph Waldo Emerson that says, "The only way to have a friend is to be one." We cannot expect the perfect friend to miraculously appear, and instantly, become one of our besties. We have to be a bit brave and put ourselves out there.

What's ONE thing you can do TODAY or this week to engage a new or old friend?

Think of TWO people to whom you will purposely reach out THIS WEEK.

1.   2.

If you're feeling set aside and alone, remember that it may just be for your good. Talk to the Lord and ask Him to show you areas of your life that you may need to let go of—maybe a fickle friendship or a relationship that is not edifying or uplifting. You might just be set apart because you're being prepared for something different and greater than your mind could even comprehend.

I am excited for you! I am excited to see how the Lord works through you to develop all that He has desired for you and from you! As we close this week, let's pray.

Heavenly Father, we thank You for helping us to recognize that who and what we surround ourselves with has an impact on our calling. Please give us the grace to steward those relationships well. Thank You, Lord, for the work You are doing within us. We love You, and we desire to honor You with our lives. It's in Your precious and holy name we pray. Amen!

HOW IS IT PLANTED?
from generation to generation...

BE *fruitful*

Here are this week's ways to DIVE DEEPER by yourself, with family, or with friends.

DISCUSS

This week we discussed how fruit is planted. Using the prompts below, start a discussion to solidify the learning!

- Retell the story of Jephthah from Judges 11. (Use the study questions to discuss lessons learned.)
- Is it necessary to be true to your word?
- Do *you* keep your promises?
- Are there any areas where you need to be better about keeping your commitments?
- Review Zechariah 4:10. Do you have a dream to do something or be something? How could you begin?
- Discuss the four soils in the Mark 4:1-9 parable.
- What comes from planting "good" or "bad" seed?
- How do those around you influence you?

DISCOVER

Visit a local farmer's market.

- Talk to the farmers about their crop. Ask them questions: How long have you been farming? What do you love most about being a farmer? What's the most challenging thing about farming?
- Try some of the market produce. Take a new-to-you fruit or vegetable home to try!

Go to a local metro park or your neighborhood park. Take a nature hike and explore. Look for all of the seeds you can find. You can even put some tape around your wrists (sticky side out) and stick your findings to yourself!

FOR THE KIDS

- "Farmer Plants the Seeds" https://youtu.be/cRhGOdqWIIo
- "Peep and the Big Wide World: Peep Plants a Seed" https://youtu.be/Yxs7P7LWzDg

DESIGN

Using the prompts below, start creating your masterpieces!

Make grape seed oil hand cream:

- You'll need 3 tbsp beeswax, ½ cup grapeseed oil, 2 tsp coconut oil, 4 Tbsp water, and 15-20 drops of your favorite essential oil (e.g., lemon or lavender).
- Instructions: In a double boiler over low-medium heat, melt the beeswax and add grapeseed and coconut oil. Mix everything well. Let it cool slightly and blend or whisk in the water. Put it in an airtight container and enjoy!

Start a garden from your kitchen:

- Use your scraps! You can use seeds from almost any vegetable you eat to start a new garden!
- Use your pantry! Find spices/beans that you can use as seed starters—many dried spices/beans can sprout new life!

If you already have a garden, go out and pull your weeds! If you are ready to start a garden, you'll have to begin by preparing the soil. Gather your supplies and get outside!

DIG IN

READ

- Visit your local library for books on seeds.
- For children, here are few books my kids enjoyed:
  - *A Seed is Sleepy* by Dianna Hutts Aston
  - *Berries, Nuts, and Seeds (Take Along Guides)* by Diane Burns
  - *The Bad Seed* and *The Cool Bean* by Jory John

REVIEW

- *Mishchah* (the physical anointing)
- *Charisma* (the spiritual anointing)
- Gethsemane: "press of oil."
- Kidron: "mournful, dark, dusky place."
- Messiah: "the anointed one."

HOW IS IT PLANTED?
from harvest to table...

BE *fruitful*

Whether you're cooking for one or having a potluck, enjoy the process of artfully putting the ingredients together to make a delicious masterpiece. Be encouraged to consider the elements of your week-long study that apply to the recipe you are preparing.

DELICIOUS DELIGHTS

SEED SALAD

Serves 6-8

INGREDIENTS FOR THE SALAD

- 1 (15-ounce) can cannellini beans, rinsed and drained
- 1 (15-ounce) can kidney beans, rinsed and drained
- 1 (15-ounce) can garbanzo beans, rinsed and drained
- 1 (15-ounce) can black beans, rinsed and drained
- ½ red onion, finely chopped (about ¾ cup), soaked in water to take the edge off the onion
- 2 celery stalks, finely chopped (about 1 cup)
- 1 cup loosely packed, fresh, finely chopped flat-leaf parsley
- 2 Tbsp hemp seed
- 1 tsp fresh finely chopped rosemary

INGREDIENTS FOR THE DRESSING:

- ¼ cup apple cider vinegar
- ¼ cup granulated sugar (more or less to taste)
- 3 Tbsp extra virgin olive oil
- ½ tsp salt
- ¼ tsp black pepper

INSTRUCTIONS

1. In a large bowl, combine the three different types of beans, celery, onion (drained of soaking water), parsley, hemp seed, and rosemary.
2. In a separate small bowl, whisk together the vinegar, sugar, olive oil, salt, and pepper. Add the dressing to the beans. Toss to coat.
3. Transfer the salad to the refrigerator for several hours to allow the beans to soak up the flavor of the dressing as they chill. Let the ingredients approach room temperature to serve.

CHOCOLATE CHIA SEED PUDDING

Serves 4

INGREDIENTS

- 2 cups unsweetened vanilla soy, hemp, or almond milk
- 4 Medjool dates or 8 regular dates, pitted
- 3 Tbsp natural cocoa powder
- ½ tsp alcohol-free vanilla extract
- ½ cup chia seeds
- ½ cup fresh berries of choice

INSTRUCTIONS

- Blend milk, dates, cocoa powder, vanilla and ¼ of the chia seeds in a high-powered blender.
- Stir in the remaining chia seeds.
- Refrigerate for 15 minutes and stir again to distribute the seeds evenly.
- Top with fresh berries.

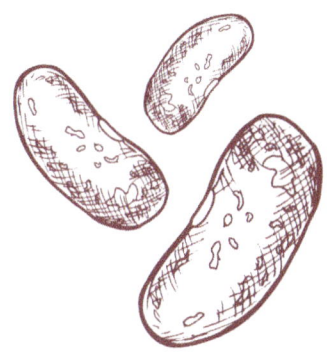

Session 4
HOW IS IT PRODUCED?

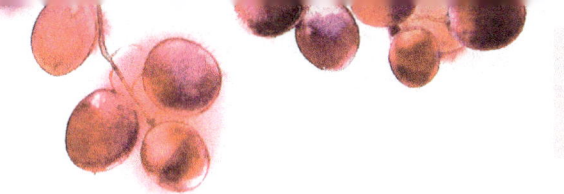

Session 4
VIDEO TEACHING

KEY VERSE

"Most important of all, continue to show deep love for each other, for love covers a multitude of sins" (1 Peter 4:8, NLT).

THE BIG IDEA

Like leaves on a grapevine, we have to be lifted up for maximum exposure so we can produce healthy fruit.

Shaded leaves are NOT good for the plant because they:

- _____ the plant's stored energy.
- Keep the grapes from _____ evenly.
- Can become the perfect environment for grape-loving _____.
- Increase the _____ to mold, fungus, rot, and other plant diseases.

Adam and Eve's first response to their sin was _____ and _____. They tried to use _____ and _____ to cover themselves and their shame.

Genesis 3:21 tells us, "And the Lord God made _____ from _____ _____ for Adam and his wife."

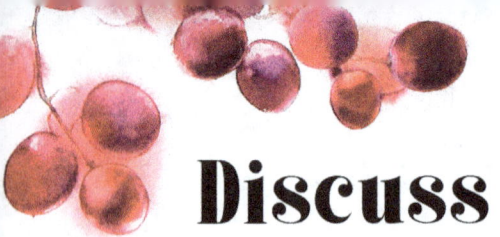

Discuss

Have you ever stolen anything?   If so, what did you steal and why?

Can you relate to finding relief when the truth is exposed—even if the truth is painful?

Why do you think there's so much tension between being truthful and extending love?

Why do you think we struggle to give both?

Day 1:
THE CANOPY

I remember summers of lying out by the pool as I slathered myself in Panama Jack and baby oil with the sole intention of broiling my skin under the sun. My girlfriends and I would stay outside for hours, crisping ourselves to a hue of bright lobster-red, hoping we'd eventually turn golden brown. Now, at forty-something, I am paying big money on all sorts of lotions and creams to reverse the signs of all the sun damage I accumulated during my ignorant youth. Let this be a warning to you twenty-somethings: Use SPF and use it liberally!

But we know the sun isn't all bad. We actually need it to survive. Without getting too scientific, the sun helps our bodies produce Vitamin D, which our bodies require for cellular growth and hormone production. Things such as our bone structure and emotional well-being are directly affected by the sun as well!

Just as our physical bodies need the sun, the earth needs the sun too. As our planet rotates around the sun, days and nights, seasons, and climates are all determined. Even a preschooler can tell you plants need sunlight to grow.

Now let's turn back to John 15:5 and fill in the blanks:

Jesus is the _____.

We are the _____.

Because Jesus described Himself as a grapevine and compared us to its branches, I wanted to learn more about this specific plant. I wanted to understand *why* He would use a grapevine for this unique lesson that is forever captured in the pages of His Holy Word. So as any reasonable researcher does, I went to the library and checked out as many "Vineyards for Dummies"-like books I could find. I poured over online articles and read blogs and other resources to educate the novice gardener on beginning a vineyard.

One summer, I even went to a local vineyard and saw the vines with my own eyes. The landscape was breathtaking, and I immediately had an intense appreciation for all of the time and labor that went into the process of cultivating and sustaining this specific crop. I spoke to a local vinedresser and listened to his fascinating stories. The vineyard was his livelihood and his life. Just like you'd expect from a *sodbuster*, everything he did was done with the vineyard in mind. One thing he said that concurred with all of my other research was that <u>sunlight</u> is the <u>most crucial thing</u> for grapevines.

Like most plants, grapes need sunlight in order to undergo photosynthesis. This is the process by which the green tissues of the plant (primarily the leaves) absorb energy from the sun to convert carbon dioxide (CO_2) to sugar. The vine then stores this sugar in its woody tissue in the form of carbohydrates or starch. The following year, these carbohydrates fuel the growth of the vine and the development of fruit.[1]

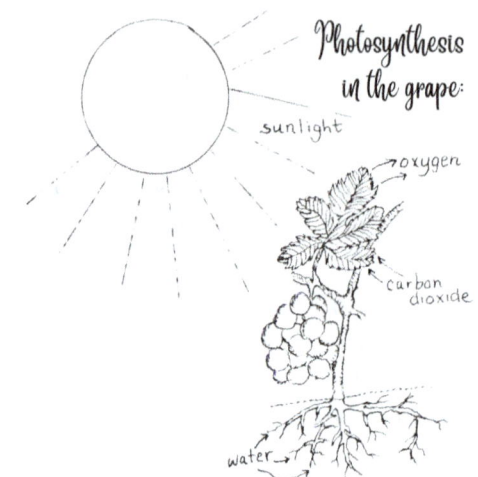

Photosynthesis in the grape:
sunlight
oxygen
carbon dioxide
water

If you've ever seen a vineyard, you may have noticed the vines are almost always on open land—or fields—where no other vegetation or structure prevents them from maximum sun exposure. Nothing can shade the vineyard. Shaded leaves are not good for the plant because they drain its stored energy. I learned that the vines need a minimum of eight hours of sunlight during the growing season, and an open canopy (the above-ground portion of the plant) allows the sun to reach the most leaves and improves the health of the entire vine.

Ultimately, the sodbuster's goal in managing the canopy is increased exposure. Through pruning and positioning, leaves are either removed or trained to help the plant produce the optimal harvest. When pruning and positioning are performed correctly, grapes can ripen evenly as sunburn, frost, mold, and disease spread can be prevented.

What words or thoughts come to your mind when you think of "exposure"?

What keeps us from wanting to be exposed?

Dig Deeper
When trained on the trellis, the vine experiences tension as it's placed in the optimal position to open the canopy and provide ideal exposure.[2]

For people, exposure requires vulnerability, and it's uncomfortable for things to be brought out into the open. It goes against our nature to be "naked" and uncovered.

Turn to Genesis 3:25.

In the perfection of the Garden, void of sin, Adam and Eve were both _____ but NOT _____.

Now turn to Genesis 3:6-8. What did Adam and Eve do after sinning?

©Alinonora /Adobe Stock

Luke 8:17 tells us, "For all that is secret will eventually be brought into the open, and everything that is concealed will be brought to light and made known to all" (NLT).

UNDERLINE what happens to all that is secret or concealed.

Look ahead to Genesis 3:21. What did God do for Adam and Eve?

Dig Deeper
The word for "hid" in Genesis 3:8 is *chaba* (khaw-baw'), and it means to withdraw or hide.[3]

Ever since the fall, our natural response has been to conceal sin and keep it covered.

Once their eyes were open to their nakedness, Adam and Eve tried to use leaves and trees to cover themselves and their shame. But due to His love and mercy, God provided an atonement before removing them from Eden. He replaced their man-made attempts to hide their sin. He provided a sacrifice. He made a covering. We aren't told what animal God used or how it was killed, but His divine restitution was a beautiful foreshadowing of things to come.

From the Old to New Testament, atoning for the redemption of sins became a recurring theme. Because Jesus loved us so much, He came into this world, sacrificed His life, and became the ultimate substitutionary atonement for the sin of humanity.

Now turn to 1 Peter 4:8. What does love do?

It can be difficult for us to fully understand how exposing sin leads to a covering of love. Love doesn't conceal to hide or to be secretive. Rather, it envelops us tenderly and compassionately to set us free from sin and shame. From Eden to Calvary, we see this love—this perfect love—covering us in every way. Still, even though we know we've been released from the ultimate consequence of our sin, we can struggle with not paying the penance.

GOD'S LOVING GRACE

We know that one way God expresses His love towards us is through His saving us from our sins. As Ephesians 2:8-9 says, "God saved you by his grace when you believed. And you can't take credit for this; it is a gift from God" (NLT).

"Grace" is a term we often hear, especially in the Christian world. Without looking it up, how would you define it?

Dig Deeper

The word describing what love does is *kaluptó* (kal-oop'-to). It means "to cover, veil, conceal, envelop or be covered over."[5]

In Greek, the word for grace is *charis* (khä'-res), and I never tire of reading the definition. It means "God freely extending Himself (His favor, grace), reaching (inclining) to people because He is disposed to bless (be near) them."[4] This means that grace is a FREE gift from God, and we did NOTHING to earn it. It is freely given to us through salvation, and Jesus' death on the cross allows us to receive grace (the unmerited favor of the Lord).

Do you struggle with extending grace to yourself? If so, why?

I think about my own journey with the Lord and how He has forgiven me of so much. I remember a great deal of my past with shame and regret, but through His grace, mercy, and love, I am redeemed, justified, and made thoroughly whole. I deserve nothing but an eternity in hell, yet through Christ's death on the cross, He took all my sin and cast it as far as the East is from the West (Psalm 103:12). The tariff for my transgressions has been paid in full.

I don't want you to miss this moment. If you doubt your salvation in any way, The Word says in Romans 10:9-10, "If you declare with your mouth, 'Jesus is Lord,' and believe in your heart that God raised him from the dead, you will be saved. For it is with your heart that you believe and are justified, and it is with your mouth that you profess your faith and are saved" (NIV).

There aren't specific words to recite, but if you feel the stirring in your heart to respond in some way, here are words for you to pray out loud:

Jesus, today I invite you to come into my life. Forgive me of my sin. I believe that you are Lord and that You died for me so I could live for You. It's in Your name that I pray. Amen.

This is single-handedly the *most* important prayer you'll ever pray, and if you just prayed this simple prayer, know that every angel in Heaven is rejoicing (Luke 15:10) and I want to hear about it too!

Now let's turn to Romans 10:13 (ESV) and fill in the blank:

"For_____who calls on the name of the Lord will be saved."

Now read 2 Corinthians 5:17 (ESV) and fill in the blank:

"Therefore, if_____is in Christ, he is a new creation. The old has passed away; behold, the new has come."

This means that if you're an everyone or an anyone, YOU are entitled to the *charis* of God. Therefore, if the God of the Universe gave His one and only Son to die for YOU and to forgive YOU of all of your sin and unrighteousness, who are you to NOT forgive YOURSELF?

Maybe you've come to the point in your walk with the Lord where you understand that His grace is sufficient for you and His power is perfected in your weakness (2 Corinthians 12:9), but what about when it comes to extending that same grace to others?

Why are we sometimes so hesitant to extend grace to others?

If you're anything like me, you're amazed at His patience and the fact that His forgiveness is always available and His grace is abundant. However, when I think about the directive in 2 Peter 3:18, sometimes I want to be whiney and dig my heels in. I want to say, "But, God, so-and-so has done this same thing to me over and over again; it's just not fair." Or, "Lord, I am sick and tired of always being the one to apologize first." And how about, "God, *they* were wrong. I should NOT have to give them any grace." As Amos 5:24 says, "But let justice roll on like a river, righteousness like a never-failing stream!" (NIV). That's what I get fixated on—wanting rivers of justice to roll over those who have wronged me!

Turn to 2 Corinthians 1:3-4.

Whom does the "Father of compassion" and the "God of all comfort" comfort first?

Why does He comfort *us* first?

We carry the story of our hurts so we can turn around and use all of it—the pain and sorrow—to give God glory. He helps us first, so we can help someone else with what we've come through. He extends grace to us first, so we can turn around and be gracious and forgive those with the same graciousness and forgiveness we ourselves have received from God.

Are you dealing with any situations where you are truly struggling to give grace to someone?

Let's be honest; if we're not struggling with this today, we probably will be tomorrow!

Now turn to Colossians 3:13. Summarize the verse in your own words here:

Do you remember the word *charisma* from our study of The Seed? This is the spiritual anointing of the gift of grace through the supernatural presence of the Holy Spirit. If we're abiding in Him and He in us (John 15:5), then we are equipped (through the power of the Holy Spirit) to be like Christ and extend grace to others—whether they deserve it or not. Giving grace to another person is simply to forgive them, unconditionally, just as God forgave us through Christ.

It's difficult to think this way, but just as we don't deserve God's forgiveness, someone you know may not deserve yours. I hate to break it to you—it doesn't matter if you feel like forgiving others. We're still commanded to forgive others and grow in grace. At the same time, I do not want to oversimplify this process. Some of us have been truly hurt and bear deep, deep scars. Though we are all called to forgive, the Lord never gives us an exact timetable for forgiveness. I will tell you this though: The sooner I give it over to God, the better I feel. When I'm experiencing the acute pain of rejection or hurts brought on by the hand of another and ask the Lord to help me see this person as He does and to remind my spirit that it's not a fleshly battle, I am bathed in a peace that is only from God. When that happens, my spirit is convicted because I have to acknowledge that I've hurt others too—both knowingly and unknowingly—because we're all sinners and we all offend (Romans 3:23). What sets us apart is our response to offense. Will we choose to move forward and extend grace to those who offend us?

EXTENDING GRACE TO OTHERS

Let's look at that specific situation/person that you mentioned earlier. With the help of the Holy Spirit, consider how YOU can extend grace and forgiveness.

If nothing comes to mind or if you're really fighting against your flesh, stop right now and ask the Lord to lead you. Seek Him first, and He will give you the steps to offer grace and forgiveness.

How is the Holy Spirit prompting you to extend grace and forgive? Write your thoughts here:

Well done. I know that was challenging because it's challenging for <u>all</u> of us. It goes against our human nature to forgive someone who has offended us. It is counter-cultural to be wronged and to extend mercy, but this is how we grow in grace.

Now read Hebrews 12:14-15.

What are we first instructed to do? (v 14)

What's the consequence of failing to follow this instruction? (v 15)

The opposite of forgiveness can become tragic because there is no middle ground. We either apply God's grace or we become corrupted by the "poisonous root of bitterness" (NLT). This root of bitterness doesn't destroy the other person. Instead, it wreaks havoc on us from the inside, and we, in turn, negatively affect everyone else.

So, let me ask you this: Have you tried to seek peace in your difficult relationships? Have you prayed for those who have offended you as much as you've complained or talked about them? You can't get over an offense if you continue to blather on about it. Some of us need to stop repeating the wrongs done to us (in our minds or out loud) because we can't walk in forgiveness and grace and still be "dishing dirt" on other people.

To see a fuller picture of the cause and effect of choosing whether to forgive, I've summarized some key verses on the importance of forgiveness:

- The Father won't forgive our sins if we don't forgive other people (Matthew 6:14-15).

- Forgiveness keeps Satan from getting an advantage over us (2 Corinthians 2:10-11).

- If we forgive others, God will forgive us (Mark 11:25).

- Letting the sun go down on our anger gives the enemy a foothold (Ephesians 4:26-27).

- Pray for and love your enemies because great is your reward (Luke 6:27-28; 35).

- Love covers offenses (Proverbs 17:9).

Turn to John 3:20-21. What are your key takeaways from these verses?

Now turn to John 8:12.

    What does Jesus say He is?

    If we choose to follow Him, what is His promise to us?

Jesus knew the immense value of comparing our humanity to life in the vineyard. Just as the canopy needs maximum exposure to sunlight for photosynthesis to occur, we, too, need exposure to The Light for complete transformation.

Let's pray to end our day.

Lord, thank You for never leaving us exposed in our sin. We are grateful Your perfect love covers us, and through the free gift of salvation, we are justified by Your grace. Thank You for the reminder that when we forgive, we follow Your example, bringing healing and growth. We thank You that You are The Light of this world, and if we follow You, we will never live in darkness. It's in Your glorious name we pray. Amen.

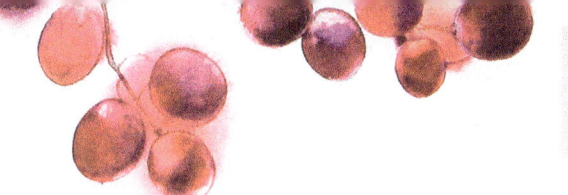

Day 2:
THE CLIMATE

One of the hot topics of our world today is the climate. On any given morning, you can turn on the news and find storms brewing, floods rising, droughts drying, and ice freezing or melting. Climate changes affect us.

Even if you've not given it any thought, you will be impacted. Food costs can spike when crops are damaged and our resources become depleted. Ultimately, the climate affects the crop.

Today, we'll discover how this same principle applies to our spiritual lives as well.

When we compare this fruit-bearing process to the grapevine, it's interesting to note that grapes don't grow in desert climates because temperatures above 95 degrees (35 degrees Celsius) shut down the photosynthetic process. On the other hand, if temperatures are less than 50 degrees (10 degrees Celsius), photosynthesis is also inhibited.[6]

Remember the seasons? Grapevines are deciduous, woody plants that go dormant in the winter to keep cold weather, ice, and snow from having a negative effect on their vines. If the grapevine is too hot or too cold, it will not produce fruit. Why?

The climate affects the vine.

The climate affects us, too.

On the next page, I'd like you to think about the evolution of our cultural climate that you've read about, witnessed, and/or experienced. Then fill in the chart with changes you've seen over time in specific areas. (I've given a few examples to get you started.)

Then...

Now...

No nudity, limited to no-profanity, family-oriented, limited choices

Biased agendas, rampant sexuality, morality presented as archaic

⟵ TELEVISION ⟶

⟵ SOCIAL MEDIA ⟶

⟵ MUSIC ⟶

⟵ SCHOOL ⟶

⟵ HOME ⟶

⟵ MARRIAGE ⟶

⟵ CHURCH ⟶

Why do you think this shift has come about?

Dig Deeper

"Boiling Frog Syndrome" is a cautionary metaphor for being aware of gradual change and not suffering undesirable consequences.

Sometimes we don't even realize the slow fade happening around us and even in us. It's the "frog in boiling water" analogy. The premise is that if a frog is put suddenly into boiling water, it will jump out, but if the frog is put into lukewarm, tepid water that is then slowly brought to a boil, the frog will not discern the danger and will be cooked to death. When it comes to our changing cultural climate, we are the frog being slowly boiled alive.[7]

Turn to Revelation 3:14-16.

How was the Laodicean church described?

What was the result of this?

I want us to understand the gravity of this concept. Being lukewarm is "a condition of the soul wretchedly fluctuating between a torpor and a fervor of love."[8] Thus, you are going back and forth between torpor (a state of physical or mental inactivity; lethargy) and fervor (intense and passionate feeling).[9,10]

Being lukewarm is somewhere between lethargy and intense passion, and it's a place that the Lord despises so much that it causes Him to spit us out of His mouth.

How does one find themselves in this place—the point of lukewarm living? Why?

GROWING IN DISCERNMENT

A famous quotation says, "The greatest trick the devil ever pulled was convincing the world he didn't exist." So, now that we know the peril of lukewarm living, how do we discern the cultural dangers so we're not slowly boiled to death?

Turn to Proverbs 18:15 (NIV) and fill in the blanks:

"The heart of the_____acquires_____, for the ears of the wise
_____ it out."

Discernment is having the wisdom to know what is true.

When I was younger in my faith, I didn't know what I know now. Years from *this* point in time, I pray my spiritual knowledge and understanding will have grown and matured exponentially. I remember when I first became a true follower of Christ, I'd read certain things I couldn't fully comprehend. However, the more I read, the more teachings I listened to, the more Bible studies I participated in, and the more time I spent in fellowship with mature believers in the Lord, the more biblical truths were revealed to me.

Turn to Proverbs 2:1-7. Write the key points of each verse.

Verse 1:

Verse 2:

Verse 3:

Verse 4:

Verse 5:

Verse 6:

Verse 7:

The New Living Translation says in verses 3-4, "Cry out for insight and understanding. Search for them as you would for lost money or hidden treasure." If we cry out for wisdom, verse 6 says, "The Lord grants wisdom! From his mouth come knowledge and understanding."

When I began working on this study, the youngest of my three children was two. I knew my time for work was limited and had to be squeezed into the nooks and crannies of my days—before the kids would wake up or during their ever-precious nap time. On one particular morning, while sitting at my kitchen table, I cried out to the Lord. I told Him I didn't have time to go back to school and get a theology degree. I told Him I didn't want my motherhood to suffer—or to be an excuse—for not knowing Him intimately. I specifically asked God to, "take me to seminary at my kitchen table." I asked for supernatural discernment of His Word. I also asked Him to reveal His heart and His truth to me like never before. I prayed, "Lord, if I truly search for insight and understanding, please give it to me." Remember, we must trust and believe that His Word is truth because, as James 1:5 says, "If you need wisdom, ask our generous God, and he will give it to you. He will not rebuke you for asking" (NLT).

If you're in this same place, I encourage you—No! I implore you—to ask the Lord for discernment and wisdom to understand His Word and His character!

STANDING FOR TRUTH IN A RELATIVE WORLD

Okay, now we know that if we ask for wisdom and discernment to know and understand the truth, He will give it to us. So what comes next?

Let's start with some additional principles. Have you heard the term "relativism" before?

How would you define it?

Relativism is defined as "the doctrine that knowledge, truth, and morality exist in relation to culture, society, or historical context, and are not absolute."[11] It is the idea that views are subject to differences in perception and consideration. According to relativism, there is no universal, objective truth; rather, each point of view has its own truth.

Why is relativism dangerous?

The Bible teaches us that there is no relative truth but rather an *absolute* truth.

Turn to John 8:32 and write it here:

In John 14:6, WHO is the truth?_____

Turning to John 17:17, WHAT is the truth?_____

If we know who and what the absolute truth is, why do Christians sometimes struggle with trying to be "politically correct" or "tolerant" of others' relative beliefs?

Maybe in your work, academic environment, or even with friends and family you fear speaking up and speaking out about your beliefs and your faith in Jesus for fear you'll be labeled a radical, a bigot, hypocritical, irrelevant, or narrow-minded. You may worry about offending others with your views, so you keep silent so as not to "stir the pot" or "make waves." In his book *Counter Culture: Following Christ in an Anti-Christian Age*, David Platt addresses this very topic: "May we not sin through silence. May we realize that not to speak is to speak. Ultimately, may it be said of us that we not only held firm to the gospel, but that we spoke clearly with the gospel to the most pressing issues of our day."[12]

We are living in a very challenging time. The climate of our culture is growing more and more anti-Christian by the day because true Christ-followers are a threat to the darkness around us. However, we will be of no threat to the darkness if we sit quietly on the sidelines, watching the climate evolve (or devolve) around us. Platt challenges us to "courageously share and show our convictions through what we say and how we live, even (or especially) when those convictions contradict the popular positions of our day."[13]

IN, BUT NOT OF

If you've made the willful decision to allow Jesus Christ to be your personal Lord and Savior, you've begun a lifelong journey of sanctification. Again, this is the process of being set apart as sacred and consecrated, and being made holy. As John 17:14-15 tells us, we are still in the world (physically present), but we are no longer of it.

Remember, this verse DOES NOT give Christians license to be ostriches and bury our heads in the sand, as we live in Christian isolation away from the wicked world. On this topic, Christine Caine writes the following:

> *Jesus didn't save us to build a Christian subculture. He didn't save us to hide from the world, avoid the world, ignore the world, fear the world, hate the world, condemn the world, or judge the world. He sent us into the world to love the world He created and loves so tenderly and fiercely.*[14]

Turn to Acts 17:24.

We have to remember that He_____the world and everything in it.

Turn to John 3:16.

He_____the world and He_____His one and only son for it.

Just as God created and loved the world, He also sent His Son, Jesus, into the world. And now, through the power of the Holy Spirit, we have been equipped to "Go into all the world and proclaim the gospel to the whole creation" (Mark 16:15, ESV).

KNOW WHAT YOU BELIEVE

How do we keep the faith and still be attractive to the world around us? How do we represent Christ and prove that what we believe is both true and relevant? We can no longer be biblically illiterate. We cannot rely on preachers, podcasts, or others to spoon-feed us The Word. While all those vehicles for learning are wonderful, we are still responsible for knowing The Truth. It's a truth that we have to personally know for ourselves so we can be set free (Acts 17:11; 1 John 2:27; 2 Timothy 2:15).

Do you know why you believe what you believe? Explain.

What will you commit to doing this week to better know and understand what you believe and why you believe it?

MODEL WHAT YOU BELIEVE

We must be an example for the world around us to follow and imitate (1 Corinthians 11:1). We cannot say that we are followers of Christ and have our actions directly oppose His instructions. We must live our lives in such a way that those who don't believe can see there is something we have that is good and wonderful—something different, something they'll be curious about, something they'll want for themselves. Remember that your life is a letter that the world around you is reading (2 Corinthians 3:3).

WHO is "reading" you?

WHAT are they reading when they see you? (Complaining? Suffering? Desiring money and the next big thing? Love? Joy? Peace? Contentment? Gratitude?)

DEFEND WHAT YOU BELIEVE — GENTLY AND RESPECTFULLY

We always have to be ready to give a defense for what we believe and not shy away from an opportunity to tell others about the Lord. However, this does not give us permission to engage in an all-out debate to win others over. How many wars of words on social media have truly convinced others of something opposite of what they believe? I'd wager to say none.

I passed a street the other day named Winsome Way, and I instantly remembered an endearing yet impactful quip: "Be winsome to win some." It's the same reminder that Peter gives us when he says, "And if someone asks about your hope as a believer, always be ready to explain it. But do this in a gentle and respectful way. Keep your conscience clear" (1 Peter 3:15b-16a NLT).

We don't have to stand outside, picketing with signs that say, "You are going to Hell!" Jesus, our perfect example, didn't use scare tactics in His ministry, but He also didn't fumble His way through the truth of the Gospel message, trying not to offend others. He was winsome; He gently and respectfully engaged others.

If you've had the opportunity to share the Gospel message, what have you found *helpful* in delivering your story?

What have you found to be a *barrier* to telling others about the Lord?

Just remember that no one can argue with <u>your</u> testimony; it's <u>your</u> story, so use it to give God glory. If we are obedient to share the truth of the Gospel message gently and respectfully, then we are not responsible for the outcome of our obedience—God is. He is more than capable of handling it.

FIND COMMON GROUND TO LEAD OTHERS TO BELIEVE

We must learn to approach people not as conversion projects but as fellow human beings who are made in the image of God. We are all imperfect, so we need to give them the same consideration that we would appreciate and desire for ourselves. This is where the relationship matters. This is where you begin building a bridge between what they believe to be true and what you know is true. When you find common ground, you must do it in a nonjudgmental and loving way (1 Corinthians 9:22-23).

Do you remember where you were (emotionally, mentally, physically) when you first came to know the Lord? Describe it:

Sometimes we have to remind ourselves of where we'd be without salvation. If you came to know the Lord at an early age, share some of your struggles and how the Lord has brought you through them. Sharing your testimony—the story of what Christ has done in your life— is one of the best ways to find common ground with a non-believer.

Can you think of any areas of common ground that you have used or can use with people in your immediate sphere of influence?

GROW AND PRODUCE IN OUR CLIMATE

Knowing that we are in the world but not of it, how do we continue to grow and produce fruit in today's cultural climate instead of falling victim to it?

Turn to 1 Chronicles 29:15 and 1 Peter 2:11. What do these verses say we are?

Depending on the translation, these two verses refer to believers in the faith as being strangers, sojourners, pilgrims, immigrants without permanent homes, temporary residents, exiles, homeless and shiftless wanderers, or resident aliens.

Billy Graham once described the "in but not of the world" essence of being a Christian in the following way:

> *Christians are like the Gulf Stream, which is in the ocean and yet not part of it. This mysterious current defies the mighty Atlantic, ignores its tides, and flows steadily upon its course. Its color is different, being a deeper blue. Its temperature is different, being warmer. Its direction is different, being from south to north. It is in the ocean, and yet it is not part of it. So we as Christians are in the world. We come in contact with the world, and yet we retain our distinctive kingdom character and refuse to let the world press us into its mold.[15]*

I love how he explained this idea. The fact is that we *do* come in contact with the world, but we *cannot* lose our distinctive, kingdom character. One of the biggest struggles of being a Christian in this world is having to remind ourselves that we are foreigners.

How would you describe a foreigner?

Dig Deeper
The Gulf Stream can be thought of as a river in the ocean. While it was first observed in 1513 by Ponce de Leon, the Gulf Stream was not charted until the early 1770s by Benjamin Franklin.[16]

If we are foreigners, then we can't talk, act, or be like the world; we need to look different from the world. To be honest, one of the greatest deceptions of our day is that Christians can have salvation without any change.

Why do some believers struggle with wanting to change?

Romans 12:2 says, "Don't copy the behavior and customs of this world, but let God transform you into a new person by changing the way you think. Then you will learn to know God's will for you, which is good and pleasing and perfect" (NLT).

UNDERLINE what we told NOT to do in the above verse.

CIRCLE what we ARE told to do instead.

PUT A STAR ☆ by **WHAT** we will **KNOW.**

1786 chart of the Gulf Stream in the Atlantic Ocean

A common misconception about Christianity is that to follow Christ is to give up all of your fun and desires. I know some people think to be a true, all-in Christian requires one to wither up, waste away into boring shades of gray, and abstain from all things enjoyable. But the end of Romans 12:2 says otherwise. It reveals we'll know how good, pleasing, and perfect life with Him really is! That's a promise—an outright guarantee! Underline and highlight it!

But we have to be all-in. We cannot straddle the line between fleshly desires and the desires of God; we cannot have one foot in the world and one out.

Turn to Matthew 7:21-23, Luke 6:46, and 1 John 2:4, and write their common theme:

If we claim to be Christians, pray, go to church, attend a Bible study, and wear our cross necklaces and Christian t-shirts, yet our lives don't mirror the Father's will, then we're fooling no one and the Lord will someday say, "Depart from me, I never knew you." I ask you to honestly examine yourself. Test yourself. Do you truly believe the gospel? As 2 Corinthians 13:5a says, "Examine yourselves, to see whether you are in the faith. Test yourselves" (ESV).

Here are a few questions you can use to examine yourself.

The climate is ever-changing, and your temperature matters. Are you living a lukewarm, casual Christian life?

Are there behaviors and activities that you find yourself participating in that look no different from the godless world around you?

If so, what needs to change?

We all struggle. Many of you have had radical transformations where you did a complete 180º turn, and your life and lifestyle choices look nothing like those of your former self. Some of you feel like your life B.C. (before Christ) is a distant memory that has all but faded away. But others of you have come to a crossroads and have to make a decision.

Are <u>you</u> all-in?

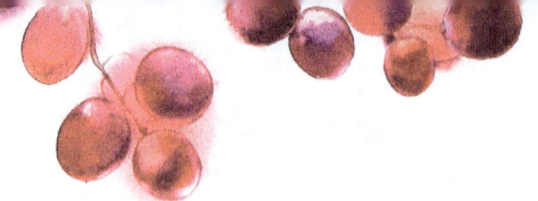

Day 3:
CORAM DEO

Every day before my three children head off to school, I pray over them. In these daily prayers, I find myself speaking a familiar phrase: "Lord, help my children remember they represent themselves, our family, and most importantly, You, Heavenly Father. Help them be mindful that You are always with them and are ever-present."

I hope and pray that my children understand they are salt and light to the world, and, as they're seen by others, God always sees them too. This isn't meant to scare or manipulate them into good behavior but rather to comfort them with the reminder that they're never alone, no matter where they are or what they do.

Have you ever thought about God's omnipresence (being present everywhere at the same time)? I can't recall how old I was when I learned about this specific characteristic of God, but it has always brought me both a sense of security and a reverential fear. It was a comfort when I needed it and a gentle prod to make an honorable choice when I was ready to head in a sinful direction.

The reality is that wherever we go, whatever we do, and whatever we think, it is all done in the presence of God. This is the essence of *Coram Deo*, which is a beautiful Latin phrase that means "in the presence of God" or "before the face of God." R.C. Sproul wrote this of Coram Deo: "To live Coram Deo is to live one's entire life in the presence of God, under the authority of God, to the glory of God."[17]

To live **Coram Deo** is more than living day-to-day with the knowledge that God is somewhere "up there" and we're trudging through this life "down here" like tiny ants, scurrying from one thing to the next. Perhaps this is part of the reason why many Christians suffer from lukewarm living—we have no reverential fear or awe of the fact that we're physically dwelling in the presence of a most-high God. We sometimes struggle with the idea that there is a difference between "God being everywhere" and understanding and truly recognizing that "God is <u>here</u>." God is present everywhere, and His desire is for us to truly dwell with Him as we abide in His presence.

Our Sodbuster's presence (God's omnipresence) is constant and never-ending. He doesn't go on vacation and ask His neighbor to water His plants in His absence. He doesn't check on us every now and then and periodically assess how we're doing. No, He is always here, there, and everywhere. We are *always* living, growing, and bearing fruit (good or bad) in the presence of God. The totality of our lives is lived Coram Deo.

Look up Jeremiah 23:23-24. Summarize the verses here:

Turn to Psalm 139:5 (NIV) and write it here:

What do you think David meant when he said, "You hem me in behind and before"?

Now write verse 7 here:

Moving on to verses 8-10, fill in the blanks (NIV):

"If I go up to the heavens,_____ _____ _____ ;
if I make my bed in the depths,_____ _____ _____.
If I rise on the wings of the dawn, if I settle on the far side of the sea,_____ _____
_your hand will guide me, your right hand will hold me fast."

If I had to select a most-loved passage in the Psalms, Psalm 139 would rank as one of my favorites because it's composed of poetic verses that sing of the omniscience and omnipresence of God. King David's words weren't that he wished to depart from God or to retreat from the Lord's presence, but they became a rhetorical song where he asks and answers the question, already knowing that no one can escape from the ubiquitous existence and observation of the Lord.

I'm not sure what David was going through when he wrote this psalm, but there is something so tender in these words. No matter what we're going through and no matter where we are, we're seen and known, and all of our life is in God's hands. We are hemmed in (some versions translate it as "hedged in") before and behind; He goes before us and follows us. This implies a protective barrier where nothing can get to us unless the sovereign will of the Lord allows it to pass through.

How do you feel knowing that God is always present, seeing, and watching?

Can you imagine a situation where God's omnipresence may make someone *nervous*?

Can you imagine a situation where it may be a *comfort* to realize we're always seen and known?

As a parent, it's much easier for me to understand our Heavenly Father's omnipresence and how it is for our good. I know my children are instantly comforted when they realize that I, my husband, or even their grandparents are watching over them (unless, of course, they are in the midst of doing something disobedient). They have no doubt of the good intentions or good will of those who watch over them. They know—and are confident in—the love and care of their parents, and our very presence brings them reassurance and solace.

Turn to Psalm 46:1 (NIV) and fill in the blank:

"God is our refuge and strength, an _____ help in trouble."

Are you dealing with anything right now for which knowing God is ever-present brings comfort?

Can you recall a time when His ever-present help brought you through a situation?

JEHOVAH SHAMMAH

Turn to Ezekiel 48:35b and fill in the blanks.

"And from that day the name of the city will be '_____ _____ _____ .'"

This Scripture translates *Jehovah Shammah* (jeh·ho·vä' shäm'·mä) as "The Lord is There." Even when you say the name Jehovah Shammah, there is something so beautiful and powerful in that name. If you can, say it aloud now: *Jehovah Shammah*.[18]

Our human minds can capture only a fraction of the description of the overflowing presence of God. The truth is, God's omnipresence exists whether we are aware of it or not. We never have to ask God to be with us if we belong to Him. We only need to ask Him for an awareness of His presence because He is already there.

I love how God knows His children so well. Sometimes He has to show up to provide a gentle reminder of what He's already promised. He has to physically manifest His presence as a reminder of His omnipresence in order to help us recognize His presence. Scripture even begins and ends with the presence of God.

In the following exercise, I'd like you to look up the Scripture references and then write how the Lord was/is/will be present among His people.

Turn to the following verses and fill in the chart:

Old Testament Scripture References	How God Was/Is/Will Be Present
Genesis 3:8	
Exodus 13:21; Numbers 14:14	
Exodus 25:8; 22	
New Testament Scripture References	
Matthew 1:23	
John 1:14	
Acts 2:1-4	
Revelation 21:1-3	

Whether He walked in the garden, was beheld as a pillar of cloud or fire, rested over an ark in the tabernacle, or came to the earth as a human baby in swaddling clothes, God gave His people a physical sign of His presence. When Jesus' earthly ministry was nearly over, He knew we would still need more of His presence, so He promised to send the Holy Spirit (John 14:16-17). The first outpouring of the manifest power of the Holy Spirit settled on the heads of believers gathered together and appeared as flames of fire. Then, in the finality of Scripture, we are promised His perpetual presence in the future establishment of a new heaven and a new earth.

God has shown, and will always show, Himself to His people.

Do you agree that God still reveals Himself to us today?

If yes, how is His presence today *similar* to His presence in biblical times?

How is His revealed presence today *different* from His revealed presence in biblical times?

How do we get to the place where we sense His omnipresence like we do the wind, where we don't always have to see Him to believe He's there?

PRACTICING CORAM DEO

Turn now to 1 Thessalonians 5:17 and write it here:

What does this verse mean? How would you explain it to a child?

Turn to Hebrews 4:14-16 and answer the following questions:

> **What is Jesus referred to as?**

> **What does verse 15 help us understand about Jesus?**

> **How can we approach God's throne of grace?**

Living in, and having an awareness of, God's presence (Coram Deo) requires communication with Him. Though we can boldly and confidently approach Him with <u>anything at all</u>, we can't just speak *at* God. It's a two-way conversation; we have to listen for Him to respond.

It'd be like us praying, "Dear God, what should I do with this situation, and please, Lord, help me with this problem, and Oh, God, I need you to show me where I should be in this issue. Thank You, Jesus. Amen." Then God replies, "Did you want to hear anything that I had to say?"

How do we get to the point of having conversational prayer with our Heavenly Father?

What do you do to practice being in His presence in your daily life?

What benefits have you experienced while practicing living Coram Deo?

Now turn to Matthew 28:20. Where is Christ?

To end today's study of living Coram Deo, I invite you to pray this prayer with me:

Heavenly Father, Your presence comforts and reassures me. I find peace in knowing You hem me in on all sides. Even though You're here right now, You're also in all my tomorrows. You already know what I've been through and what's to come. I know I don't have to ask You to be with me, but help me be aware that I'm not alone. I'm grateful You're a compassionate and ever-present help.

You, Jehovah Shammah, will never leave me or forsake me. Whether I'm washing dishes, paying bills, engaging in a heated conversation with someone, or sitting quietly at home, I can live this life before the face of an Almighty God. I'm thankful to know Your presence is in—and all around—me, and I can boldly and confidently come to You with anything. You are a faithful Father who will always be there for me, even until the end of the earth. Thank You. I love You, Lord. In Jesus' name I pray. Amen.

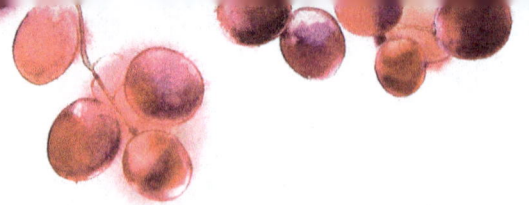

Day 4:

THE CONNECTION

Have you ever noticed that funerals bring all sorts of people together? Some come to honor the dearly departed, and others who may not have known the deceased come to support those left in the wake of loss.

A few years ago, I attended two funerals for the fathers of two of my college friends. I knew both men, and while they were very different in life, both of their tragic deaths occurred at their own hands—by suicide.

At each service, I couldn't help but notice that, despite such a horrific demise, so many people were paying their respect to the families left behind to sort through the sorrow, confusion, and despair. For one, it was a funeral home, and for the other, a church, yet both locations were overflowing. It would be no exaggeration to say that hundreds of people came to say their last "goodbyes" to these men who were sons, brothers, uncles, fathers, grandfathers, and husbands.

Not long after, I had lunch with my friend Kendra, the daughter of one of these men. At one point, our conversation turned to discussing the masses of people at her father's funeral. That's when Kendra made a profound statement: "He was so loved but felt so alone." Through tears, she said, "I just don't understand suicide, and I don't think I ever will."

I am not a mental health professional, but I believe it's safe to say that no one will ever fully understand the mental anguish that these two men must've endured before they resolved to end their own life. But one thing is certain: They felt alone.

They felt disconnected.

It's been said that this generation is the most interconnected yet also the most disconnected. As a culture, we're the most socially connected we've ever been, yet many of us still feel completely alone.

How can we be surrounded by people but still feel alone?

As you sit and read this, can you think of a time when you've felt disconnected and alone?

When we're out in public, my husband and I love to people-watch. Over the years, we've developed a silly go-to game where we assign names and even accents to those passing by. We narrate elaborate stories and scenarios for the unknowing participants in our game and describe where they're going or what they're doing. It's truly an entertaining way to pass the time when you're waiting at a restaurant or anywhere for that matter! But the reality is, our game is just childish make-believe, and we have no clue who these people are or what they're doing. Still, even if we don't know who they are or what they're going through, God does.

We walk alongside people in the line at the grocery store, we're pressed together with other parents in school pickup huddles, and we rub shoulders with people sitting next to us in the cafeteria, on the subway, on buses, and even in the pew at church. Yet we may never be aware of the struggles, inner turmoil, and anguish they may be enduring. If we're honest, some days (maybe even today) we might be those very people—the desperate, the hurting, and the lonely.

I want us to work together to paint one of the most beautiful pictures that Scripture gives us when it comes to being surrounded yet feeling completely alone. Nevertheless, even in a pressing crowd of people, our Lord knows us, sees us, and will never neglect us.

Look up Mark 5:21-24 and answer these questions:

What is Jesus on His way to do?

Who was with Jesus?

I like to use my imagination when I read Scripture. Sometimes I'm reading to study, but at other times I'm reading for the narrative. In those moments, my mind fills in the blanks of what The Word does not share. For instance, I imagine that it was the middle of a hot Mediterranean day when we find Jesus on His way to attend to the needs of a sick and dying twelve-year-old girl. At this point in His earthly ministry, He had likely grown accustomed to the throngs of people who surrounded Him. Since stories of Jesus feeding the 5,000 are recorded in each of the gospels, I imagine thousands of people followed after Him on this day as well. All the while, they tread on His garments, pushing and shoving their way to gape at Him, trying to get within earshot of His teaching or witness something miraculous. Yet outside of this passage, Scripture never mentions Him taking notice of something that happened to Him in the crowd this particular day.

Using Mark 5:25-26, answer the following questions:

Who specifically was mentioned to be in the crowd that day?

How long had she been suffering?

What does verse 26 tell us of her financial status and how she'd gotten to this point?
(See Luke 8:43 for additional information.)

Now turn to Leviticus 15:25.

What does Mosaic law tell us about this woman?

Given the information that the Bible tells us about her, how would you describe her (*i.e. physically, emotionally, mentally*)?

From a physical and medical perspective, anyone who's been hemorrhaging for 12 consecutive years is going to be severely anemic, tired, exhausted, and sickly. Her emotional and mental status were likely fragile and suffering as well because she was probably living in isolation and without much human touch since she was ceremonially unclean. If that were not enough, Scripture tells us that she was destitute and penniless because she'd spent everything she had to pay doctors in an attempt to find a cure.

Turning back to Mark 5:27-34, answer the following questions:

What did the woman do to Jesus?

What IMMEDIATELY happened when she did this?

In verse 30, why do you think Jesus asked, "Who touched my clothes?"

In verse 33, what was her response to the realization of what had happened to her?

This poor, apprehensive woman had been made timid by 12 years of illness, failed hopes of a cure, and poverty. She felt alone and isolated, yet she still had faith. Mark 5:28 says, "For she said, 'If I touch even his garments, I will be made well'" (ESV).

She had nothing to lose and everything to gain.

After she told Him what she had done, what was Jesus' response to her?

I love the end of this story.

So often the Bible gives us exact names of people or places because there is so much that can be revealed in the definition of a name, but in this instance, the *absence* of the woman's name has meaning too. In some versions, she is simply referred to as "the woman with the issue of blood." Her imperfection and diagnosis became her identity. Her uncleanness, her isolation, and her suffering were how the world saw her.

But Jesus saw her differently. He knew her. He saw past all her fear, sadness, loneliness, and pain, and He called her "DAUGHTER." In Greek, this word is *thygatēr* (thü-gä'-tar) and means "a daughter, a daughter of God, acceptable to God, rejoicing in God's peculiar care and protection."[19]

This woman who had suffered in isolation and loneliness was the <u>only</u> woman in all of Scripture whom Jesus addressed by such a name. He let her know through His tender words that she was accepted, and at the same time, she was given peace, brought out of isolation, and made whole. From the moment she reached out, she connected herself to The Vine—The Messiah—and was never the same again.

Her earthly name was never mentioned in this story, but her heavenly name was "Daughter." Her faith in Jesus made her whole on this side of Heaven and secured her a place in eternity. I wait with joyful expectation for the day when I can hear Jesus call me "Daughter," too.

WHILE WE WAIT, WE REMAIN

Let's go back and reference our foundational Scripture in John 15, specifically John 15:4.

What one word is repeated in this verse?

The repeated word comes from the Greek word, *menō*, which is translated as "remain, abide, dwell, continue, tarry, and endure."[21]

Dig Deeper
Malachi 4:2 prophesies of "healing in his wings." This word for wings is *kraspedon* (kras'-ped-on), and it's also found in Numbers 15:38, Matthew 9:20 and 14:36, and Mark 6:56. This word describes the hem or the borders of Jesus' garment.[20]

©Shannon Witrenga /"Reach of Faith"

Now I'd like you to review John 15:4-11. HIGHLIGHT each time you read the word "remain," "abide," or "dwell" in this passage.

    How many times did you see it written in these verses?

    Why do you think it was repeated so many times?

When we study this word in context, it has three meanings:

1. **A PLACE.** It means to sojourn or tarry, not to depart, to continue to be present, or to be held or kept continually.
2. **A TIME.** It means to continue to be, not to perish, to last, to endure, to survive, or to live.
3. **A STATE or CONDITION.** It means to remain as one or not to become another or different.

For our study today, I want us to focus on the third definition: to remain as one. So how do we, as branches, get to the point where we can remain, dwell, and abide as one with The Vine?

Read Romans 11:16-18. Summarize verse 17 in this passage in your own words:

Strong's *Concordance* summarizes Romans 11:16-18 in the following way:

> *In these passages, Paul likens the heathen who by becoming Christians have been admitted into fellowship with the people for whom the Messianic salvation is destined, to scions from wild trees inserted into a cultivated stock.*[22]

Ultimately, this means that even Gentiles (non-Jewish descendants of the house of Israel; Jeremiah 31:33) can be grafted into the vine to produce fruit and can share in the full spiritual inheritance of the Kingdom of Heaven.

What exactly does it mean to be "grafted into the vine"? Grafting is a technique used in the plant world and in medicine. In medicine, a portion of living tissue is surgically transplanted from one part of an individual to another part or from one individual to another individual, for adhesion and growth. In plants, specifically grapevines, grafting is the delicate process of connecting two varieties to create a plant that produces the fruit and above-ground growth of one variety with the root system of another.[24]

Dig Deeper

There are multiple ways to graft a new grapevine onto an old one, but some of the easiest and most successful include cleft grafting, bark grafting, and whip grafting.[23]

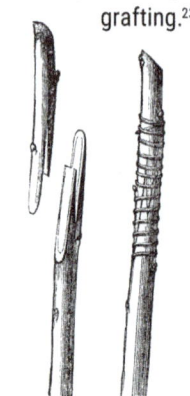

Grafting is done for many reasons. Can you think of any?

In medicine, in its most simplistic definition, grafting is done for healing—to remove the damaged or diseased tissue and replace it with healthy, vital tissue. The grafted tissue will never be the same as it once was, but it has the opportunity to function and be restored. Many things can be grafted: skin for burn victims, hair for the follically challenged (a.k.a. bald) patients, veins and arteries in cardiac patients, nerves, bones, and more.

In the horticulture world, there are several ways to graft different species of plants together.

When we look specifically at grapevine grafting, all the techniques begin with two steps:

1. **CUTTING** a section of a stem (the scion) with some leaf buds (the fruit-bearing part) from one variety and then
2. **ATTACHING** it to the cultivated rootstock of an existing grapevine of a different variety.

The grafted portion is placed in specific alignment so that the vascular tissues (or cambium) of both pieces match up. That way, the grafted portion is able to receive nutrients from the stock. Increased cambium contact (surface areas that touch) between the scion and the cultivated rootstock increases the likelihood of successful grafting. Once grafting is complete, the grafted sites are bound together, secured, and sealed so the incision site can heal. Grafting is a time-consuming process that requires patience and practice.

You might be thinking, *Okay, thank you for that science lesson, but how does this relate to me?*

Thinking about the grafting process, answer the following questions:

How is the grafted portion obtained?
(Hint: What is the first step in the grafting process?)

Is the grafted portion (the scion) different from the rootstock to which it is connected?

Dig Deeper

"Fruit salad trees" are multi-grafted trees with different fruits from the same family that are all grafted together onto a single tree. All the fruits retain their own characteristics, such as flavor, appearance, and ripening times.[25]

After a successful grafting, what does the grafted portion share with the rootstock?

Now think of yourself being grafted into The Vine. What did/do you first have to be cut away from?

Once you're connected to The Vine, what type of "nutrients" do you receive?

Turn to John 17.

On the night before His crucifixion, Jesus prayed a prayer that is recorded in Scripture. If you have time, I encourage you to read the entire passage, but at a minimum, I'd like you to read how Jesus closes His prayer in John 17:23-26.

In verse 23, what does Jesus say we are being perfected into?

Write the last phrase of verse 26 here:

Jesus is more than just the forgiver of our sins and some untouchable lofty deity. We are just like the woman who suffered in isolation and disconnectedness for 12 years because He wants to make us whole too. He never wants us to feel disconnected and alone. Our Heavenly Father desires a close relationship with us, one where abiding is mutual—if we abide in Him, He will abide in us. If we have faith and reach out to Him, we will find our connection.

Let's end today with a prayer; I invite you to pray with me.

Heavenly Father, I am amazed that the Savior of the world wants to be perfectly united with me! I am thankful to be separate from my former sin and in alignment with You. I am grateful I no longer have to live surrounded by other people, feeling completely alone.

Lord, I know You want me firmly grafted into You, and, in the process, You will secure me so I may be healed and nourished by Your Holy Spirit. Through this connected life, I can bear much fruit for Your glory! In Jesus' name I pray. Amen.

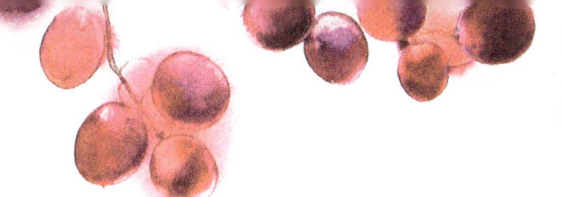

Day 5:
THE CONSIDERATION

In March 2020, the United States declared a state of emergency for a global pandemic—a disease that spread worldwide.

To give you a little background on the word "pandemic," the three letters in the prefix of this word (pan) originate from the demonic god Pan.[26] From this pagan god, we get the word "panic," which means "the sudden, unreasoning terror often accompanied by mass flight."[27]

Our country—and the world around us—was placed into a multi government-mandated state of emergency. Major sporting events, concert venues, restaurants, gyms, schools, air travel, international borders, and even places of worship were closed and shut down. The government shut down any industry where more than ten people convened. We learned new terms such as "social distancing" and began isolating ourselves from others in an effort to mitigate the spread of disease. An ultramicroscopic agent, SARS-CoV-2, a strain of coronavirus, caused the entire world to shut down.

Our generation had <u>never</u> experienced anything like this before. Today we live in unprecedented times, and our human efforts use our limited knowledge to control what we can. But in the midst, we must pause and remind ourselves that <u>God</u> <u>is</u> <u>in</u> <u>control</u>.

Though we may battle against diseases that spread fear worldwide, we serve a God who does not want us to fear evil. He gives us constant reminders in the Scriptures to "FEAR NOT," and if we are in covenant with Him, abiding with Him, then we can have *perfect peace*—a fruit of His Holy Spirit living in us.

Turn to Isaiah 9:6 and write who God is:

Isaiah 26:3 says, "You will keep in perfect peace those whose minds are steadfast, because they trust in you" (NIV).

In the passage above, <u>UNDERLINE</u> what we will have if we fix our minds on Christ and trust Him.

Dig Deeper

Pan was the half-goat, half-man Greek god of the wild. His unseen presence aroused panic in all who traversed his realm. He was known to let out an angry, blood-curdling shout that inspired a sudden sensation of fear and anxiety in everyone unfortunate enough to hear it.[28]

In our discussion of Coram Deo, we learned that *nothing* can come to us except through the permissive will of our Sovereign Lord. That means **nothing** is a surprise to God. Nothing about whatever you are going through is a surprise to God.

Turn to Isaiah 55:8-9. Write what these verses mean in your own words.

I am comforted and relieved to know that God's ways are so much higher than my own, and even though you and I do not know what tomorrow holds, He does. This is why we <u>must</u> live life connected to Him.

Yesterday we discussed what a life of connectedness looks like. Today I want to take some time to consider what a disconnected life looks like and how we can return to abiding with The Vine.

VIVIPAROUS LIVING

Years ago, some tomatoes on the vine were sitting in a bowl on my kitchen counter (because my mother taught me long ago never to refrigerate tomatoes for optimal flavor). One evening, I went to grab one of these tomatoes for dinner. To my shock and awe, the tomato had begun to self-germinate and had worm-like sprouts shooting out from its own skin!

I quickly googled this phenomenon and gave myself a crash course in the botanical term "vivipary." Then, of course, I felt my entire social network needed to see this disturbing anomaly, so I posted a picture of it on Facebook. Halfway down the comment thread filled with, "*Ew, gross!*", "*What the heck is that?*" and "*It's an alien tomato!*", my dear friend, Jenny, commented, "*Sounds like the making of a lesson!*" At the time, I just thought it was a crazy-cool-looking tomato, but after I did some research, I found that it is a peculiar development. And, yes, Jenny was right—there *is* a lesson to be learned.

I discovered that these new seedlings could be potted and could grow into tomato plants, even producing tomatoes themselves. However, what's fascinating is the fact that these sprouts will <u>NOT</u> produce exact replicas of the parent plant; the DNA of the self-germinating seeds is entirely different from that of the parent plant.[29]

Dig Deeper

Vivipary is derived from the Latin word *viviparous*, which means "live birth." It is the term for plants that begin growing while still inside or attached to the parent plant. The seeds break their dormancy cycle and grow in warm, moist conditions from within.[30]

Actual picture of my viviparous tomato!

Now turn to John 15:5 and write the last sentence of the verse here:

I think the lesson of my viviparous tomato (aside from maybe learning a new scientific term) is the fact that life apart from Christ might produce something for a while, but eventually, it will be nothing like Him. To say it another way, we will be nothing like Him.

Today I'd like you to consider your own life.

Can you recall a time when you were living life apart from Christ?

What did living apart look like?

How was your prayer life?

How was your worship?

What did your fruit look like? Good or bad?

What did you experience both mentally and emotionally?

Now turn to James 1:21. What does this passage tell us to do and WHY?

The Word of God is alive, and it has the power to save. In order for us to have this salvation, we have to get rid of things in our life that separate us from God.

I'd like you to take some time and think about things that cause us to be separated from God. List them here:

I have a personal testimony of having a willful time of walking away and separating from the Lord. In my 20s, caught up in the freedom of college, I made choices that resulted in a disconnection from God. However, because I'd been connected to The Vine for many years of my early life, I never had complete peace about my lifestyle choices when I was in the midst of my sin. No relationship, party, or drink could nourish me like Jesus did. I tried to dull the still-small voice that would caution me or prompt me to make a better choice, and every time I would try to drown out any nudge from the Holy Spirit, I never had peace. I felt duplicitous.

I professed to have faith in Jesus Christ, yet my life was hardly a mirror of His image. I felt like a fraud. I felt like a hypocrite. I had so many conflicting emotions, but I was caught up in a cycle that I just couldn't figure out how to stop. At the time, I was not deeply rooted in God's Word to truly understand His love for me, so I constantly battled the fallout of my detachment from the Lord.

It's never easy to examine and consider our own experiences of a separated life. Thank you for trudging through that part of your own life. It's important to realize none of our story is wasted. God can redeem every part of it. Now let's look to the Bible to study other examples of detached living.

THE GARDEN AND THE CROSS

Turn to Genesis 3:23. What happened in this verse?

At one time, Adam and Eve spent daily time in the presence of the Lord. What separated them?

Now turn to Mark 15:34. What did Jesus cry out?

Billy Graham once wrote this of Jesus' words from the cross:

> *His words point...to the fact that when Jesus died on the cross, all our sins—without exception—were transferred to Him. He was without sin, for He was God in human flesh. But as He died all our sins were placed on Him, and He became the final and complete sacrifice for our sins. And in that moment He was banished from the presence of God, for sin cannot exist in God's presence. His cry speaks of this truth; He endured the separation from God that you and I deserve.*[31]

We have the free will to want to be connected to Him. We have the free will to seek Him. We have the free will to desire a relationship with Him. Because of His love, we have the continual choice of willful connectedness, but because God is perfect and holy, He cannot condone sin. Even when Jesus, who was perfect and blameless, willfully carried the weight of all the world's sin on the cross, He endured separation from God the Father, for sin cannot exist in God's presence.

WHEN SEAWEED SURROUNDS

Turn to Jonah 1:1-2. What does God tell Jonah to do?

In the very next verse, what did Jonah do?

What do the sailors say to him? (v 10)

Dig Deeper

Seaweed refers to thousands of species of marine algae. The smallest seaweeds are only a few millimeters, while the largest routinely grow to a length of 100-165 feet.[32]

Even the heathen sailors knew better than to try to run away from the Lord! If only Jonah had done Day 3 of this session's study, then he would've known he could NEVER flee from Jehovah Shammah. He could never run away from the omnipresence of the Lord!

Even though God spoke directly to Jonah, a Hebrew, and told him to deliver a specific message to a Gentile nation, Jonah still made a deliberate choice to turn and run in the opposite direction; he willfully disconnected himself from God. Jonah's story, albeit a short one, is written for our edification. God knew we needed a four-chapter book to succinctly give us instruction and understanding for our lives today. So let's work now to uncover some of this revelation together.

Turn to Jonah 1:4-16.

What was the first thing to happen as the result of Jonah's direct disobedience?

Who else was affected by Jonah's decision?

When Jonah made the willful choice to turn away from his calling, the storms began to rage all around him. Similarly, when you live apart from the perfect will of God, you never have perfect peace. You may be able to fool yourself for a while, but only a surrendered life can experience any sort of peace in the middle of a storm. A surrendered, connected life still receives nourishment from the stable rootstock of The Vine. The Vine is the anchor to the ground, and this anchor remains in the midst of the raging storms. Like Jonah, when life's difficult or when sorrow-filled times come, you may feel like crying out:

> *You threw me into the ocean depths, and I sank down to the heart of the sea. The mighty waters engulfed me; I was buried beneath your wild and stormy waves...I sank beneath the waves, and the waters closed over me. Seaweed wrapped itself around my head. I sank down to the very roots of the mountains. I was imprisoned in the earth, whose gates lock shut forever. But you, O LORD my God, snatched me from the jaws of death! (Jonah 2:3;5-6, NLT)*

Dig Deeper

Shalom (sha-lome') is perfect peace that is complete, whole, and lacking nothing.[33]

As I was typing these words, an instrumental version of the song "Oceans (Where Feet May Fail)" began to play. To most people that doesn't mean anything, but to me, it is divine. You see, in the spring of 2014, my dear friend Julie walked through one of the darkest storms of her life, and this specific song was a source of profound comfort to her while she felt like she was drowning.

Unlike Jonah's story, Julie's story was not about a willful decision or detachment that brought about the consequence of her storm. Because we live in a fallen world, we *will* experience suffering, and there *will* be times when we are confused and unsettled. There will be times when God allows us to go through situations where we feel buried beneath the wild and stormy waves with seaweed wrapped around our heads.

Though Julie's story is not my own, I experienced sorrow for her like never before. Julie was 38 weeks pregnant with her third son, Archer, when she stopped feeling him move inside of her. On May 27, 2014, our Bible study group heard the devastating news that he had passed away in her womb; he no longer had a heartbeat. Even as I write these words, I am overcome with emotion and sadness at the life that never was. I remember being alone in my room on that day when I learned that Julie was headed into her induction. Our entire group began praying as she was in labor, delivering Archer as a stillborn.

Then, on June 4, 2014, just seven days later, Julie wrote these words on her Facebook page:

> *I felt anxious leading up to today (knowing that today was the scheduled induction day for Archer). Today was supposed to be a day of joy and excitement. The day we finally meet Archer. Our God is so powerful because today I have peace, peace that can only come from God. I really appreciate all your prayer as I know that your prayer is working. God's hand is working in this in so many ways but one very observable way is the peace I have right now. I miss Archer deeply and long to hold him in my arms again but I know that he is being held in Jesus' arms and his arms are a much better place to be than mine.[34]*

I share Julie's story because I had a front-row seat to witness a perfect example of a surrendered life in the midst of a raging storm; it was a place where perfect peace still remained. Whether it's a novel virus that wreaks havoc on the entire world around us or as we experience great pain, sorrow, loss, and devastation in our own world, we can have a peace that can come only from Jesus—The Prince of Peace.

He is Jehovah Shalom, God our Peace (Judges 6:24).

Dear Friends, we are not just studying this book—the Bible—because we enjoy reading an ancient text. No, we study it because its words have the power to deliver us.

Now turn again to John 15:4-6 (but still keep your spot in Jonah) and complete these statements:

A severed branch produces _____

Apart from The Vine we can do _____

Anyone who parts from The Vine is _____

We may be able to get through this life living viviparously for a time, but we will never experience all that the Lord has for us. Whether we're willfully turning and running in the opposite direction or we're engaged in a slow process of disconnecting from God, the result is still the same: a disconnected life cannot receive nourishment, cannot produce fruit, and will wither away.

Now let's go back to see what Jonah did next. Turn to Jonah 2:7-10.

What did Jonah do?

At the end of verse 9, what does Jonah say?

In verse 10, how did God answer Jonah's prayer?

Jonah's decisions had consequences, but God is always faithful to His Word. Because He never leaves us or forsakes us, He heard Jonah's cry and saved him.

Sometimes our answered prayers look nothing like what we imagine. I'd like to think that God was using a creative brushstroke when He enlisted the help of a whale to teach Jonah (and us) the valuable lesson of redemption and second chances. I'm grateful I didn't have to spend three days in the belly of a giant sea creature when I was willfully living separated from God. However, God did get my attention in other ways, namely through the wise words of my mother and specific friends who saw me headed in the opposite direction of my calling.

Throughout this entire week, we've worked to bring about the process of producing our fruit. During our time today, I've specifically asked you to consider your connection to The Vine. If you are already connected, I hope you have been challenged to remain so. If you are not, then turn back and hold tight to your source of life. But please know—regardless of your circumstance—that God is the God of second chances.

Remember my friend Julie?

I don't want to end today without giving you one of the best parts of her story. Her testimony is a beautiful example of second chances because, in June 2015, she gave birth to her fourth son, who was healthy and whole. Julie and her husband, Andy, chose to name him Canaan because, like the Israelites' promised land, *he* was a long-awaited promise fulfilled.

God never abandons His children. He is always in the business of redemption and restoration. As we end this day and this week, I'd like to close with a passage and a prayer.

Isaiah 43:1-3 is a beautifully constructed work of poetry and is the perfect anthem for anyone's journey through grief and sorrow. I am certain some of you will find solace in the profound reminder of whose we are.

> *"Fear not, for I have redeemed you;*
> *I have called you by name, you are mine.*
> *When you pass through the waters, I will be with you;*
> *and through the rivers, they shall not overwhelm you;*
> *when you walk through fire you shall not be burned,*
> *and the flame shall not consume you.*
> *For I am the LORD your God,*
> *the Holy One of Israel, your Savior" (ESV).*

Let's pray.

Lord, we thank You that when the world around us may be in a panic, we belong to the giver of perfect, shalom peace—a peace that we can experience only in a storm. We praise You for who You are, and we rest in Your word that though the waters may be deep and the fire hot, You are always with us, and we will not be consumed.

Father, we desire a truly submitted heart that is connected, nourished, and sustained by—and in—You. Lord, if any of us lacks peace, we pray that You reveal the areas of disconnectedness in our lives. We thank You that Your promises are true. In Your compassion, You give us gentle (and sometimes not-so-gentle, whale-like) reminders that You are a God of second chances, redemption, and restoration. We love you. In Jesus' name we pray. Amen.

HOW IS IT PRODUCED?
from generation to generation...

BE *fruitful*

Here are this week's ways to DIVE DEEPER by yourself, with family, or friends.

DISCUSS

This week we discussed how fruit is produced. Using the prompts below, start a discussion to solidify the learning.

- Have you ever had to give someone else grace?
- Have you ever been given grace from someone else?
- Do you ever struggle with giving yourself grace?
- Discuss the "frog in boiling water" analogy and relate it to the changing climate of our culture.
- Is it difficult to share your faith with others? Why or why not?
- Who in your circle of friends/family/influence is watching you and your behavior? Who is studying you?
- How do you sense God's presence in your life? How do you know God is always with you?
- Have you ever felt alone, even in a crowd? Relate your sense of disconnection to the woman with the issue of blood.
- Given the reference to suicide in Day 4 of this week, I'd like to provide the National Suicide Prevention Lifeline number: 988

DISCOVER

- If you have houseplants, notice how they grow toward a window or natural sunlight.
- Explore your local garden centers and see if they sell "fruit salad" plants. Sometimes you can find grafted plants ready to take home!
- Visit a local vineyard and explore the trellising and grafting process.
- Check out YouTube videos on vine grafting and vivipary.

FOR THE KIDS
- YouTube search Superbook:
  - "In the Beginning" and "Jonah"

DESIGN

Using the prompts below, start applying your learning from this week.

- Use Pinterest to find age-appropriate Jonah and the Whale crafts.
- Send a card to a friend from whom you've been disconnected.
- Send a "hello" text to someone who's been on your mind. Let them know you're praying for them.
- Invite a friend or family member to go on a long walk. Connect while you exercise!
- If you can, have a "walking meeting" at work. Get the blood and ideas flowing!
- Bring flowers to your local nursing home residents (Carnations are inexpensive.) Ask if you can hand them out. Some residents never get visitors.

DIG IN

READ
- Go to your local library and find books on grafting to understand the process.
- For children, here are a few books my kids have loved:
  - *Everywhere I go, God is With Me* by Mikal Keefer
  - *I AM: The Names of God for Little Ones* and *I AM: 100 Devotionals About the Names of God* by Diane Stortz

REVIEW
- Lukewarm living
- Absolute truth vs. relative truth
- *Coram Deo* - in the presence of God
- *Jehovah Shammah* - The Lord is there
- *Meno* - to remain, abide, dwell, continue, tarry, and endure
- "Viviparous" - live birth

WEHOW IS IT PRODUCED?
from harvest to table...

BE *fruitful*

Whether you're cooking for one or having a potluck, enjoy the process of artfully putting the ingredients together to make a delicious masterpiece. Be encouraged to consider the elements of your week-long study that apply to the recipe you are preparing.

DELICIOUS DELIGHTS

ROASTED ROOTS
Serves 6-8

INGREDIENTS

- 1 large yam or sweet potato, peeled
- ¾ lb red potatoes scrubbed clean, with the peel
- ½ lb beets (red or golden), trimmed and cleaned
- ½ lb large carrots, peeled and halved lengthwise
- 1 medium parsnip (4-5 oz), peeled and halved lengthwise
- ½ red onion, peeled
- 6 whole garlic cloves
- ¼ cup extra virgin olive oil, divided
- 2 Tbsp fresh thyme leaves (or 2 tsp dried thyme)
- 5 sprigs fresh rosemary (or 3 tsp dried rosemary)
- 1 tsp ground cumin
- 1 tsp kosher salt or more to taste
- ¼ tsp black pepper or more to taste

INSTRUCTIONS

- Preheat the oven to 400 degrees F.
- Slice all vegetables into chunks roughly 1½ inches wide.
- Place cut vegetables into a large mixing bowl. Add 3 tbsp olive oil, fresh thyme leaves, ground cumin, kosher salt, and black pepper. Stir until all vegetables are evenly coated with the oil, spices, and herbs.
- Brush a large-rimmed baking sheet with the remaining 1 tbsp olive oil. Spread the vegetables out evenly on the baking sheet. Place the rosemary sprigs on top of the vegetables evenly across the sheet.
- Roast the vegetables in the oven for 15 minutes.
- Stir the vegetables and continue to roast them until the largest chunks are tender and the edges turn golden/dark (15-25 minutes).
- Remove the roasted rosemary sprigs and stir the vegetables.
- Serve warm or at room temperature.

DECONSTRUCTED DOLMAS (STUFFED GRAPE LEAVES)
Serves 4

INGREDIENTS

- 1 cup white or brown rice
- 1 cup chopped grape leaves from a jar
- 1 cup sugar snap peas, coarsely chopped
- ½ cup chopped dill leaves
- 1 lemon, juiced
- 1 Tbsp extra virgin olive oil
- 1 tsp black pepper, or to taste
- ¼ cup crumbled feta (optional)
- ¼ cup pine nuts (add more if you like)

INSTRUCTIONS

- Prepare the rice as instructed on the package. While it is cooking, place the chopped grape leaves in a sieve and rinse them under running water to remove excess salt. Squeeze out any excess moisture and add the leaves to the simmering pot of rice.
- Toast the pine nuts over low heat for five minutes, occasionally turning them until they are golden and aromatic.
- Stir the cooked pot of rice to mix in the grape leaves. Transfer everything to a mixing bowl and add all the remaining ingredients except the pine nuts. Adjust the seasoning if necessary.
- Garnish with toasted pine nuts and serve warm, cold, or at room temperature.

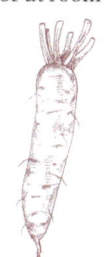  

Session 5
HOW IS IT PROTECTED?

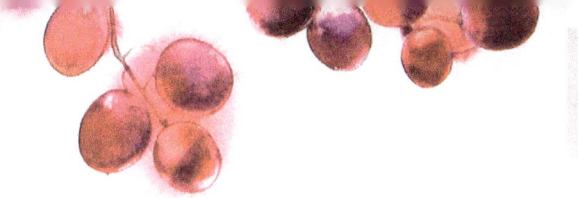

Session 5

VIDEO TEACHING

KEY VERSE

"Put on the full armor of God, so that you can take your stand against the devil's schemes" (Ephesians 6:11, NIV).

THE BIG IDEA

Regardless of our fruit's developmental stage, it will always be under attack, so we have to be armed and ready with our strategic barriers and offensive weapons to combat the devil's targeted attacks.

Three things are essential for protecting our fruit:

1. _____.

2. _____.

3. _____.

We have to _____ what we've been given.

We have to actively _____ and actively _____ what we've been called to produce.

We have to be _____ and on _____!

_____

_____

_____

_____

Discuss

Considering the three essential things for healthy fruit production *(preparation, prevention, and maintenance)*, is there an area you need to focus on right now?

What are the cares (the weeds and thorns) of your world that try to creep in and choke out your future fruitfulness?

What specific attacks does the enemy commonly use against you?

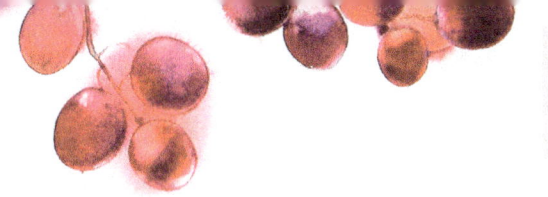

Day 1:
THE PREVENTION PLAN - PART 1

Nursing was a second career for me. I initially had an interest in it; however, the college I chose didn't offer it as a major. So, as a young 18-year-old fresh out of high school, I landed on a bachelor of science in wellness as my first degree of study. From there, I went on to earn a master's degree in public health and concentrated on health education and promotion. I don't share this to wave my resume around but rather to share a bit about my earlier passion: wellness, health promotion, education, and disease prevention.

In the '90s, this concept of disease prevention and health promotion was relatively new. But today, most people understand the idea of disease prevention as it is the driving motivation to get annual physical exams, exercise regularly, take vitamins, eat nutritious food, get adequate sleep, have a good work-life balance, and so on. The question is, why do we work to achieve these things?

The answer is largely because we don't want to become sick.

No one wants to get heart disease, diabetes, or cancer, and no one wants to be overweight, experience depression, or develop a co-morbidity. Therefore, if we value our well-being, then we make choices that support a healthy and fulfilling life, doing what we can to help mitigate disease—and much of this includes preventive measures.

And guess what? The concept of prevention is biblical.

Using the Scripture provided below, answer the following questions:

"Don't you realize that your body is the temple of the Holy Spirit, who lives in you and was given to you by God? You do not belong to yourself, for God bought you with a high price. So you must honor God with your body" (1 Corinthians 6:19-20, NLT).

What does Paul say is the temple of the Holy Spirit?

To whom do you belong?

What are we to do with our bodies?

Turn to 2 Corinthians 5:10. Summarize this verse in your own words:

Prevention relates to the concept of stewardship. Since our bodies are not our own, we have been entrusted with the careful and responsible management of them. We do our part to take care of what's been given to us: one body and one life. In other words, we are called to steward what we've been given and to steward it well.

Now let's take a look at the Scriptures to see how this lesson of prevention and stewardship can be applied to other areas of our life. In Matthew 25 and Luke 19, Jesus specifically teaches us about preparation and the need to live ready for the day He returns.

Using Matthew 25:14-30, answer the following questions and fill in the chart below:

Who does the Master/King represent?

Whom do the servants represent?

What do the silver/talents in Matthew and the gold/minas in Luke represent?

What do you think the Master/King's property represents?

	What did the Master/King give each servant?	What did each servant do with what he was given?	What was the Master/King's response to what each servant did?
Servant 1			
Servant 2			
Servant 3			

Why do you think the first two servants invested the talents? What was their motivation?

When YOU invest your gifts, talents, time, money, or spiritual gifts, what is YOUR motivation?

In Matthew 25:25, what is the third servant's reason for NOT investing what he was given?

Can you think of a modern-day reason that someone would be afraid to invest what he or she has been given?

Sometimes we allow fear to paralyze us and prevent us from moving forward in our calling. As we work through bearing our fruit, ask yourself if there are things that have prevented you from investing what you've been given.

In Matthew 25:28, what did the Master/King tell the servants to do?

What finally happened to the third servant?

This parable is about lifelong stewardship. It's about what we do with what we've been given. The third servant didn't so much waste the master's money as he wasted an opportunity. In the end, he was cast out of the kingdom and thrown into outer darkness (Matthew 25:30).

The master could've left his money where it was, and it would have remained unchanged until he returned. However, he graciously chose to give his servants specific amounts to invest. He wanted them to grow and multiply what had been apportioned to them to advance his kingdom in his absence. Just like his servants, we will also be held accountable for what we've been given. There <u>will</u> come a day—either when we die or when Christ returns—when we all must give an account of how we stewarded what was entrusted to us. Did we multiply our investment for the Kingdom of Heaven, or did we waste it, never moving forward in our calling because we were paralyzed by fear and anxiety?

What did you think about the fact that the servant who multiplied his talents the most received the original investment of the third servant (Luke 19:24, NLT)? Like the other servants, did you think he had received enough already?

Did you find a parallel between the FIRST servant and our mandate to bear fruit?

Each fruitful servant was given more, but the one who produced <u>the MOST</u> was entrusted with <u>EVEN MORE</u>. We've seen this concept before: Those who bear much bring the Father glory (John 15:8).

Perhaps Jesus wanted to illustrate that there are certain things we've all been given the same amount of, such as the same number of minutes in an hour, hours in a day, and days in a week. These things "level the playing field" of life. No one has more seconds in a minute than any other person, so how we steward our time and priorities matters.

How are you stewarding your time? Are you investing it well? Are there priorities (e.g., sleep/wake time, time spent on social media or watching TV, etc.) you've been challenged to change?

The master in this story demonstrated an interesting principle by giving varying amounts of talents to his servants. The master understood that the one-talent servant was not capable of producing as much as the five-talent servant. The lesson here for us is that we are all created uniquely—not equally.

To be clear, the unequal gifting of talents isn't a measure of fairness because, ultimately, the reward for each is the same. Even though we're not created equally with regard to the talents we're given, there is equality in this lesson. Each faithful steward put effort and energy into multiplying his unique investment, and those who were able to multiply their talents received the *same* response from the master: "Well done, my good and faithful servant. You have been faithful in handling this small amount, so now I will give you many more responsibilities. Let's celebrate together!" (Matthew 25:21, 23, NLT).

I don't want to miss the fact that, when each of the servants were initially given their entrusted treasure, they didn't wish they'd been given what the other had. We do a disservice to ourselves when we negatively compare our gifts, talents, situations, or whatever it may be, and long for what someone else has.

In Session 4, Day 2, we talked about people reading us. We have to recognize that we read others in the same way. However, we must be careful to NOT make negative, rash assumptions about them. They may seem perfectly polished and put together, but they may have struggled and sacrificed to get to where they are. Or maybe they seem like a hot mess, and we just caught them on an atypical, bad day. Because we are human, we intrinsically make rapid judgments about others—what they are like, what their socioeconomic status is, and whether they are educated, competent, trustworthy, or attractive—the list goes on.

Psychological Science published an article that revealed that all it takes is a tenth of a second to form an impression of a stranger from his or her face, and that longer exposures do not significantly alter those impressions (although they might boost your confidence in your initial opinion).[1] Even though this tendency to judge quickly is intrinsic, we should never judge a person's story by the chapter that we walk in on. Still, we can't beat ourselves up too much for succumbing to our human nature (our sin nature) because even Jesus had to put one of His closest disciples in check when he started comparing himself to another.

Now turn to John 21:15-25 and read the passage. What was Jesus' instruction for Peter in verse 22?

I have told this story to my children, and now in our house, we use the phrase, "Worry about yourself," to paraphrase what Jesus told Peter. Simply put, Jesus' lesson to Peter was: Don't concern yourself with anyone else's future. You cannot compare yourself with what anyone has been given because YOU will stand and give an account of YOUR life and what YOU did with it. We are not accountable for anyone else's gifts/talents and what they do or don't do with them; we are accountable only for our own.

Turn to Matthew 12:36-37. What will we have to give an account for?

Though it may not be a question of our eternal salvation, there will come a day when we stand before a holy God in righteous judgment for every word we've spoken, every thought we've had, every dollar we've spent, and every use of our spiritual gifts, talents, time, and energy (and our motivation behind each act).

Now turn to 1 John 2:17 and answer the following statement:

Whoever does this: _____ , will do this:_____.

This is why we can't sit idly by. If we do the will of God, we will abide forever. But this takes action and stewardship on our part, and our action (our mandate from God) is to bear fruit with selfless motivation.

Throughout the first few weeks of this study, we've worked through the concepts of defining, planting, and producing fruit. As we've worked through stewarding what we've been given, the idea of prevention is an essential element in protecting our fruit. Before the sodbuster ever begins planting his vineyard, he takes certain preparatory steps. He takes preventive measures to ensure his crop will be protected. Tomorrow, we will take some time to understand those steps and how they can apply to us in our everyday, fruit-bearing lives.

Let's close this day with a prayer.

Lord, I know I need to trust You and do good. Please give me clarity on the "doing" part. I don't want to function in a dead work, and I don't want to bury what You've given me. Help me move forward even if I'm afraid. Help me walk in boldness, knowing Your perfect love casts out all my fear. Your Word says You direct the steps of the godly, and You delight in every detail of my life. Though I may stumble, I will not fall because You hold me by my hand (Psalm 37: 23-24). Lord, I thank You for infusing me with talents, gifts, and dreams. Please help me steward them well. I want to hear, 'Well done, good and faithful servant.' Let me trust You with everything. I don't want to miss an opportunity. I know I'm called to do Your work, so use me exactly how You need me to be used. Help me have a life of integrity that honors You. I love You. In Jesus' name I pray. Amen.

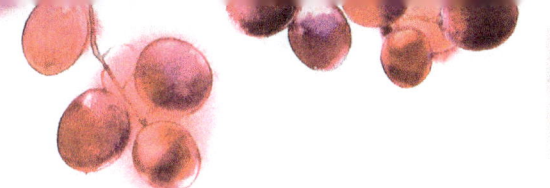

Day 2:
THE PREVENTION PLAN - PART 2

There are physical measures that we take to ensure our fruit will be safe from those who would want to eat, overtake, or destroy it. <u>Strategic barriers</u> are specific methods we implement to obstruct anything that jeopardizes the success of our fruit production.

In my backyard, it would be foolish of my husband and me to begin planting without taking any preventive measures to ensure the safety of the vegetation. Remember the open field in my backyard that I mentioned in Session 2, Day 4? Well, this open landscape brings every type of wildlife native to central Ohio. We've looked out our windows and seen wild turkeys, coyotes, foxes, rabbits, groundhogs, deer, raccoons, and even a family of skunks! Just the other day, I was startled to look out on my back patio and see a white-tailed deer snacking on some of the new spring growth in my flower bed. I ran out like a crazy person, shouting at the deer to get away from my plants.

We need a barrier to prevent these overgrown rodents from helping themselves to their own personal salad bar. Just as we take preventive measures for our health, we must also implement strategic barriers that are the proactive measures put into place *before* we ever have a problem with our fruit.

In the plant world, the prevention plan for protecting fruit includes planting cover crops, laying mulch, applying pesticides, erecting fences, using netting or tarps, and placing decoys among crops. All these methods involve creating a barrier or halting the problems that destroy our fruit. But what does this look like when we apply it to our personal ministry? How do we implement strategic barriers to stop the enemy from attacking and destroying our fruit? How do we steward through prevention?

PUT ON THE ARMOR

Turn to Ephesians 6:10-18. *(Put a bookmark here because we'll be coming back to this passage throughout the next section.)*

In verse 10, whose strength do we use?

In verse 11, what is the very first instruction?

This is a general command to be strong in the power that God has already given to us. Next, we are given a specific command (an action verb) that reveals something that *we* do. We are instructed to "*put on.*" This requires effort on our part, and it implies that we have a responsibility to act. In the parable of the talents, the master condemned the third servant with words like "wicked and lazy" because he did not *do* anything to advance his gifts. Clearly, God does not want us to remain in the same condition that we started in; He wants us to grow and mature. He wants us to multiply our gifts exponentially, similar to a profitable financial investment. Note that when the productive servants received their reward, the master said, "Well done..." This phrase implies completion. They had done something with what they were given and saw it through to the end.

Now that we know we are instructed to put on armor, *whose* armor are we putting on?

According to Ephesians 6:11-13, why do we need the armor Paul refers to?

Armor is the protective barrier worn by soldiers or warriors to guard their physical bodies in battle. Verse 11 says, "Put on the full armor of God, so that you can take your stand against the devil's schemes" (NIV). The word "schemes" is *methodeia* in Greek, and it is defined as cunning arts, deceit, craft, and trickery.[2] Paul understood that we are in a daily battle through which we wage war against the powers of darkness and wicked spirits in the heavenly realms. He instructs us to use EVERY piece of God's armor in our spiritual prevention plan. We have to combat the devil's schemes with spiritual strategies of our own.

THE FIRST PIECE OF ARMOR

In Ephesians 6:14, what is the first piece of armor we're instructed to put on?

Why do you think outfitting ourselves with the truth is the first step in putting on our armor?

We have to know the standard against which to measure everything. Do you recall our discussion of relativism versus absolute truth? If we know that Jesus is the way, THE TRUTH, and the life, then we know where the boundary of absolute truth begins and how to <u>guard, protect, and put a barrier around it</u>. With truth, we are able to frame our thoughts, desires, and emotions as well as the investment of our talents within the margins of a God-honoring life.

For example, when your reality says, "*You have cancer*," THE TRUTH says, "*I am Jehovah-Rapha, your healer*" (Exodus 15:26). When your reality says, "*You've lost your job*," THE TRUTH says, "*I am Jehovah Jireh, your provider*" (Genesis 22:13-14). When your reality says, "*Your marriage is in shambles*," THE TRUTH says, "*I am El Moshaah, the God who saves and I am El Shaddai, the All Sufficient One*" (Psalm 68:20, Genesis 17:1). Thus, when we gird ourselves with THE TRUTH, we align all the other pieces of our armor with who we are in Christ. When the little foxes that seek to spoil our vines begin lurking (Song of Solomon 2:15), we'll be ready to prevent their attacks from succeeding by knowing and operating in THE TRUTH.

THE SECOND PIECE OF ARMOR

After we surround ourselves with truth, what does verse 14 tell us to use?

What does the breastplate guard?

Now turn to the following verses and fill in the blanks:

Proverbs 4:23 (NIV)
"Above all else,_____ your heart, for everything you do flows from it."

Luke 6:45 (NIV)
"A good man brings good things out of the good stored up in his_____, and an evil man brings evil things out of the evil stored up in his_____. For the mouth speaks what the _____is full of."

Luke 8:12 (NIV)
"Those along the path are the ones who hear, and then the devil comes and takes away the word from their_____, so that they may not believe and be saved."

In these three passages, two Hebrew words (*leb* and *kardia*) are used for "heart;" however, both words have the same meaning: *the soul or mind; the seat of our thoughts, passions, and desires.* They refer to our inner man, conscience, will, and emotions.[3]

Why is it important for our spiritual breastplate to protect the center of our innermost being?

Turning back to Ephesians 6:15, what piece of armor is next?

Last week, we discussed peace at length, but I want to remind you that as a believer in Jesus Christ, you already have the gift of peace within you as a fruit of the Holy Spirit (Galatians 5:22). Through this free gift, we have the peace of God. We can have peace with God too; however, this peace requires our action. We have to put it on—just like the warrior's shoes—and keep it on so that we may be able to both stand firm and move forward.

Using the following verses, <u>UNDERLINE</u> the action required of us for achieving peace.

"Turn from evil and do good; seek peace and pursue it" (Psalm 34:14, NIV).

"If it is possible, as far as it depends on you, live at peace with everyone" (Romans 12:18, NIV).

The pursuit of peace is a lifelong challenge. At more times than I care to admit, I've felt the quickening of the Holy Spirit to stop whatever I'm doing and send a text message, write an email, or make a phone call to seek peace in a relationship. Maybe I owe the other person an apology, or perhaps there just needs to be a conversation to work out hurt feelings on both sides. Whatever the situation, it is NEVER easy. Sometimes the outcome doesn't end in the way I had hoped. Sadly, you may experience situations where there is no reconciliation, but we have to remind ourselves that we are responsible for our part.

Many years ago, I participated in a Bible study called *Resolving Everyday Conflict*.[4] One of the key takeaways for me was that it's *my* job to admit my mistakes and apologize, even if the other person is 98% wrong and I was only 2% wrong. I still have to take responsibility for my 2%, regardless of whether the other person ever admits his or her mistakes.

Remember, we will ALL stand and give an account for *ourselves*—no one else.

Once in a while, our peace-seeking is one-sided. You may have suffered at the hand of another, and reconciliation is absolutely not an option because distance is necessary or the person is a danger to you (mentally, physically, emotionally, or spiritually). Or that person may no longer even be alive. How do we put on peace in these situations? We forgive even though we may never have reconciliation because forgiveness and reconciliation are two separate things. We need to forgive those who sin against us because it sets us free. Forgiveness is something that takes place between the one who has been hurt and God. We seek forgiveness so that a bitter root doesn't take up residence in us and destroy our fruit.

Reconciliation, on the other hand, is when both sides of the damaged relationship seek healing and restoration. Ultimately, reconciliation is desired but not required. We are, however, required to forgive and put on peace.

THE FOURTH PIECE OF ARMOR

Read Ephesians 6:16 below and write what we need next.

After reading the verse below, can you CIRCLE the difference in the instruction for this piece of armor compared to the rest?

"Above all, lift up the [protective] shield of faith with which you can extinguish all the flaming arrows of the evil one" (AMP).

The shield that Paul wrote about referenced the large Roman soldiers' shields designed to protect the entire body. These shields had an iron frame and were covered in several layers of canvas and leather. When soaked in water before a battle, the shields could put out the fiery missiles thrown at them by the enemy, but they were HEAVY![5]

This piece of armor was not worn on the body. It was an extension piece used only in warfare. The shield can protect you only if you actually lift it up.

Perhaps Paul needed to explain the necessity of the shield's importance because, otherwise, no one would want to hold onto such cumbersome equipment. However, it's totally worth the effort because, once we are safely behind this strategic barrier, we can hold tightly to our faith, girded in the truth, and move forward in peace.

Hebrews 11:1 says, "Now faith is confidence in what we hope for and assurance about what we do not see" (NIV).

Using the above verse, how do YOU explain faith?

Have you experienced an *increase* in your own faith as you've matured in your relationship with the Lord? If yes, how so?

Dig Deeper

The *scutum* was likely the shield referenced in Ephesians 6, and it was approximately 22 lbs, 41.5 in high, 16 in wide, and 12 in deep.[6]

©2dmolier /Adobe Stock

The apostles needed help with understanding how to increase their faith. In Luke 17:5-6, Jesus was teaching on forgiveness, and the disciples felt completely defeated by the idea of always having to forgive those who have offended them. They didn't believe they had it within them to carry out this lifelong assignment, so they said to the Lord:

> *"Show us how to increase our faith." The Lord answered, "If you had faith even as small as a mustard seed, you could say to this mulberry tree, 'May you be uprooted and be planted in the sea,' and it would obey you!" (NLT).*

It's not about how *much* faith you have or how much faith you have *compared to someone else* because even the smallest amount of faith can help you move forward. The real issue is in WHOM do you have your faith. Do you believe that God is who He says He is? Jesus Himself said, "Anything is possible if a person believes" (Mark 9:23, NLT).

I'll be honest: When those fiery darts attack or when those critters and pests start to destroy my fruit, I can struggle. I've often had to pray, "I do believe, but help me overcome my unbelief!" (Mark 9:24, NLT). If I'm not operating in faith, then it's fear, and fear is not of God. Remember that fear was the very thing that kept the third servant from investing his talents. Fear will keep you from moving forward in your calling, and fear will hamstring you after you've taken a bold step forward in your faith, working hard to knock you back. So be prepared for the enemy to attack before (and after) you move. The enemy does not want you to succeed.

Let me remind you that we overcome the enemy by the blood of The Lamb and the word of our testimony (Revelation 12:11). Every time I hear a testimony, it encourages my spirit and strengthens my faith. When I receive a praise report from someone for whom I've been interceding, I am encouraged and my faith increases. The next time I offer up a prayer, I can go with confidence because I know God answers prayer. More specifically, I know He answers <u>my</u> prayer.

Dig Deeper

Research suggests that *Salvadora persica* is the plant described in the parable of the mustard seed. Called *khardal* by the Arabs, the mustard tree is a true tree growing to about 25 feet in height.[7,8]

THE FIFTH PIECE OF ARMOR

Now that we've got our shield up, what does Ephesians 6:17 say to put on next?

What does this piece guard?

There is a direct correlation between our mental status and our helmet wearing.

Just do a simple web search, and you will find a plethora of books related to your mind and how you think. Seminars and self-help courses help us understand how to rewire, awaken, change, silence, open, stimulate, and play games with our minds. Our culture has a deep desire to understand how to overcome our constant mental warfare. So many people have been under attack; they've suffered blow after blow in the space between their ears. I think about the crushing assaults on our thinking, and I am tired of it. I am tired of the mental victimization. I want to use my defensive barrier and flip the script. I want to go on the offensive. But how do we do this? We look to the Holy Word as our ultimate self-help book.

Look up the following Scriptures and match them with their central theme:

Romans 12:1-2	Have the same mindset as Christ Jesus.
2 Corinthians 10:4-5	Let God transform you into a new person by changing the way you think. Then you will know His perfect and pleasing will for your life.
Philippians 2:5	Use godly weapons to knock down the strongholds of human reason, destroy false arguments, and take every thought captive to the obedience of Christ.

We can go on the offensive by casting down every thought that does not align itself with the truth of the Word and by renewing our minds so we can have the same mindset as Christ.

Let's look at a biblical example of how helmet-wearing affects our outcome.

Turn to 1 Samuel 17.

In this chapter, the Israelite and Philistine armies are facing one another on opposite hills with the valley of Elah between them. Then, in verse 4, we're introduced to Goliath, a giant of a man.

After reading verses 5-8, describe Goliath's armor.

Throughout 1 Samuel 17 (vv 8, 16, and 24) we find that Goliath has been tormenting the Israelite troops for 40 days and nights. He's been taunting them incessantly, trying to goad them into battle. Then, in verses 32-40, David steps onto the scene. This ruddy and handsome shepherd boy had just been anointed as the future king of Israel (1 Samuel 16:12-13), and Scripture says that from the moment the anointing oil bathed over his head, "The Spirit of the Lord came powerfully upon David from that day on" (NLT). As David heard the taunts of this pagan giant who was insulting the name of the Most High God, he was instantly affronted and made the decision to go on the offensive.

When David was questioned about his ability, he testified to all the prior times God had helped him succeed over an enemy attack. He had been anointed with the physical and spiritual presence of the Holy Spirit, and he was able to move forward in the truth of who the Lord Almighty was to him, shod with (and in) peace, and covered by faith as his defensive barrier.

What happens next in verses 38-39?

Man-made armor will never compare to the spiritual armor of God. This is why all the self-help books will never compare to the help that comes from the Lord, the Maker of heaven and earth (Psalm 121). Though Saul's armor was made from the exact same material as Goliath's—a helmet of bronze and a coat of mail—it was ill-fitting and restrictive for David. So David proceeded with what he knew to be tried and true: his shepherd's staff, sling, and five smooth stones.

In verses 41-44, what is Goliath's reaction to seeing David approach him?

Isn't that predictable? It's so typical of an opponent to trash-talk and use scare tactics. However, David had his mind fixed on God and was able to see through the ploys of an unworthy adversary. King Saul may have cowered in fear for 40 days, but David wasn't going to let the blasphemous insults continue. In verses 45-47, David combatted the lies with THE TRUTH. God had been faithful to protect him in the wilderness against lions and bears, and David had NO doubt that God would be faithful to protect him again.

Now read verses 48-51 and answer the following questions:

Where did David hit Goliath?

To secure his victory, what did David do to Goliath's head?

Goliath had a shield, but someone else was carrying it. Goliath wore a helmet, but it was his own. With one smooth stone strategically launched past a worthless shield and expertly aimed at the exposed part of Goliath's forehead, David sent the giant tumbling to the ground, face-first. The lesson here is that no matter what giants we face (whether physical, mental, emotional, or spiritual), we have to employ our weapons of strategic warfare to establish a defensive barrier around ourselves.

There is no fair fighting in a spiritual battle.

In fact, there was nothing fair about these two opponents. Their weight class, training experience, physical armor, and weapons were unequal. But we have to think supernaturally, as David did, and remember that we have the full armor of God at our disposal and the battle is won only through the strength and power of the Lord God Almighty. The more we guard our minds by putting into place the protective spiritual barrier, the more our thinking, emotions, and desires align with the perfect, sovereign will of our Heavenly Father. As a result, the enemy's insults, scare tactics, and full-frontal assaults will not prevail against us.

Now that we understand the strategic barriers we have the authority to employ, let's not forget the last two pieces of armor—our offensive weaponry.

THE SIXTH PIECE OF ARMOR

Turn back to Ephesians 6:17. What is the next piece of armor we are to utilize?

Hebrews 4:12 says, "For the word of God is alive and active. Sharper than any double-edged sword, it penetrates even to dividing soul and spirit, joints and marrow; it judges the thoughts and attitudes of the heart" (NIV).

UNDERLINE the characteristics of The Word of God in the Scripture above.

What's the significance of a double-edged (or some versions say two-edged) sword?

The Word of God is likened to a two-edged sword that cuts in both directions. This weapon is effective on both the foreswing and on the backslash, but it's also used with precision.

Like the surgeon's scalpel, we need complete accuracy when making incisions between viable and damaged tissue. We need a razor-like distinction between good and evil, and the most potent offensive weapon we have in this effort is the piercing and dividing Word of God.

I find it supremely poetic when I read of David's final act toward Goliath in 1 Samuel 17:51. Using Goliath's own sword, David cut off his head, piercing through flesh, physically dividing his joints and marrow (Yes, it's graphic, I know!) The final judgment had been rendered, and victory was the Lord's! How can we, like David, use The Sword as a tool in our prevention plan?

Using the following Scriptures, <u>UNDERLINE</u> the language that pertains to The Word.

Psalm 119:11

"Your word I have treasured and stored in my heart, that I may not sin against You" (AMP).

Psalm 119:105

"Your word is a lamp to my feet and a light to my path" (AMP).

2 Timothy 3:16-17

"All Scripture is God-breathed and is useful for teaching, rebuking, correcting and training in righteousness, so that the servant of God may be thoroughly equipped for every good work" (NIV).

The Sword is more than a lethal weapon. It's also a guiding and training tool. To be a Christian is to be a trained, weapon-wielding warrior. The weapon specifically mentioned in these passages requires close combat. We use The Sword as an offensive weapon when the enemy is within arm's reach.

Remember that the enemy will work to attack us before we ever step out in our calling. Even Jesus did not elude the unoriginal tactics of the devil. Jesus hadn't even begun His earthly ministry yet, and Satan was already working to prevent Him from fulfilling His Messianic destiny. Jesus had been fasting and praying in the wilderness for 40 days and nights, and He was hungry. The devil thought he had an obvious win—a tired, hungry, easy target. However, with every temptation that Satan launched, Jesus answered, "It is written" and quoted Scripture in context, using The Word with razor-sharp precision. After three rounds of spiritual combat, verse 11 says, "Then the devil left him, and angels came and attended him" (NIV).

Dig Deeper

In Greek this "sword" is translated from *machaira* (mä'-khī-rä), and it's the same word for Peter's weapon on the night of Jesus' arrest (John 18:10). Peter was a fisherman, not a soldier. A fisherman's *machaira* was used for killing animals and cutting up their flesh with precision.[9]

Charles Spurgeon wrote the following regarding our spiritual battles:

> *To meet the powers of darkness is no sham battle... Nothing but your eternal damnation will satisfy the fiendish hearts of Satan and his crew...If you are to live through this fight, and come off victorious, no form of conflict will suffice less sharp and cutting than sword-work.*[10]

As the Scriptures reveal, Jesus was ready and prepared when the devil tested Him. He combated the enemy's lies with the truth of the Word He had hidden in His heart and enlisted the power of prayer and fasting long before the enemy came lurking to destroy His fruit. Because we have the mind of Christ, we too must be prepared. We must READ, STUDY, and SPEAK The Word to defeat our enemy.

THE FINAL WEAPON

Once we have on our armor with sword in hand, ready to slice, what do we do next?

Paul's final instruction is to "Pray in the Spirit at all times and on every occasion. Stay alert and be persistent in your prayers..." (Ephesians 6:18, NLT). Prayer is our final weapon.

This topic of prayer leads us to tomorrow's lesson. When we implement our prevention plan and stand alert and on guard, we can swiftly recognize anything amiss with our fruit. We will aptly determine any fruit-bearing problems and be able to move forward with a <u>diagnosis</u> and <u>treatment plan</u>.

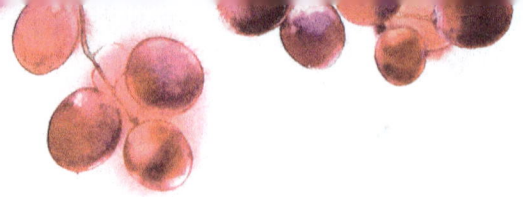

Day 3:
PHYSICAL EXAM & PRESENTING PROBLEM

It was the summer of my junior year as an undergraduate, and I decided to take courses at the local community college. I didn't normally attend that school, but I needed a close-to-home option to make up for switching my major at the tail end of my four-year program.

So, on a hot July afternoon, I walked into Psychology 101 and sat in a seat at the front of the class. I was early, and there weren't many other classmates in the room yet. My professor walked over to me and said, "I need your help with something today." Half-freaked-out and half-excited, I said, "Sure, what's up?"

He replied, "Ten minutes after class starts, I need you to stand up, slowly push in your chair, grab your stuff, and walk out of the classroom."

"Okaaaay?" I said, not fully understanding what was going on.

Then he said, "Wait out in the hall, and I'll call you back inside. We're going to do a little class experiment."

So, at 2:10 p.m., I stood up in the front of the room while my teacher was talking. I grabbed my belongings, pushed in my chair, and with a downward gaze, slowly walked out of the room. After about ten minutes, my professor peeked out into the hall and said, "Okay, Angela, you can come back in!" I grabbed my stuff and headed back into the room. As soon as I opened the door, I heard comments of, "Oh, man! She's got brown hair!" and "I was right; she is tall!" Needless to say, I was very confused.

As I sat back down in my seat, I must've had a look of complete and utter bewilderment because my professor quickly explained that he had done an experiment on the validation and reliability of eye-witness testimony. He went on to say, "After you left the room, I asked everyone to write down your description." He collected the intel from around the room, and my classmates had compiled a profile indicating that I had short, blond hair and blue eyes, and I was roughly 5'1" (for reference, I have long, brown hair and hazel eyes, and I am 5'7"). Some of the other students were a bit closer, but none of them had a 100% accurate description of me. They did not know me.

Now, let me present you a completely different scenario.

On April 13, 2015, the jewelry company Pandora released a video advertisement called *The Unique Connection*.[11] In the ad, six children were asked to try to find their mothers—while blindfolded.

One by one, the children were escorted into a room where their six moms all stood in a line. Some of the small children tugged on the women's hands to pull them down to their level. With their sense of touch, each child felt their clothes, hands, faces, and even hair. Some of them even smelled the women in order to find their mom. When each child approached their own mother, they'd nervously or excitedly nod, smiles beaming across each of their faces. Almost all the moms were tearful as they removed their child's blindfold, which resulted in an excited embrace. I have cried every time I've watched it. Well done, Pandora. Well done. You got me. You've successfully tugged on this mama's heartstrings with this tearjerker of a commercial.

After I watch something like this, I find myself asking, "Could my children identify me if I were in a line-up of other moms?" "Would my nose, my lips, or the expression lines on my face give me away?" "Would they know me by my hands?" "Would they know me by my scent?" I hope so. The bond between a parent and child is intense. That's why Isaiah 49:15 has always been one of those verses that repeatedly makes me pause and consider the weightiness of the words:

> *Can a mother forget the baby at her breast and have no compassion on the child she has borne? Though she may forget, I will not forget you. (Isaiah 49:15, NIV)*

Personally, I struggle to grasp the depth of these words because I have a mother who loves and supports me. I can't even begin to imagine putting any of my three children out of my mind and forgetting them; in fact, the very idea of that pains me. But I know some of you have experienced great suffering from someone who was meant to have compassion for you. So the promise of this Scripture may intimately resonate within your spirit. Even if we are abandoned and forgotten by those who are supposed to care for and love us most, <u>God</u> <u>NEVER</u> <u>will</u>.

He knows us.

My prayer is that we will know Him too.

Turn to John 10:14 and write it here:

Now turn to John 10:27 and write it here:

How does the shepherd know his sheep?

How do the sheep know the shepherd's voice?

Dig Deeper

Contrary to popular opinion, sheep aren't dumb. They know who feeds them, protects them, and cares for their needs. Sheep can distinguish their keeper's voice from others.[12]

©bernardbodo /Adobe Stock

Each human being has a voice that is distinctively different from everyone else's. To know someone's voice, you have to hear it over and over. The sheep recognize the shepherd's voice because they have heard it day in and day out. Because the shepherd has been a faithful master and guardian, they follow him without hesitation. Just like the Pandora commercial, they have a "unique connection." He knows His own sheep, and they know Him.

To build on how we ended yesterday's discussion, let's work through how to recognize if anything is going awry with our fruit. How can we become valid, reliable, and expert eye-witnesses of the condition of our crop? How do we vigilantly protect our fruit?

In the horticulture world, grapes can suffer from many problems. If the prevention plan were never implemented or there were a failure or defect in the strategic barrier, then fruit production would be plagued by a multitude of challenges.

Just like a faithful vinedresser, we have to observe and know our crop.

As fruit bearers, we have to physically examine the branches (ourselves) and our fruit (our ministry) to determine if there is a presenting problem. Romans 12:11 says, "Never be lazy, but work hard and serve the Lord enthusiastically" (NLT). We cannot afford to be lazy like the third servant. We have to be ever-vigilant and on guard to have an accurate, intimate knowledge of our fruit.

In her book *The Armor of God*, Priscilla Shirer writes this about laziness:

> *The call to victorious Christian living is a wake-up call out of laziness, urging you to rise up and take serious action. The strength you need for resisting and standing firm depends on it. Satan and the demons of darkness are hoping you'll be disengaged and disinterested instead of alert, aware, and active.*[13]

In this next section, I want you to look up specific verses that will teach and train us so we may be thoroughly equipped to be alert, aware, and active.

Look up the following Scriptures and fill in the chart. (I used the NLT.)

Matthew 7:7
"Keep on _____ , and you will receive what you ask for. Keep on seeking, and you will find. Keep on _____ , and the door will be opened to you."

Mark 13:33
"And since you don't know when that time will come, be on_____! Stay_____!"

Acts 12:5
"But while Peter was in prison, the church prayed very _____for him."

Ephesians 6:18
"_____ in the Spirit at all times and on every occasion. Stay_____ and be _____ in your _____ for all believers everywhere."

Philippians 4:6
"Don't worry about anything; instead, _____ about_____. Tell God what you need, and _____ him for all he has done."

Colossians 4:2
"Devote yourselves to_____with an_____mind and a thankful heart."

1 Thessalonians 5:17
"Never stop_____."

James 5:16
"Confess your sins to each other and_____for each other so that you may be healed. The_____ _____of a righteous person has great power and produces wonderful results."

1 Peter 5:8
"Stay_____! _____out for your great enemy, the devil. He prowls around like a roaring lion, looking for someone to devour."

Do you notice any common themes in these passages?

When we engage in perpetual, earnest, specific, and fervent prayer, we are able to expertly oppose the meticulous ploys that the enemy uses to take us out. When we compare this to a life lived on the vine, we can ask ourselves questions such as: Is the growth of our fruit weak or excessive? Are shoots curling? Are leaves eaten or scarred? Has the color changed? Is there a distortion of the leaf surface? Are insects present? Is the problem localized or is it scattered throughout the vineyard? When we examine our fruit, we can discern whether there are problems.

Taking time to know the condition of our fruit enables us to see issues that may need addressing. Once we've identified the enemy's schemes, we can stay alert and put into place strategic barriers to counter the presenting problem(s) and appropriately protect our fruit.

I want to challenge you to think about the condition of your fruit right now.

Is there anything that you know to be plaguing your fruit production?
(Is anything going on in your life right now that you know to be attacking your calling?)

Think about all of your God-given gifts, talents, and interests and how you can use them to glorify the Lord. Be ready because you will suffer the greatest attacks when you are functioning within this realm. You have to prepare to guard the areas of your greatest influence because the enemy does not want you producing good fruit to advance the Kingdom of Heaven. Remember that wildlife and critters do not want to eat rotten, moldy, or dead fruit. If given the option, they'll go for the juiciest, most succulent fruit on the vine—the fruit that is an indication of a thriving, productive life.

What are YOUR areas of greatest impact and strength? Where is YOUR fruit the healthiest?
(Your faith? Your relationships? Your prayer life? Your perseverance? Your testimony?)

Have you experienced any attacks in these areas? If so, please describe.

Now think about the weeds and thorns that you wrote about in Session 3, Day 3.

What are the cares and anxieties of YOUR world that, given the right conditions, will creep in and choke out YOUR fruit? (Fear? Rejection? People-pleasing? Resentment? Anger?)

How has the enemy used these triggers to set you off, thwarting your ability to produce good fruit?

The enemy will use any sensitive, hot-button issue specific to you to derail you from your calling. Ephesians 6:11 tells us that Satan and his legion of demonic forces will use "all the schemes and the strategies and the deceits of the devil" (AMP) wherever and whenever he can. *The Message Bible* says it this way: "This is no afternoon athletic contest that we'll walk away from and forget about in a couple of hours. This is for keeps, a life-or-death fight to the finish against the Devil and all his angels."

The hallmark of the devil is that he wants to keep us oppressed and depressed. He has studied us and knows the exact places to pull the snagged thread of our emotions to make us unravel. He wants us condemned, doubting, and discouraged. He does NOT want us to rise up and live the life we are called to live. He wants to choke us out before our lives even have a chance to blossom into anything that remotely resembles good fruit. In addition, if we are walking in our calling, he is going to deploy strategic attacks to poison, eat, corrupt, trample, and ultimately destroy our healthy fruit from being harvested. We must be alert and on guard—armed and ready with our strategic barriers and offensive weapons to combat his targeted attacks.

Turn to Genesis 50:20. Write the Scripture here:

Summarize what this verse means to you.

Do you have a personal story of something the devil meant for evil that God used for good?

It is time for each one of us to flip the script and become a threat to the kingdom of darkness. Let's go on the offensive and be prepared to fight when the enemy starts using his tired, old tactics against us. As Max Lucado paraphrased Genesis 50:20, "In God's hands, intended evil becomes eventual good."[14]

KNOWING THE PRESENTING PROBLEMS

Now that I've given you a snapshot of how the enemy uses his schemes against me, I want you to work through developing strategic barriers against common attacks that the devil uses against YOU, so you can be armed and ready to protect YOUR fruit.

First, you have to know your fruit to know the presenting problems.

As we end today, I'd like you to work through the common presenting problems that we face as believers. Some problems might be more of an issue to you than others. Remember, Satan is a cunning adversary who's studied you, so certain presenting problems are most likely his tired, old schemes repeatedly and specifically being used against you. Most likely, you've experienced all the problems listed in some way, shape, or form. Let's prepare a battle plan to ward off the enemy's unoriginal strategies. When we see them start to creep in and try to destroy our good fruit and our future, we will be prepared.

In the following problems, I've given a synopsis of how the enemy specifically attacks and how each issue might present itself in our lives. It may take some time to work through this, but do the work up front so you're not caught off guard. Remember that Noah didn't start building the ark when the rain began—He prepared for the storms far in advance!

Read through the presenting problems and (CIRCLE) the enemy's hallmark calling cards for you.

PRESENTING PROBLEM #1: DECEPTION
(Genesis 3:1-5; John 8:44; 2 Corinthians 2:11, 11:3, 11:14; Revelation 12:9)
These are lies we accept or lies we commit. Just as with Adam and Eve in the Garden of Eden, Satan manipulates the truth to deceive us into believing relative truths versus the absolute truths of what God's Word says. He also deceives us into thinking that our own half-truths, white lies, or lies of omission aren't harmful to the point that we sometimes justify our sin.

PRESENTING PROBLEM #2: DECOYS
(Luke 4:13; 1 Thessalonians 3:5; 1 Corinthians 10:13; Matthew 4:3, 26:41)
Like a shiny fishing lure skimming across the surface of the water, Satan wants to bait you into temptation. For example, images on your computer or a co-worker's comforting words amid marital strife could make you believe you can engage in certain activities without suffering consequences.

PRESENTING PROBLEM #3: DEJECTION, DETACHMENT, DISCORD, AND DISTRESS
(1 Peter 5:8; Ecclesiastes 4:9-10, 12; 1 Timothy 2:8; Proverbs 6:14, 19; Titus 3:9-11; 2 Corinthians 2:10-11; 1 John 2:10; Hebrews 12:14-15; Ephesians 4:30-32)
Satan loves for us to feel rejected and isolated. We become like the weakest animal in the herd, falling behind the pack, and he can single you out and attack you when you're alone and vulnerable. When relationships deteriorate, you know the enemy is at work.

PRESENTING PROBLEM #4: SELF-DETERMINATION
(Proverbs 3:5-6; Jeremiah 9:23; Philippians 2:3; Romans 9:16; Ephesians 2:8)
This is when our own self-determination or self-reliance takes preeminence over our dependence on God. We believe that we can accomplish things using our own talents and skills, and pride keeps us thinking that we don't need God. We lean on our own understanding and our own merit.

PRESENTING PROBLEM #5: DISCONTENTMENT AND DISDAIN
(Colossians 3:5; James 3:16, 4:2-4; Romans 13:9)

We see others' achievements/failures, and we begin to compare our life to theirs. Satan flashes others' picturesque Facebook and Instagram profiles in our faces, and we believe they have a better life than we do. Discontentment can lead to jealousy or envy of others—their homes, spouses, families, jobs, appearance, etc.—and we feel inferior and insecure. Or maybe we feel superior to them, and arrogance and pride creep in, further disconnecting us from God.

PRESENTING PROBLEM #6: DISGRACE
(Romans 8:1; Zechariah 3:1; John 3:17-18; Revelation 12:10)

Satan makes you feel shame, regret, and condemnation for past mistakes. The enemy constantly reminds you of your poor choices and past sins to make you feel unworthy of the redemptive blood of Jesus. He reminds you of your past to keep you from moving forward in your future.

PRESENTING PROBLEM #7: DISTRACTION
(Deuteronomy 5:15; Psalm 23:2, 46:10)

Satan steals our joy by overloading us with the busyness of life. This is when our attention is diverted from God to other things, such as hobbies, social media, and TV. It's when we repeatedly spend hours on other things instead of spending time with God. We wake up to Facebook alerts and a full email inbox, and before our feet hit the ground in the morning, we're inundated with calendar reminders and an activity-packed day. These things are not inherently evil, but they take our focus away from the Lord. They are distractions from our time spent with God—time that He deserves.

PRESENTING PROBLEM #8: DOMESTICATED PETS
(Proverbs 22:3; Psalm 51:10; Romans 13:14; Galatians 6:8; 1 John 2:16)

No, these aren't dogs, cats, and fish. These are the "pet sins" we feed without truly realizing we are preventing our own fruit production from flourishing. When we gossip, use foul language, tell crude jokes, are gluttonous or lazy, repeatedly procrastinate, or slander others, we are actually causing harm to our character and inhibiting our own growth.

PRESENTING PROBLEM #9: DOUBT
(Genesis 3:1-13; John 8:44; John 20:27)

This is when you begin to question whether God has really called you. Thoughts of fear, anxiety, and worry creep in, and you begin to feel apprehensive about the ministry He's entrusted to you. You doubt what you have been given and who you are in Christ.

PRESENTING PROBLEM #10: DULLED DESIRE
(Ephesians 1:17-19; 2 Corinthians 4:8-10)

Here, every day is more of the same, and your life becomes some variation of *Groundhog's Day*. You find that another day has gone by without prayer or quiet time spent with the Lord. Your passion and desire for spiritual things have been dulled. Over time, your desires and dreams are slowly eroded by the monotony of the days, weeks, months, and years. You are no threat to Satan because you are fruitless and barren.

After reading through these presenting problems, ask yourself: How will YOU be prepared to guard against these schemes? WRITE what you plan to do when you recognize the invasion. (For example, you can cite Scripture you'll quote or people you'll seek for counsel, or you can write out your fervent prayer.)

Let's pray to end this day.

Father, I am so grateful that You know me—even better than I know myself. Lord, I ask that You would reveal the areas of my life that need Your tender care. Examine me and expose any hidden problems that have hindered me from truly knowing You and producing fruit. Please use anything the devil meant for evil against me for Your good. Let my life glorify You. In Jesus' name I pray. Amen.

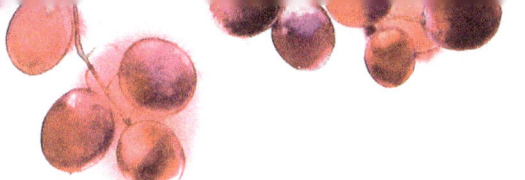

Day 4:
THE DIFFERENTIAL DIAGNOSIS

Let me tell you about *Daktulosphaira vitifoliae*—no, that is not a typo. This is the extremely long and difficult-to-pronounce scientific name for the North American aphid.[15]

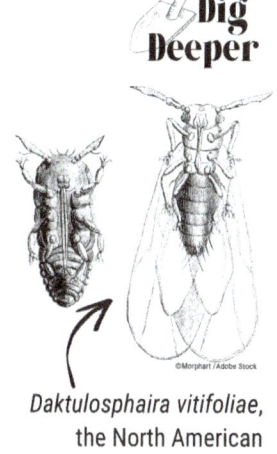

Daktulosphaira vitifoliae, the North American aphid

In the late 1850s, the North American aphid—also known as the *grapevine phylloxera*—made an unannounced Atlantic crossing and laid waste to the famous vineyards of France. It destroyed 40% of French grapevines over a 15-year period and put every vine in Europe at risk. These almost microscopic, pale, yellow, sap-sucking insects feed on the roots and leaves of grapevines. They climb onto the grape leaves and lay eggs inside a gall (an abnormal leaf growth) that they create by injecting their saliva. Nymphs then hatch from these eggs and quickly move to nearby leaves. Eventually, they make their way to the roots, where they inject a toxin and suck up the vine sap. This causes the small roots to swell and die quickly, and the injected poison eventually kills the entire vine.[16]

Legions of aphids went unnoticed by the French vinedressers because, once their toxin begins its lethal work on the root system, the sap level in the plant falls and the aphid moves on to seek a better source of food. A vinedresser digging up a dead vine would never find the culprit. The vinedressers finally diagnosed the problem when they dug up a dying vine and saw the small, yellow insects attached to the roots.

Although the aphid was eventually identified as the culprit, the damage had already been done. This tiny insect destroyed approximately two-thirds of all European vineyards. Vinedressers were forced to switch their entire crop because the regions were so blighted by phylloxera that they never recovered.

Now let's turn our focus to a biblical perspective. How does the lesson of the 1850s aphid infestation relate to the spiritual attacks on our fruit? In medicine, the term "differential diagnosis" means "the process of differentiating between two or more conditions which share similar signs or symptoms."[17]Generally, a differential diagnostic procedure is a method used to identify the presence of disease for which there is more than one potential cause. (For example, high blood sugar can result from a faulty pancreas or the ingestion of too many oral steroids.) When we look through Scripture, we can identify two specific reasons for attacks by insect invaders. We can identify the culprit as either an extrinsic (from outside) or intrinsic (from within) factor. However, we must know which it is in order to differentiate the diagnosis and, like the 1850s French vines, avoid total ruin.

Let's begin unpacking how extrinsic factors can affect our fruit.

Turn to Ephesians 2:1-2. How does this passage explain/describe Satan?

Ephesians 6:12 (NIV) says, "Our struggle is not against flesh and blood, but against the rulers, against the authorities, against the powers of this dark world and against the spiritual forces of evil in the heavenly realms."

In the verse above, <u>UNDERLINE</u> WHO our battle is truly being waged against.

Where is this unseen enemy located?

In high school, many of us read William Golding's allegorical novel *Lord of the Flies*. Although this book is now featured on the American Library Association's list of the most banned books ever, the book's title is a direct reference to Satan.[18]

When I think about a fly, I naturally cringe in disgust; they are a nuisance. I genuinely detest them because they breed and feed on human food, and during this process, they soften the food with their saliva and deposit their feces.[19] It's simply repulsive. Other than waste management, I cannot think of any benefit these disease vectors offer to our world. This is why Satan is called the lord of the flies; he is a disease vector to our world.

Now read Matthew 12:22-28.

In the following verses, <u>UNDERLINE</u> whom Jesus was accused of being in league with:

> "But when the Pharisees heard this, they said, 'This man casts out demons only by Beelzebul the ruler of the demons'" (Matthew 12:24, NASB).

> "But some of them said, 'He casts out demons by Beelzebul, the ruler of the demons'" (Luke 11:15, NASB).

"Beelzebul" or "Beelzebub," translated as "lord of flies," was derived from the name of the dung-god of the Ekronites (2 Kings 1:2), who had the power to drive away troublesome flies. Most scholars believe the Jews transferred the name to Satan in contempt.[20]

Because the Pharisees did not have eyes to see Jesus as the true Messiah, they ascribed their limited human understanding to the miracles they witnessed. Though others saw the miracles and experienced awe and wonder, the Pharisees were offended. To justify their offense, they applied their flawed logic, polluted the truth, and suggested that Jesus' supernatural acts must be from Beelzebul (or Satan), the "ruler of the demons" and "lord of the flies."

Now turn to John 8:44. Write all of the descriptions of Satan below:

In medicine, we cannot always see the cause of an affliction, and this is called an *unknown* etiology. Sometimes our human eyes cannot physically see the organisms that infect, the emotional wounds that scar, or the pathology (the cause and effect) of the disease or condition.

In such cases, we work backward from the symptoms.

Guess what? This same concept can apply to the symptoms we experience in our spiritual lives. Remember that our struggles are not against flesh and blood. The father of lies, the accuser of the brethren, the tempter, the ruler of the demons, and the lord of the flies is the extrinsic factor at work "in the heavenly realms" (Ephesians 6:12).

Every symptom or presenting problem, that we experience is evidence that there is a spiritual reality behind a physical, mental, or emotional one. We need to train our minds to acknowledge that, like phylloxera, even though we may not see the cause of our problems with human eyes, it is there.

The enemy is there—he is the *known* etiology.

Now turn to Psalm 23:5. Write it here:

In his book *A Shepherd's Look at the 23rd Psalm*, William Keller gives a shepherd's insight into David's 23rd Psalm. In the context of our discussion, Psalm 23:5b says, "You anoint my head with oil." If we look at this Scripture through the lens of a shepherd, we will find that this profound poetic line is a metaphorical reference to the devastation that insects can cause. Keller further explains that a number of parasites trouble sheep and make their lives miserable. These parasites include warble flies, bot flies, heel flies, nose flies, deer flies, black flies, mosquitoes, and gnats. Still, sheep are especially troubled by the nose fly. He writes the following:

These little flies buzz about the sheep's head, attempting to deposit their eggs on the damp mucous membranes of the sheep's nose. If they are successful, the eggs will hatch in a few days to form small, slender, worm-like larvae. They work their way up the nasal passages into the sheep's head; they burrow into the flesh and there set up an intense irritation accompanied by severe inflammation. For relief from this agonizing annoyance sheep will deliberately beat their heads against trees, rocks, posts, or brush. They will rub them in the soil and thrash around against woody growth. In extreme cases of intense infestation a sheep may even kill itself in a frenzied endeavor to gain respite from the aggravation...Because of all this, when the nose flies hover around the flock, some of the sheep become frantic with fear and panic in their attempt to escape their tormentors.[21]

Where do the flies attack?

Does this remind you of anything from our lesson on Day 2 of this session?

As a former shepherd, Keller shares that at the very first sign of flies among the flock, the shepherd must apply an antidote to the flies. He explains, "I always preferred to use a homemade remedy composed of linseed oil, sulfur, and tar, which was smeared over the sheep's nose and head as a protection against nose flies." Keller notes, "Once the oil had been applied to the sheep's head, there was an immediate change in behavior. Gone was the aggravation, gone the frenzy, gone the irritability and the restlessness. Instead, the sheep would start to feed quietly again, then soon lie down in peaceful contentment."[22]

What I find interesting about the analogy of the sheep is that they did nothing to invite the flies. Rather, their very existence attracted the flying invaders. When I apply this to my life, I am reminded that sometimes I will be attacked just because I am a child of God. You and I will be a target for the enemy because we belong to the Lord.

In the following table, we read that sometimes attacks, persecution, and temptation from the enemy—the extrinsic factors for our suffering—are evidence of a life that is truly serving the Lord well.

Look up the following Scripture references and match them with their message:

Matthew 5:10-12	Blessed are those who are persecuted, insulted, and falsely accused because of Jesus.
Matthew 10:22	You will be arrested, punished, and even killed. Because of me, you will be hated by people of all nations.
Matthew 24:9	Everyone will hate you because of me. But whoever holds out to the end will be saved.

When we are being attacked by Satan—the lord of the flies, the extrinsic factor, the *known etiology*—we have to saturate ourselves, specifically our minds, with the anointing oil. We have to thoroughly soak in the presence of the Holy Spirit. We live in a fallen world, so we must recognize there *will* be times when the attacks and suffering we experience are evidence of our lives bearing good fruit for the Kingdom of Heaven. Through our suffering, we can bring our Father glory.

When you recognize that you are being plagued by the "flies" of this fallen world, how do you apply the antidote of the Holy Spirit?

Recall the strategies you worked through yesterday to combat the presenting problems. In the space below, describe the methods you frequently employ that bring you peace.

If you've been struggling with this, write something that you will do today to invite the presence of the Holy Spirit.

ANALYZING THE INTRINSIC FACTORS

Now that we've determined that the aggravated assaults we endure are sometimes caused by the mere fact that we are The Good Shepherd's sheep, let's look at some of the *intrinsic factors* that can bring about the plaguing pests that wreak havoc on our lives.

Throughout Scripture, we find many recorded accounts of insects plaguing the land. Whether they were swarming invaders or a solitary pest, they caused tremendous irritation and complete destruction.

Using the Scripture references provided, complete the following table by indicating the type of pest, the reason for their infestation, and the result of their presence.

	The Pest	The Reason	The Result
Exodus 8:16-24		Pharaoh hardened his heart and did not let the Israelites go.	
Exodus 10:12-20			They devoured everything!
Amos 4:9		The Israelites had turned their backs on God. They had abandoned their first love.	

Insect infestation was historically a sign of God's judgment on a nation or people group. God protects and blesses *and* sends disaster and pestilence when it accomplishes His righteous purposes on earth. Whether it was a plague against an enemy nation brought about by Pharaoh's hardened heart or insect infestations sent to punish the rebellious Israelites for their ongoing idolatry and disobedience, God has used insects as a punishment for sin. For example, the Israelites rebelled against the Lord, grieved His heart, tested His patience, and frustrated Him. They forgot about His power and how He had rescued them from their enemies. Like any good father, God uses discipline to help us come into alignment and to turn the hearts of His children.

Although not every plague is the direct judgment of God, the Bible indicates that specific instances of insect infestation have been a punishment for sin. Because of this, we have to differentiate the cause of the infestation.

Turn to 2 Chronicles 7:13-14 and write verse 14 here:

Revelation 2:4-5 was written to the church in Ephesus and says, "But I have this against you: You have abandoned your first love. Therefore, keep in mind how far you have fallen. Repent and perform the deeds you did at first. But if you do not repent, I will come to you and remove your lampstand from its place (BSB)."

According to this Scripture, what was their intrinsic issue?

What was their instruction?

Ezra 8:22b-23 says: Our God's hand of protection is on all who worship him, but his fierce anger rages against those who abandon him. So we fasted and earnestly prayed that our God would take care of us, and he heard our prayer (NLT).

Within this passage, CIRCLE the prescription to combat an enemy attack.

Now turn to Joel 2:12-13. What did the prophet instruct the people to do?

It's not a complicated formula. The strategy for getting rid of an *internal* insect infestation requires us to:

1. **RETURN to our First Love.**
2. **REPENT.**
3. **REND our hearts.**

When we see the insect invaders start to creep in—be it aphids, locusts, or a solitary fly buzzing around—it is time to seek the Lord and ask Him to help us in the areas where we need Him most, whether it's an external or internal issue. We have to be ready to hear and receive what the Lord has to say. If we differentiate between the two factors, extrinsic or intrinsic, we'll be able to use the antidote of the Holy Spirit to protect and treat us. If you've been experiencing internal attacks, it's time to return to your First Love, repent, and ask God to rend (or break) your heart for what breaks His.

To end the day, let's pray by asking for open minds and hearts to be receptive to The Great Physician's treatment plan, which has been expertly designed to heal and make us whole.

Lord, thank You for exposing areas of my life that need Your intervention. I know I will suffer attacks simply because I have committed my life to serve You, but I'm reassured Your Holy Spirit protects me. When my choices bring suffering, help me quickly sense the lack of peace and realize my behavior needs correction because I never want to grieve You. I am grateful that You are a merciful and compassionate Father who is slow to get angry and is filled with unfailing love for me. I truly desire to please and honor You with my life. I love You. In Jesus' name I pray. Amen.

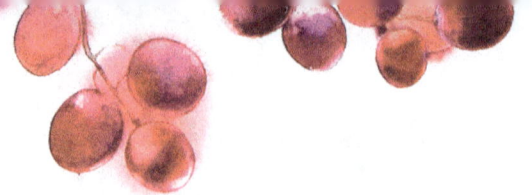

Day 5:
THE TREATMENT PLAN

In medicine, a treatment plan is "*a detailed plan with information about a patient's disease, the goal of treatment, the treatment options for the disease and possible side effects, and the expected length of treatment. A treatment plan may also include information about how much the treatment is likely to cost and about regular follow-up care after treatment ends.*"[23]

A treatment plan establishes a <u>partnership</u> between the patient and all those involved (doctors, nurses, other specialists, etc.) in the selected strategy for the best course of action. It also creates accountability for the patient and those providing the medical care. In addition, the treatment plan outlines the patient's responsibilities for his or her own care. A patient who decides to forgo personal responsibility is considered *noncompliant*. Noncompliance can happen for a number of reasons. Perhaps the patient needs to purchase food instead of costly medication, or disregards a follow-up test because they are unable to take the time off from work or cannot find transportation to and from the appointment. No matter the age, culture, or education of a patient, the healthcare professional must understand the person, and not just the diagnosis, before prescribing a treatment plan.

I am thankful our Heavenly Father knows us intimately and we can trust that whatever He asks of us is for our good. We don't have to worry about it costing too much because He'll always provide everything we need to be fully restored. Furthermore, His focus is not on a single dimension of healing; He provides a comprehensive treatment plan. God desires restoration of the whole person—mind, body, and spirit—to Himself.

We've previously studied presenting problems. After we've differentiated a diagnosis based on our presenting problems, how then do we move forward in establishing a treatment plan?

STEP 1: ALLOW THE GREAT PHYSICIAN TO WORK.

Turn to Exodus 15:26. Who did God declare Himself to be?

In Hebrew, *Jehovah Rapha* (rä·fä´) means "the God who cures, heals, repairs, and thoroughly makes whole."[24]

Turn to Psalm 103:2-3. Write the verses here:

Now turn to Psalm 147:3. Write it here:

Look up 1 Peter 2:24. How does it say we are healed?

What does this mean?

Maybe I have a unique lens regarding physicians because I am married to one, but we all know there are good and bad doctors. Some doctors have an amazing bedside manner, phenomenal medical knowledge, and expert skill; however, not all doctors possess these attributes. Nevertheless, God, our Healer, is the whole package all the time. When God tells His chosen people that if they listen carefully to Him, do what is right in His eyes, pay attention to His commands, and keep all of His decrees, then He will keep them from disease, this isn't an arrogant physician touting his success rates and surgical stats. No, this is THE Great Physician providing a 100% guarantee—it is a sure deal. There is no doctor on the planet with a 100% success rate. Yet through His suffering and death on the cross, <u>Jehovah Rapha</u> has paid the price, and by His stripes, we have been healed. Not *will be* but *have been* healed. It is already done. Our Great Physician forgives our sins, binds our wounds, and heals our disease; we just have to allow Him the authority to do so.

STEP 2: ACKNOWLEDGE.

In Mark 2:15-17, we read:

> *Once again, Jesus went to the shore of Lake Galilee. A large crowd gathered around him, and he taught them. As he walked along, he saw Levi, the son of Alphaeus. Levi was sitting at the place for paying taxes, and Jesus said to him, "Follow me!" So he got up and went with Jesus. Later, Jesus and his disciples were having dinner at Levi's house. Many tax collectors and other sinners had become followers of Jesus, and they were also guests at the dinner. Some of the teachers of the Law of Moses were Pharisees, and they saw Jesus eating with sinners and tax collectors. So they asked his disciples, "Why does he eat with tax collectors and sinners?" Jesus heard them and answered, "Healthy people don't need a doctor, but sick people do. I didn't come to invite good people to be my followers. I came to invite sinners." (CEV)*

After reading this passage, <u>UNDERLINE</u> Jesus' response to the Pharisees.

In his commentary, R.C. Sproul discussed the necessity of recognizing one's sinfulness:

> *Spiritual blindness to our own condition must be overcome if we are to be saved from sin. As long as we do not believe we are sinners, we cannot receive the cure, for only those who know they need a cure will receive it. In order to move closer to God, we first have to confess how far away we are from Him.*[26]

In your own words, to WHOM has The Great Physician come to cure, heal, repair, and thoroughly make whole?

Using the ESV, turn to the following verses and fill in the blanks:

Romans 3:23
"For_____have sinned and fall short of the glory of God."

Ephesians 2:1
"And you were_____in the trespasses and sins."

James 5:16
"Therefore,_____your sins to one another and pray for one another, that you may be_____. The prayer of a righteous person has great power as it is working."

John 3:16
"For God so loved the world, that he gave his only Son, that _____believes in him should not perish, but have eternal _____."

These verses illustrate that because of our sins we are ALL given a death-sentence, but if we simply confess our sins and believe in Jesus Christ, we will have eternal life.

Charles Spurgeon said this about Jesus' ability to heal us from our sin:

> *Jesus is able to heal all the mischief that sin has worked...because He Himself took our sin upon Himself by His sacred Substitution. Sin is the root of our infirmities and diseases and so, in taking the root, He took all the bitter fruit which that root did bear.*[27]

What must we do first for complete healing to begin?

When we finally come to the point where all of our internet searches and home remedies are no longer cutting it and we realize we are so spiritually sick that we truly need a doctor, that's when we can finally begin taking the necessary steps to be healed. When we truly ACKNOWLEDGE the fact that we are in need of The Great Physician, He can remove the bitter fruit and bitter root and make us healthy and whole. Let's be honest: Whether we acknowledge it or not, He already knows our condition. Find peace and freedom in that truth.

STEP 3: BE ACCOUNTABLE.

We must be accountable, or responsible, for our role in the healing process.

In John 5:1-9, we read of Jesus healing a man by the pool of Bethesda in Jerusalem.

Turn to this passage, read the account, and fill in the chart:

Where was the pool of Bethesda?	
What kind of people were found in the five porches surrounding the pool?	
Why were they there?	
In verse 5, we read of a certain man. How long had he been there?	
What did Jesus ask the man?	
What was the man's response?	
What three things did Jesus command the man to do?	1. 2 3.
In verse 9, what three things happened?	1. 2 3.

This situation has beautiful significance when we study it more deeply. For years, this man had lain on a mat near the sheep gate by the pool of Bethesda, and the sheep gate was the one-way entrance for sacrificial lambs being led to the slaughter. Further, the word "Bethesda" in Hebrew means "house of mercy."[28]

The Scriptures provide additional insight into the significance of this moment at Bethesda in John 10:7-9 when Jesus says:

> Truly, truly, I say to you, I am the door of the sheep. All who came before me are thieves and robbers, but the sheep did not listen to them. I am the door. If anyone enters by me, he will be saved and will go in and out and find pasture. (ESV)

Jesus, the spotless, sacrificial lamb (1 Peter 1:19), went to the "house of mercy" and sought out the lame man in order to save him and make him whole. When Jesus asked this man, "Do you want to get well?" instead of just saying, "YES!" he gave an excuse and blamed others for why he hadn't been healed. I love how Jesus didn't even respond to his excuse. He just moved on to the issue at hand—a total boss-move!

My imagination takes over when I picture this exchange. I instantly think of my children and the common occurrence of my asking a point-blank question about a situation and immediately being met with the excuse, "Well, I was just..." I often respond with something like, "Oh, I know 'you were just,' and I'm not questioning your intention, but you have to take accountability for your actions." Then I think about myself and how I struggle with an apology sometimes.

Remember the Sunday fights I mentioned earlier in our study? Well, let me give you an example of my own struggle with accountability. My entire family was packed in the van and headed for church while my husband and I were in the throes of another Sunday fight. Of course, I can't even recall what the argument was about, but I knew I was wrong. I even know the exact spot on our drive when I felt the nudging conviction of the Holy Spirit. I was having a complete, inner battle, an all-out wrestling match between my flesh and the Holy Spirit. I really did NOT want to concede my position, even though I knew I'd messed up. But I felt the still, small voice of the Holy Spirit finally say, "Don't let the enemy win today." So I looked out my window, gritted my teeth, and said to my husband, "I am choking on the words I am about to say, but...I. Am. Sorry." He instantly burst out laughing, and immediately the argument was diffused. Once I accepted accountability and apologized—even though it wasn't the prettiest apology—we were able to overcome, and the enemy did not get a foothold.

Why do we struggle with accountability?

STEP 4: ADHERE.

In John 5:8, why do you think Jesus wanted the man to pick up his mat and carry it with him?

Now turn to Luke 5:17-26. What does Jesus instruct in verse 24?

What happens in verse 25?

I love the fact that in both of these accounts, Jesus told both men to "pick up" their mats; neither man was told to leave it behind or throw it away. Both were told to first pick up their mats and then walk. The mats signified their testimony. By carrying the mats wherever they went, these men could give Jesus all the acknowledgment and credit for His miraculous work. In addition, the mats were a historical reminder of what they had come from and been through. To think of it another way, others need to witness our "mat story" for His glory. Others need to see the outcome of our accountability, faith, and adherence to what the Lord asks of us.

After the man who was lowered through the roof was healed, the very next verse says, "Everyone was gripped with great wonder and awe, and they praised God, exclaiming, 'We have seen amazing things today!'" (Luke 5:26, NLT) As this story illustrates, others need to see and hear about *our history* to be encouraged for *their future.* This is the power of the testimony. We need to make what Jesus did for us greater than anything else that has happened to us.

A friend recently posted on social media that she felt so broken by her depression and wondered if she'd ever be "put back together the right way again." I'm careful in my public responses to people's sorrow, but I shared that I felt her words were profound in that it's not that we'll be put back together the *right* way or back to what we once were, but rather, put together in a *different* way. Through our brokenness, *Jehovah Rapha*, God our Healer, can put us back together in such a way that our scars tell a story. Through every *test*—every mat we've lain on for years—we can have a *testimony.* Others can see the healed scars and be comforted through our triumph over sorrow and suffering. If we allow the treatment plan to work and do our part, our perspective on the *right* way will be changed forever.

Speaking of doing our part, in medicine, there is a term called "concordance."[29] It's the ideology that patients will have better compliance with (or adherence to) medical treatments if they trust that their beliefs and wishes are being respected. It's a collaboration between patients and healthcare professionals to choose treatment and medical care. Occasionally, our part in God's treatment plan seems ludicrous or downright impossible. Yes, He truly cares about our desires, but sometimes we are asked to do difficult things without knowing or understanding the reason behind the request.

Have you ever felt God ask you to do something that you knew was for your good—His treatment plan—but it just seemed impossible to carry out?

What made it so challenging?

Were you able to follow His plan? If so, how did you do it and what was the outcome?

If you've struggled to find a personal example of how God's treatment plan may seem challenging but eternally rewarding, I'd like to give you an example from the Bible to help illustrate God's mysterious ways.

Turn to 2 Kings 5:1-19 and answer the following questions:

Naaman was a mighty warrior, but from what disease did he suffer? (v 1)

Whom was Naaman encouraged to see? (v 3)

What was he instructed to do? (v 10)

What was his initial response? (vv 11-12)

What did Naaman's officers say to reason with him? (v 13)

What was the outcome of Naaman's obedience? (v 14)

Naaman's story is a profound lesson in having complete faith in the Great Physician and His treatment plan. Pain, suffering, and not-so-great medical diagnoses are not without purpose. This is made clear in the Scriptures through verses such as Psalm 46:10, which says, "Be still, and know that I am God. I will be exalted among the nations, I will be exalted in the earth!" (ESV). Also, Romans 8:28 says, "And we know that for those who love God all things work together for good, for those who are called according to his purpose" (ESV).

These Scriptures all proclaim that He is God and we are not.

If we love Him and are walking in accordance with His will, then He will make every crooked path straight (Isaiah 45:2) and illuminate our path (Psalm 119:105). Like the caring vinedresser that He is, He can look down at a broken or wounded branch and see with expert eyes why our fruit is suffering injury and harm. Then, in His omniscient way, He expertly crafts a treatment plan to restore us.

We just have to do these things:

1. **ALLOW** Him to work.
2. **ACKNOWLEDGE** where we are injured or broken.
3. **TAKE ACCOUNTABILITY** for our part in the healing process.
4. **ADHERE** to His will.

Sometimes the treatment is as simple as weeding. Perhaps wild plants have taken over and are competing for sunlight, water, and nutrients—everything you need to have a successful harvest. In that case, the plan is simple: Physically remove the foreign invaders, plant cover crops, and lay mulch. Or maybe a vine branch just needs to be lifted off the ground so it doesn't become riddled with mold or fungus from the soil and surrounding vegetation. The vinedresser knows that weak or stressed plants are more subject to predation and become an easy target for critters that troll the vineyard. He'll take an injured branch, lift it, and tether it to a stronger branch on the vine until it is healed. As Psalm 143:7 says, "He heals the brokenhearted, and binds up their wounds" (NIV). He doesn't chop off an injured branch if it's producing fruit. He restores it.

Whatever the treatment plan is, The Great Physician uses it to illustrate that He alone deserves the credit. Our trials make it obvious to the world that we are not in control. Everyone can see that we don't have the capacity to fix ourselves or resolve our problems. Like Naaman dipping in the Jordan River seven times, when God reveals His handiwork, He gets all the glory—not us!

As we close this week, I want you to always remember that God's ways are infinitely higher than our own, but we have to partner with Him to be restored to complete wholeness. We may never be restored to our former selves, and that's okay. In fact, it's actually better this way. Though the treatment plan may require sacrifice and may seem impossible, and you may come out looking different, it is necessary for total healing and restoration.

Dig Deeper

Kintsugi is the Japanese art of taking broken vessels and mending them with gold. The method sees breakage and repair as part of the history of an object rather than something to cover up and disguise. The vessel is restored yet forever changed, but it has more value than before.[30]

To end the day, let's pray.

Lord, thank You for teaching us and revealing Yourself to us. Though there may be pain in the process, we want to be transformed to be more like You every day. Thank You for using every part of our story to be glorified. You use the dusty old mats and broken pieces of our lives to reveal Your handiwork. We allow Your presence to lead us, acknowledge that You are God and we are not, and take accountability for our part in Your masterful plan. We love You. Thank You. In Jesus' name we pray. Amen.

HOW IS IT PROTECTED?
from generation to generation...

BE *fruitful*

Here are this week's ways to DIVE DEEPER by yourself, with family, or with friends.

DISCUSS

This week, we discussed how fruit is protected. Using the prompts below, start a discussion to solidify the learning.

- How are you stewarding your time right now? Are there areas where you've been challenged to change your priorities?
- Is there any area of your life where you need to "put on peace"?
- Is there any relationship for which you need to seek and pursue peace?
- What are your cares and anxieties that tend to creep in and choke out your fruit?
- Discuss the 10 presenting problems. Which ones do you struggle with most?

DIG IN

READ

- Dig deeper with:
  - *The Armor of God* by Priscilla Shirer
  - *A Shepherd's Look at the 23rd Psalm* by William Keller
- For kids, here are a few books mine have loved:
  - *Joseph and His Coat of Many Colors* by Rachel Elliot
  - *Unseen: The Armor of God for Kids Younger Kids Activity Book* by Priscilla Shirer
  - *David and the Very Big Giant* by Tim Thornborough

REVIEW:

- *Methodeia* - cunning arts, deceit, craft, trickery
- *Machaira* - "sword" or a "large knife"
- "Beelzebul" or "Beelzebub" - lord of the flies
- *Jehovah Rapha* - God our Healer
- *Bethesda* - House of Mercy
- "Kintsugi" - mending broken vessels with gold

DESIGN

Using the prompts below, start applying your learning from this week!

- If you have a garden, make a homemade decoy.
- Represent the armor of God by using an orange and a cup of water:
  - Use two clear cups of water.
  - Place an orange *without* the peel in one cup.
  - Place another orange *with* the peel in the other cup.
  - Watch the peel-less orange sink to the bottom.
  - When we take off the armor of God, we sink!
- Search Pinterest for crafts, activities, and object lessons about the parable of the talents, the armor of God, the mustard seed, David and Goliath, and Elisha and Naaman.
- Make your own kintsugi.
- Make your own fly repellent.

DISCOVER

- Check out these free personality profiles:
  - https://www.16personalities.com
  - https://assessment.yourenneagramcoach.com
- Check YouTube for Pandora's *The Unique Connection*

FOR THE KIDS

- YouTube the following *Superbook* episodes:
  - "Joseph and Pharaoh's dream"
  - "A Giant Adventure"
  - "Jesus in the Wilderness"
  - "Naaman and the Servant Girl"

HOW IS IT PROTECTED?
from harvest to table...

BE *fruitful*

Whether you're cooking for one or having a potluck, enjoy the process of artfully putting the ingredients together to make a delicious masterpiece. Be encouraged to consider the elements of your week-long study that apply to the recipe you are preparing.

DELICIOUS DELIGHTS

ARMOR OF GOD SALAD
Each of these ingredients helps the body, head to toe.
Serves 4-6
INGREDIENTS

- 8 ounces orzo
- 2 cups frozen peas
- ¼ cup chopped red onion
- ¼ cup chopped cauliflower
- ¼ cup olive oil and vinegar dressing or your favorite Italian dressing
- 1 Tbsp lemon juice
- ¼ cup freshly chopped mint leaves
- ½ - 1 Tbsp chopped garlic
- 1 package (4 ounces) of crumbled feta (optional)

INSTRUCTIONS

- In a large pot of boiling, salted water, cook orzo per package directions. When orzo is al dente, remove from heat and add frozen peas, red onion, and cauliflower to the cooking water. Let sit for 1 minute.
- Drain and transfer it to a serving bowl.
- Stir in the remaining ingredients.
- Serve warm or cold.

FEEL BETTER PHO
Serves 4-5
INGREDIENTS

- 4.5 oz rice noodles, white or brown (or soba noodles)
- 1 Tbsp sesame or olive oil
- 1 green onion, sliced; stem and stalk separated
- ½ cup mushrooms, chopped
- 4 cups reduced sodium vegetable broth
- 1 handful basil
- 1 lime, quartered
- 1 jalapeño, sliced thin for garnish
- 1 Tbsp peanuts, chopped for garnish

INSTRUCTIONS

- Cook the rice noodles per the package directions. Then drain, rinse, and set aside.
- In a soup pot on medium-high, heat the oil. Add the green onion (stem) and mushrooms; sauté until tender and fragrant.
- Add the vegetable broth and increase the heat. Bring the mixture to a boil. Then reduce the heat and allow it to simmer for 5 minutes.
- To serve, divide the cooked noodles evenly into two or three soup bowls. Pour the broth and vegetables over the noodles. Top with basil, lime, jalapeño pepper slices, peanuts, and green onion (stalk).

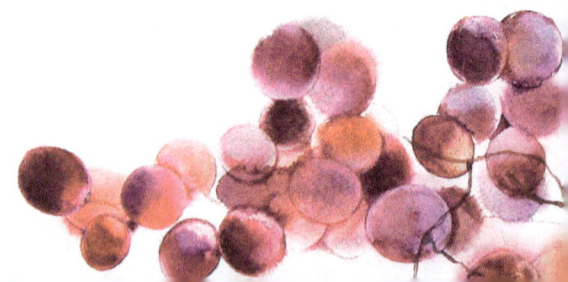

Session 6
HOW IS IT PRUNED?

Session 6

VIDEO TEACHING

KEY VERSE

"He cuts off every branch of mine that doesn't produce fruit, and he prunes the branches that do bear fruit so they will produce even more" (John 15:2, NLT).

THE BIG IDEA

The pruning process is a painful but necessary process for our good and future fruitfulness.

- **The principle of heavenly economics where _____ becomes_____.**

- **_____ _____ branch that does NOT bear fruit is _____ _____ and removed.**

- **_____ branch that DOES bear fruit is _____.**

- **Regardless of the fruitfulness of the branch, The _____ does the pruning.**

- **God will use _____ tool _____ to get our attention.**

Video sessions available at warriorraiser.com/fruitful   #FruitfulBibleStudy
Answers: *less/more; Every single/cut off; Every/pruned; Vinedresser; any/necessary*

190   FRUITFUL

Discuss

How does it make you feel, knowing everything we experience—the good and bad—passes through God's permissive will?

What are your thoughts about God's sovereignty and trusting Him with everything we experience?

When you consider the biblical stories of pruning—Joseph, Job, and Saul—can you relate to any of the pruning processes they went through?

Can you recall a time when the art of *your* becoming was a painful but necessary process?

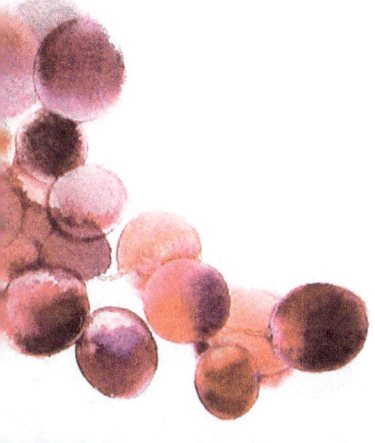

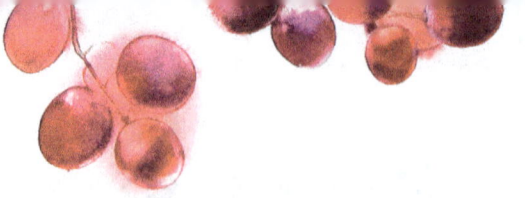

Day 1:
THE TAKEAWAY

Today we begin our discussion of pruning. No, I don't mean what happens to fingers and toes when you've been submerged in water too long; I mean *the selective process of removing the unwanted parts of plants.*

We will discuss the *takeaways* for why we *take away* targeted portions of our fruit-bearing branch. We will look at the process of pruning and the necessary reasons it is done.

For many casual gardeners, pruning is underrated. Personally, I never gave much thought to the timing and technique of pruning until I had a rose bush that began dying. I wanted to save it, so naturally I began watching YouTube videos on the proper ways to prune and even what tools to use. I was serious about saving my precious roses!

As I began my search, I found that pruning is a highly scientific process. Pruning is not done haphazardly but rather methodically—with precision—to ensure the optimal survival and productivity of the plant. And grapevines are no different. They require regular pruning to produce fruit.

Let's go back to our key Scripture and specifically review John 15:1-2. The Amplified version says,

> *I am the true Vine, and My Father is the vinedresser. Every branch in Me that does not bear fruit, He takes away; and every branch that continues to bear fruit, He [repeatedly] prunes, so that it will bear more fruit [even richer and finer fruit].*

What happens to EVERY branch that does NOT bear fruit?

Why do you think this is done?

What happens to EVERY branch that DOES bear fruit?

Why is this done?

When verse 2 says that every branch that does not produce fruit is "taken away," this is *airō* (i'-ro) in Greek. It means "to move from its place; to take from among the living, either by a natural death, or by violence; to cause to cease."[1] This means there are no more chances to produce a harvest tomorrow, next month, or next year. It is permanent.

Every single barren branch is cut off and thrown away.

What does this mean for us? We cannot afford to procrastinate. We MUST bear fruit. Not someday, eventually, when you can finally afford it, once the timing is right, or when you are confident you will succeed—but today.

Turn to James 4:14. Rewrite the verse in your own words.

Now turn to James 4:17. What does this verse mean to you?

We are now five weeks into this study, and if you haven't been stirred to move forward in your calling yet, I encourage you—no, I IMPLORE you—to step out in faith and take action. If you've lived long enough, you've seen the world around us change and you've probably witnessed things that we never expected to see in this lifetime. Our life is but a vapor (a passing moment in history), and if we know what to do but willfully choose not to do it, then we are guilty of sin.

In the following passages, <u>UNDERLINE</u> or HIGHLIGHT the concepts that relate to a FINITE LIFE. (All verses are taken from the NIV)

John 2:17
"The world and its desires pass away, but whoever does the will of God lives forever."

John 9:4
"As long as it is day, we must do the works of Him who sent me. Night is coming, when no one can work."

Mark 13:32-33
"But about that day or hour no one knows, not even the angels in heaven, nor the Son, but only the Father. Be on guard! Be alert! You do not know when that time will come."

1 Peter 3:8-11

"But do not forget this one thing, dear friends: With the Lord a day is like a thousand years, and a thousand years are like a day. The Lord is not slow in keeping his promise, as some understand slowness. Instead he is patient with you, not wanting anyone to perish, but everyone to come to repentance. But the day of the Lord will come like a thief. The heavens will disappear with a roar; the elements will be destroyed by fire, and the earth and everything done in it will be laid bare. Since everything will be destroyed in this way, what kind of people ought you to be? You ought to live holy and godly lives."

What are your thoughts after reading through these verses?

Dear Friends, we don't have the luxury of endless, infinite time on earth. Yes, the Lord is patient with us, but there will come a day when we have no more chances. It is time to do something—do anything. Just make forward progress, even if you do it while being completely afraid. An old German proverb says, "Begin to weave, and God will give you the thread." We will never succeed at bearing any fruit if we never take action.

We have to change our mentality and train our minds to at least try—even if we fail. When I played college basketball, my coach frequently quoted Wayne Gretzky: "You miss 100% of the shots you don't take."[2] Sometimes we hit the mark, and sometimes we miss. Thankfully, we have the Holy Spirit to help redirect us and keep us headed toward our target. God can work with a willing and pliable spirit, but not a hardened, immovable one.

In his book *Failing Forward: Turning Mistakes into Stepping Stones for Success*, John C. Maxwell writes, "Everything in life brings risk. It's true that you risk failure if you try something bold because you might miss it. But you also risk failure if you stand still and don't try anything new."[3] So let's risk it. Let's try something new because it might bring the greatest reward yet! And even if it doesn't, we can still learn something from the experience.

STOP KICKING AGAINST THE GOADS

Read Acts 26:9-18. Write your key takeaways from this passage here:

In this passage, we see a man who was *becoming*. Saul couldn't see what God had planned for him. In fact, NO ONE would've imagined that Saul—a man who did everything he could to oppose Christians—would eventually come to love people, share Jesus everywhere he went, and write much of the New Testament.

Dig Deeper

Today "to goad" means to provoke or annoy (someone) so as to stimulate some action or reaction.[4]

In Acts 26:14, Jesus said, "Saul, Saul, why are you persecuting me? It is hard for you to kick against the goads" (ESV). Goads were made from slender pieces of timber that were blunt on one end and pointed on the other. Farmers used the pointed end to urge oxen to move. Occasionally, a stubborn ox would kick at the goad, causing itself pain and sometimes injury. To phrase it another way, Jesus was asking Saul, "How long will you kick against what I want you to become?" Some versions even say, "It is useless for you to fight against my will" (NLT).

Saul had traveled a destructive path, but God had a plan for his life the entire time. Even with Saul's evil past (imprisoning and taking part in the murder of Christians), God was able to reveal His majestic glory through him. What a profound testimony! When the world saw Saul's (a.k.a. Paul's) heart change, it could have been only a display of God's handiwork.

The process of "becoming" can be difficult and challenging, and sometimes you have to take responsibility for the parts of you that aren't so pleasant. But the truth is, this "becoming" will never happen if we leave it up to ourselves. The Holy Spirit prunes us to shape and sometimes goad us into becoming all that our Heavenly Father has called us to be and do. The reality is that we are pruned to become the best version of ourselves, which, ultimately, is a truer reflection of God.

God may be calling you to become a serious Jesus follower, a stronger parent, or an influencer in your circle. God may be calling you to become a storyteller so you can tell someone else where you were on the road when *you* met Jesus. Whatever the assignment, know that He will provide all the thread you need to weave the tapestry of your life.

Who or what has God used to refine or shape your life?

Have you ever felt like you were "kicking against the goads"? Explain.

How has God used YOU to refine or shape others?

Let's revisit John 15:2 again, but this time, let's look at the end of the verse:

> *And every branch that continues to bear fruit, He [repeatedly] prunes, so that it will bear more fruit [even richer and finer fruit]. (AMP)*

Being in the midst of a pruning process is not fun. Sometimes it's downright painful. But it is necessary, and God always has a reason for it because He wants us to bear even richer and finer fruit.

Without intervention, grapevines grow into a bushy, tree-like mess of leaves and branches. Meticulous pruning and training help the vines stay organized and focus their energy on growing good grapes.

In the following exercise, look up the Scriptures provided and fill in the <u>main idea</u> from the verse.

Job 5:17-18

Psalm 94:12

Jeremiah 31:18-20

Hebrews 12:5-11

When something within us is not God-honoring, it must go. It has to be cut away because it will either divert energy from the fruit-bearing process or infect the rest of the branch, causing death and ultimate destruction.

Once we've diagnosed and removed the factors that cause injury or disease to the vine, there will likely be cracks and crevices in the branch. A sensitive vinedresser will use wax or tar to fill the wounds. However, if this is done without finding and removing any foreign invaders, disease could be encapsulated. Though it may look maintained on the outside, the infection can continue to grow and spread internally. When disease runs rampant, there is no precision to what it lays waste. There is widespread destruction with no methodical touch.

However, the surgeon's incision is precise. The borders are not jagged, and the wound is brought together with sutures and is well approximated. The healing of the surgeon's incision is still a wound that results in scarring, but it is done so that we may be made completely well. As Job 5:18 says, "For he wounds, but he also binds up; he injures, but his hands also heal" (NIV).

That's why it's so important for us to allow the Great Physician to treat us and expertly and lovingly prune us, removing all remnants of disease or decay. As C. S. Lewis once said, "A good surgeon would not stop a procedure because a patient dislikes being operated upon. A good surgeon works to make sure all the diseased elements are removed and the patient thoroughly treated."[5] Thus, even though surgery can correct a problem and even save a life, most patients would not gleefully sign up to "go under the knife." No one relishes medical appointments or surgical procedures. As such, we must remind ourselves that as long as we are being pruned, we still have life. We still have the capacity to become even richer and fuller. We still have the ability to produce a peaceful harvest of right living (Hebrews 12:11).

God loves us too much to leave us where we began. Hopefully, we can have the strength to endure the process and rest in the knowledge that whatever The Vinedresser takes away will never diminish us but will produce more in us and through us.

Now I'd like you to consider YOUR pruning process.

Is there anything that you've had *taken away* from you that was painful but NOW you know was purposeful?

Is there anything that needs to be *taken away*, but you've been fighting the pruning process?

Thank you for working through that. Self-reflection can be challenging at times, but I pray it will be eternally rewarding. Let's pray together as we end this day.

Father, I know this life is but a vapor, so I don't want to waste one moment. Stir my spirit to action. Help me have ears to hear You; I don't want to miss You in everyday moments. Bring revelation to my mind so I can move forward in obedience. Lord, You are the Master Vinedresser, pruning me into Your likeness. As I remain in You, I know things will need to be cut off and taken away from me. Help me recognize that Your pruning is for my good. Take away anything—in, on, or around me—that doesn't look like You, so I may continue to grow and produce a full harvest for Your glory. Thank You that Your loving and precise cut makes me whole. I love You. In Jesus' name I pray. Amen.

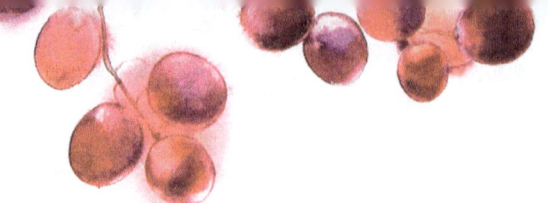

Day 2:
THE TIMING

One afternoon, I sat at the patio table in my backyard, scrolling through Facebook while my children ran around shouting and wrestling with one another. I was thoroughly engrossed with my newsfeed when, suddenly, I was startled by an intrusively blaring and rattling engine. I quickly looked up and found my husband wielding a hedge trimmer. With a smile and a thumbs-up, he began to hack away at the overgrown, eight-foot-tall lilac bushes that flank the side of our home.

I immediately jumped up and ran toward him. Using my best theatrical pantomime gestures, I made every effort to communicate for him to stop. The lilacs still had flowers, and I didn't want him to get rid of the beautiful, fragrant blooms. Plus, if he were to cut back the bush before it finished flowering, it might not bloom the following season.

Somehow, he was able to understand my crazy gesticulations and turned off the hedge trimmer's engine. He told me he'd done his research and felt it was worth cutting them back now in order to preserve the integrity of the house (they were scraping against our siding) even though pruning them too early would likely compromise the plant's future. Some say it can take three years for a lilac to bloom again if it's pruned too early (or too late), but this was the sacrifice we had to make because, up to this point, we had not properly pruned them and they were well on their way to growing completely out of control.

That's why the timing of pruning matters—it affects the plant's future.

Because my husband is a practical fixer of problems, he saw that the lilacs were becoming overgrown and getting too close to the house, and he wanted to remedy the situation. To Derrick, it was a simple a + b = c issue: The lilacs are too big; therefore, cut them, and they won't be too big anymore.

One thing Derrick and I both discovered in the process was that, though our lilac bushes were huge, they weren't flowering in proportion to their size. When I looked at pictures of the bush from earlier years, it had been full of flowers. How had I missed the fact that it was slowly losing blooms year after year? Because we hadn't correctly pruned them, the leaves, stems, and shoots had become the majority of the bush. The small scattering of flowering buds left on the uppermost branches were the plant's feeble attempt to let us know it was still a lilac bush. However, the lack of appropriate pruning over the years had left the plant a shadow of its former self, barely able to produce any flowers.

For the average plant owner, the process of pruning can sometimes be overwhelming. There is so much to learn just to become a mediocre gardener. Maybe that's why there has been an increase in faux plants over the past few years. People like the idea of plant ownership but don't want to deal with the maintenance. They willingly sacrifice the real thing for the ease and simplicity of an artificial replica.

I am thankful that, when it comes to me, the Lord doesn't trade me in for a fake ficus. I am grateful He still sees the potential in each of us, even if we haven't fully matured and even if we aren't producing fruit yet. I am comforted that our God is an expert in taking away the things that don't belong. He knows the exact timing of how to remove them so we can continue to grow and thrive. Thus, when The Vinedresser prunes us, it is done with intentionality and purpose. He understands the environment and what we are able to endure during different seasons of our lives. He is gentle with His cuts, but they are cuts nonetheless. Just like the vine, if we are not producing fruit in an area of our lives, that area may need to be cut away.

In the Session 2 of our study, we discussed the different amounts of fruit each of us is producing at any given point in our lives: *none*, *some*, *more*, and *much*. How do we get from none to some? From some to more? And from more to much?

We do this by His PRUNING.

David wrote this in Psalm 27:13-14: "Yet I am confident I will see the Lord's goodness while I am here in the land of the living. Wait patiently for the Lord. Be brave and courageous. Yes, wait patiently for the Lord" (NLT).

In addition, David wrote this in Psalm 31:14-15a: "But as for me, I trust in You, O LORD, I say, 'You are my God. My times are in Your hand...'"

CIRCLE what David did and encourages us to do in the above passages.

UNDERLINE what David believed to be true of his life.

Turn to Proverbs 16:9 and WRITE it here:

Turn to Proverbs 20:24 and explain this verse in your own words:

Now turn to Jeremiah 29:11 and fill in the blanks below.

"They are plans for_____ and not for _____, to give us a_____and a _____ ."

Regardless of the version you read, Scripture tells us that God knows His plans for us. When we read and study the Bible, we see there's a purpose in God's timing and in His plans for us, but we have to wait on Him. Grasping this concept will help us trust that the pruning period and process is for our good—it's to give us a hope and a future.

Allow me to explain this concept another way. For most of us, the exact time we were born was recorded. As a nurse, I spent a portion of my career in labor and delivery, where we time everything: the contractions, when the bag of waters ruptures, the time of delivery of the baby, the time of delivery of the placenta...everything. We do so because if the baby is born too early or too late, there is an increased risk to both the mother and the baby.

That's why understanding the timing is <u>essential</u>.

If we get ahead of the process and start hacking away with a hedge trimmer, we could potentially destroy our future fruit. However, if we procrastinate and take too long, we might be left with a bunch of suckers (shoots growing from the base of the plant that "suck up" needed energy) and with leaves that take over. Eventually, we will bear no fruit at all.

Again, that's why the timing of *our* pruning is <u>crucial</u>.

With grapevines, almost all of the transformative pruning is done during the dormant season, but a significant amount of pruning is necessary during the growing season as well. Let's take a deeper look at this concept and compare it to our spiritual lives.

DORMANT PRUNING

In Session 3, we studied seasons at length. If you recall, the winter season is a dormant season when grapevines are mainly pruned. Physically, this is done so that the plant's wounds from the pruning cuts have enough time to close before the next growing season. If they become callused and form a scar before the weather turns, then complete healing can occur and any potential of disease transmission is inhibited. That's why a vine pruned at the wrong time of year will be more susceptible to a fatal disease. If the vinedresser pruned them before they were fully dormant, it could interfere with the ability of the vine to enter into a phase of rest and nutrient storage, increasing the potential for injury.

When I think of this concept and compare it to my own life, it makes sense that some of my most fruitless times were seasons of dormancy. During these times, I was acutely aware of the pain of pruning. Conceptually, I recognized that the Lord was masterfully shaping me—taking some things away, pinching off a piece here, snipping a bit there—so the stored energy of my branch could be directed to where it needed to go. Still, this process brought a lot of suffering, tears, and trials. When you're in the midst of the cutting, it's difficult to remind yourself that you will flourish in springtime.

Can you recall a time (or times) when you were in a dormant season? If so, can you describe it?

Did you recognize the pruning process? If so, why do you think you needed to be pruned?

At times, we cannot make any sense of what happens around us; these are the moments when we ask questions and wonder, "Why?" In situations such as these, we must be like David and trust God. We have to have faith that, though we are imperfect people, we are being conformed and transformed to look more like a perfect God.

Maybe you're in the midst of a dormant season right now, and you're totally rolling your eyes at this idea. I get it. The other day, I looked over at a sign that said, "Bloom where you are planted," and I saw that simple quip for the first time from a different perspective. I began to think: *What if you're in a dormant, fruitless season where you physically CAN'T "bloom where you're planted"? What if the environment is wrong, the temperatures are too cold, or you've been planted just recently? No one blooms when they are dormant.*

What comes to mind when you think of the phrase, "Bloom where you are planted"?

Does it inspire you or does it frustrate you when you're in a season of dormancy?

I asked some of my friends this very question, and the feedback I received was so good. Most of them could see the concept for its intended purpose—to encourage and uplift no matter where you are or what you're going through. But some mentioned the fact that the blooming would not always be instantaneous, and sometimes you have to endure fruitless seasons patiently because God is preparing you for a purpose.

Let's go back to that verse in Jeremiah that we looked at earlier. Most of us are familiar with the hallmark passage (Jeremiah 29:11), but it's important to understand *why* the Israelites needed those important words of encouragement.

Turn to Jeremiah 29:4-14 and answer the following questions.

Where were the Israelites?

What did God tell them to do? (vv 5-7)

How long were they told they'd remain in exile? (v 10)

What were the conditional statements God gave them (the if/then promises)? (vv 12-14)

Though we may not always be able to immediately "bloom where we are planted," we will always be able to "grow through what we go through." If we allow the pruning process to change us, then we can count on God's promises.

The Message version of the Bible describes Jeremiah 29:10-11 like this:

> *This is God's Word on the subject: "As soon as Babylon's seventy years are up and not a day before, I'll show up and take care of you as I promised and bring you back home. I know what I'm doing. I have it all planned out—plans to take care of you, not abandon you, plans to give you the future you hope for."*

Did you catch that? <u>Not</u> a <u>day</u> <u>before</u> <u>the</u> <u>time</u> <u>was</u> <u>right</u>! God knows what He's doing. He has it all planned out. We cannot rush the process.

My friend, Pastor Michael Oldfield, once said, "There is an anointing and grace in obscurity. Don't let the devil rob you of your development because you couldn't discern that obscurity was actually for your good." Like a dormant vine, there will be times when we're in a season of obscurity, exile, forced rest, and transformative pruning. Though we may not understand the timing of it all, we must trust The Vinedresser and remember that ALL of it can be used for our good.

Now that we understand we're transformatively pruned during dormant seasons, let's look at the pruning that happens during the *growing* seasons.

DEVELOPMENTAL PRUNING

When Jesus gave His last lesson to His disciples on the way to Calvary, He used a living, dynamic, fruit-bearing plant as the analogy for our eternal assignment. But what if the message had been about cutting away pieces of stone rather than pruning vines? What if the lesson had been about how to be chiseled into a statue rather than a fruit-bearing branch?

Perhaps you've heard the story of Michelangelo taking marble that had been discarded and abandoned for 25 years and, with his discerning eye, envisioning and producing a masterpiece from the remnant scrap. He created a famous work of art, but once the stone was shaped and formed into the statue of David, the marble had lost all capacity to be changed or altered. Stone cannot grow anew. Crafted vessels and carved structures have their purpose, but they cannot produce fruit.

When we endure the pruning process, we still show signs of life. We aren't made of inanimate stone. If we're still being pruned, it proves we still have the capacity to grow and be cultivated to produce a harvest. The Vinedresser knows we can handle the cuts if we don't fight the process. Just as Michelangelo took that six-ton slab of Carrara marble and chiseled and chipped away every bit of stone that didn't look like David, the Vinedresser does the same to us.[6] He uses His pruning tools to snip, cut, and strip away anything that doesn't look like the masterpiece He sees in us. This is why Jesus said, "I am the true Vine, and My Father is the vinedresser. Every branch in Me that does not bear fruit, He takes away; and every branch that continues to bear fruit, He [repeatedly] prunes, so that it will bear more fruit [even richer and finer fruit]" (John 15:1-2, AMP). It's a perpetual process so we can grow and bear even more good fruit.

Turn to John 3:30 and write it here:

It's so much easier for me to write these words than to live them because this concept is entirely counter-cultural. We live in a world that believes more is better: more money, more material, more equity, more "likes," more "followers," more "friends," more of everything. But sometimes more isn't better. Sometimes, more is just more. Sometimes, more is clutter, which gives rise to disorder, chaos, disarray, confusion, and mess.

In 1 Corinthians 14, beginning in verses 25-33, we find Paul speaking of congregational worship. But in this passage, Paul used specific words to describe God and tell of His character—no matter what the situation.

Turn now to 1 Corinthians 14:33. What words did Paul use to describe God?

Does your life have an area of excess (e.g., material possessions? Time spent on social media? Relationships that clutter and bring chaos to your life?) that needs pruning?

Have you thought, "I really need to prioritize 'xyz' better"? What's the 'xyz' you've been putting on the back burner? *(Reaching out to that friend you keep thinking about? Calling to enroll into a new program? Applying for that job? Reaching out to a counselor to have some much-needed conversations?)* **Where do YOU need order?**

Even though most of the pruning of our lives is done when we are in a dormant season, at times, we must be shaped with pruning cuts while we are actively producing fruit.

Why do you think removing viable parts of the vine is important to its overall health?

Grapes tend to go wild with growth as they approach late summer, and it can be challenging to figure out what is going on in the green trellis maze. During this time, grape stems, leaves, and even the smallest bunches must be thinned. An overgrowth of the canopy renders the vine vulnerable to a host of diseases and affects the internal chemical balance of the fruit. Shading increases the humidity inside the vine canopy and reduces airflow, creating ideal conditions for mildew. Also, shaded leaves turn yellow and deteriorate prematurely, becoming utterly useless to the vine.

The reality is, sometimes, even good things must be removed because they're not the best thing. Like my lilacs, without pruning, we become all leaves, shoots, and no blooms. We become all foliage and no fruit.

Have you ever had to be pruned of a seemingly "good thing" because it wasn't the "best thing"?

In his book *The Fruit of Christ's Presence*, Harry Poe said this of overgrown foliage in our lives:

> *Since Adam and Eve...people have liked having plenty of foliage in their lives to hide behind. Spiritual foliage is an outward show. It covers up who we are sometimes. It creates a costume for being something other than what God wants us to be. Unless a Christian is careful, the show of foliage can become a substitute for the substance of fruit.[7]*

Until I realized my lilac bush wasn't producing substantial blooms, I thought it was healthy because it was still full and green. I was ignorant of the concept that pruning the foliage would produce more fruit—more blooms. This is the same struggle that many of us experience in our spiritual lives. We don't like the discomfort and pain of pruning and eventually become overgrown in seemingly "good areas" of our lives. Inevitably, this overgrowth keeps us from bearing good fruit. Our lush foliage becomes a "form of godliness" or a substitute for genuine, good fruit.

Read Matthew 21:18-19 and answer the following questions:

Describe the fig tree that Jesus found on the side of the road.

What did He say to the fig tree?

What happened to the fig tree?

Jesus had no use for a fig tree that didn't bear fruit. He ultimately cursed it, and it withered up and died. The barren fig tree, though replete with leaves, represented how useless we are without any substance. Without faith (or fruit), our works (our overgrown foliage) are dead, barren, and withered up (James 2:14-26). That's why Jesus prepares us for repeated pruning. He wants us to understand that we must endure it to produce more fruit. We cannot allow the leaves and suckers to take over. We cannot have a form of godliness because it is like an artificial plant—incapable of growth or real fruit production.

Read the following passages and explain them in your own words:

Matthew 6:1-4

Matthew 6:5-8

Matthew 6:16-18

Dig Deeper

The fig tree is the second specific tree mentioned in the Bible (Gen 3:7). Figs are technically not a fruit—they are inverted flowers, and most are pollinated by female fig wasps. The wasp crawls inside the fig, lays her eggs, and dies inside shortly after. Many edible figs have at least one dead female wasp inside! Thankfully, the fig releases an enzyme called ficin to break down the wasp into protein.[8]

We live and breathe for God and God alone—not the approval of man. That's why Jesus took time to teach us about the motivation of our hearts. While each thing (giving to those in need, praying, and fasting) is good and pleasing, the appearance of piety or godliness is merely a form of religion that Jesus expressed a zero-tolerance policy for. There is no eternal reward for substitute fruit (Matthew 6:2b, 16b).

Now turn to Matthew 7:15-20 and answer the following questions:

How will we recognize true godliness?

A good tree CANNOT bear what? _____ _____.

A bad tree CANNOT bear what? _____ _____.

How are we ultimately recognized?

In Romans 8:18, Paul said, "Yet what we suffer now is nothing compared to the glory he will reveal to us later" (NLT). In 1 Corinthians 4:17, Paul also wrote, "For our present troubles are small and won't last very long. Yet they produce for us a glory that vastly outweighs them and will last forever!" (NLT). These passages remind us that we must be pruned as we grow so we can produce more fruit. Sometimes, we suffer because we are reluctant to give up things that inhibit our growth. We must understand that pruning does not detract from us but improves us. If we endure the pain and suffering of our spiritual pruning, then the overgrowth of our branch—our excess—will be diminished and God will ultimately become greater.

Pruning removes parts of us and, in the process, changes who we are. We are changed to look more like Christ. Whether we endure The Vinedresser's pruning cuts while dormant or actively developing, the process, though uncomfortable, is necessary. He knows the exact cuts to make so we can produce an abundant harvest, a harvest of good and authentic fruit that reveals His glory in and through us.

Be confident that He knows exactly what He is doing.

His timing is perfect.

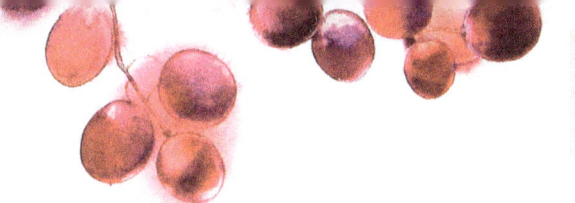

Day 3:
THE TOOLS

If you needed to cut paper, you wouldn't grab a wrench, and if you needed to see in the dark, you wouldn't turn on a blender. You use the tool necessary to complete the task at hand. This same principle applies to the pruning process of our spiritual lives. Sometimes we just need a little snip of pruning, and sometimes we need a full, slash-and-burn clearing.

Recognizing which tools The Vinedresser uses helps us understand the types of pruning we endure. From simple to complex methods, understanding the tools helps us to be "pinched" in private before we're "lopped" in public! There are many tools for pruning, but we will limit our study time to the following:

- Pinching and pulling
- Pruning shears
- Loppers
- Prescribed burn

As we work through today's lesson, we will discuss the way the Lord uses these tools to prune and shape us into His likeness.

PINCHED AND PULLED TO GET PLUMPER

Grapevines must be pinched and pulled in three main areas of unnecessary growth: sucker shoots, excess leaves, and some immature fruit. This type of pruning is done during the active growing phase to direct the energy of the plant toward quality fruit production rather than superfluous plant growth. This technique is relatively simple: The vinedresser sees the extraneous growth and, with a quick pinch of his fingers, pulls off the excess. Also, when the first fruits start to form, if he removes some of them, the vine produces even larger, plumper fruit. It's that heavenly principle being applied again! <u>Less is more.</u>

Can you think of something that's been pinched or pulled off of YOU in the pruning process?
(It doesn't have to be something major. It could be little things that needed to go, such as saying "no" to extra things on your calendar, putting time limits on your use of technology, not watching a specific show, or not listening to specific music.)

Turn to Proverbs 3:9-10.

>What are we to honor God with?

>What will happen if we do?

Now turn to Malachi 3:10.

>What are we instructed to do?

>What will happen if we do this?

Dig Deeper

Only seven species were listed as acceptable Temple offerings of first fruits: wheat, barley, grapes, figs, pomegranates, olives (oil), and dates (honey) (Deuteronomy 8:8).

Did you catch that? More conditional statements! If we honor Him, then He will bless us. In Malachi, God even challenges us to TEST HIM! If we give Him the first fruits (the tithe, the first 10% of whatever we produce), then He will pour out a richer, plumper blessing than we could ever comprehend, imagine, or even contain!

Though pinching and pulling is usually a quick process, it still stings. We often have trouble giving things up because we fear being left empty-handed. In actuality, the Lord says, test me and see if I don't show up and shell out!

Now turn to Job 1:21b and write it here:

We must remember to hold onto things in this life with an open hand. The Lord gives, and He also takes away. He can repeat the cycle with an even fuller, more abundant blessing than we could ever have hoped or dreamed (John 10:10). If we stubbornly decide to close our fists around what we have now, we'll never be able to receive more. A closed fist will never hold a new gift.

SHEARED TO PERFECTION

Pruning shears are to grapevines what a scalpel is to a surgeon—a tool for precision. Swift cuts with the one-handed tool minimize the exposed surface area. However, when that shearing blade comes to chop off the parts of you that must go, it will not be without pain.

Similarly, when the vinedresser uses his pruning shears and cuts off thicker overgrowth during the active growing phase, the vine actually weeps. If done correctly, the sap bleeds out away from the budding fruit, and in approximately two weeks, the wound calluses over—scarred but completely healed.

Have you ever wept over the cuts made by The Vinedresser's pruning shears?

I love how wonderfully poetic David is in his Psalm 56:8 prayer to God where he discusses his own weeping:

> *You keep track of all my sorrows.*
> *You have collected all my tears in your bottle.*
> *You have recorded each one in your book. (NLT)*

The root of the word "tears" in this passage is *dimah* (dim·aw), which means "to weep, tears."[9] It is a beautiful metaphor for the juice from olives or grapes that, when cut into or crushed, "weep" their tears or juices.[10] I love the image of our Heavenly Father collecting every tear we've ever cried while being crushed or cut. He remembers them all. When we require a pruning cut that leaves us shedding tears, we must remind ourselves that it is for our good.

Turn to Psalm 30: 5 and write it here:

Dig Deeper

A "tear-catcher" or a lachrymatory (from the Latin *lacrima*, or "tear") is a small vessel in which Jewish women used to store their tears in times of grief and lament. It would even be buried with the dead.[11]

The word for "weeping" in this passage describes a lamentation, and there is true sorrow behind these tears. When the pruning shears have to be applied, we often find ourselves in a position of mourning and deep distress. This sorrow is a necessary response for divine joy to come, giving us strength to continue growing.

Pruning shears are most often used during the dormant season. Once grapevines drop their leaves and fade into the cold, winter landscape, 80-90% of the branches are cut off. To the untrained eye, the nearly naked vines may appear dead and without hope for the future. But when we look at the vines with our heavenly lens, we again see that less is more. Come spring, these pruned vines will produce a healthy, balanced, and abundant crop!

Have you ever experienced a pruning that felt like a MAJOR loss?

What did it look like?

What did it feel like?

What was the outcome?

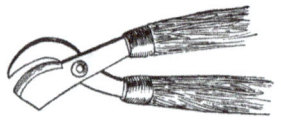

LOPPED TO LESS

Loppers are large pruning shears that require two hands to operate and are necessary for medium to large cuts. If you consider each of these tools, there is a progression in their utility and size.

1. *Pinching and pulling* are <u>very intimate</u>. These pruning methods are up-close and personal. The cut is swift, the pain doesn't last long, and the pruning site <u>heals quickly</u>.

2. The *pruning shears* are a bit <u>further removed</u>. A small, one-handed object is now necessary to cut smaller branches that could not be pinched or pulled off. The injury site <u>takes a bit longer to heal</u>, and the pain of this pruning brings weeping and sorrow.

3. Then there's the <u>lopper</u>. It requires a <u>much longer extension</u> to gain more leverage to chop off the thick, woody branch. Even more space is created between the branches and The Vinedresser. A tar or salve is applied to the injury site to protect it from rot and infection.

By the time we require the loppers, I think it's safe to say that we've ignored some of the earlier signs of overgrowth, excess, and dead portions of our branch. If we resist, rebel, or resent the pruning process while also failing to take the necessary time to heal, then we will require a more corrective tool to shape and develop us into the person God has designed us to be.

Turn to Proverbs 13:18.

What happens when discipline (some versions say instruction or criticism) is ignored?

What happens when you accept discipline or correction?

Proverbs 15:2 says, "If you reject discipline, you only harm yourself; but if you listen to correction, you grow in understanding" (NLT).

Do you see the two conditional statements in the previous passage? CIRCLE the "IF" statements and <u>UNDERLINE</u> the "THEN" statements in the above verse.

If we don't get the memo by the time the loppers have been applied, The Vinedresser may have to resort to drastic measures to get our attention!

BURN, BABY BURN

Fire is a tool used only by humans. Every other creature on the planet fears it, but we've been given the unique ability to harness its energy to enhance our lives. Prescribed burns are not used directly IN the vineyard but rather AROUND the vineyard. In regions where vineyards pervade the land, this controlled method is used to prevent fires (i.e., forest fires) that could potentially destroy crops without measure. Essentially, fire prevents fire. Applying a controlled fire to an area of overgrowth can prevent the dry, decayed foliage from auto-igniting and causing an uncontainable natural disaster.

Turn to Lamentations 3:21-23. Write this verse in your own words.

Now turn to 2 Peter 3:9.

What does Peter say the Lord is purposefully doing?

Why is He doing this?

What does the very next verse explain (2 Peter 3:10)?

Turn to Revelation 20:11-15 and answer the following questions:

What future event is being described in these passages?

What will happen to EACH one of us?

What happens if our name is NOT found in the Book of Life (v 15)?

Prescribed burns are an agent of renewal and transformation. Experts describe the tool this way:

> *Forest management practices such as thinning and prescribed burning create healthier, more productive forests. Overcrowded trees often struggle to survive, weakening them against insects or disease. Thinning competing trees allows remaining trees to grow faster and be more resistant to pests. Prescribed burning removes competing vegetation, improves habitat for wildlife, and reduces dangerous buildup of combustible forest fuels.*[12]

In our world, fire is a necessary part of life. It heats, lights, protects, and purifies. When it's used as a pruning and cleansing tool, it is life-giving, life-directing, and life-changing.

MATCH the Scripture with the verse (all are taken from the NLT):

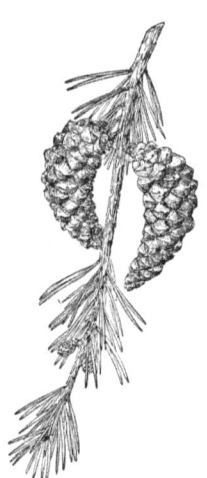

Daniel 3:27	"We went through fire and flood, but you brought us to a place of great abundance."
Psalm 66:12	"When you go through deep waters, I will be with you. When you go through rivers of difficulty, you will not drown. When you walk through the fire of oppression, you will not be burned up; the flames will not consume you."
Isaiah 43:2	"The fire had not touched them. Not a hair on their heads was singed, and their clothing was not scorched. They didn't even smell of smoke!"

Fire is a catalyst for change—it alters ANYTHING it comes into contact with. That's why the topography is completely different after a prescribed burn. When a forest is burned, what comes back does not resemble what was lost, as second-growth forests look very different from what they replaced. This is a perfect metaphor for the prescribed burns that we go through. Every time we are refined in the fire, we come out changed and purified to look more like Jesus.

Dig Deeper

Some species, like the lodgepole pine, jack pine, eucalyptus, and banksia, have cones/fruit that are completely sealed with resin and actually require fire for their seeds to sprout. They can release their seeds only after the heat of a fire has melted the resin.[13]

If you are in a season where everything around you is being burned up, my heart aches for you because I have been there. Wisdom tells me that if I'm not acutely aware of the ongoing need for pruning, my flesh (and areas of overgrowth in my life) will be torched in the refining fire again.

Do you trust that you won't come out charred and destroyed?

Can you remember a *refining fire* moment in your life? If so, describe it.

Did you come out burnt to a crisp? Or did you become healthier, cleaner, purified, and singe-free?

Long before the final judgment, we will have many chances to be transformed by The Vinedresser's pruning tools—even a prescribed burn. Let us be saved by a transient, refining fire rather than being perpetually burned in an eternal damnation fire, as fire will automatically separate God from those who don't believe in Him. Thankfully, because of Jesus, we don't have to fear fire. Instead, we pursue the consuming fire of God, knowing that it purifies and changes us.

To end the day, let's pray.

Father, I thank You for Your relentless love. I thank You for continuously seeking to develop us into the masterpiece You have designed us to be. Help us not resist the pruning process. Please help us see that it is for our good. Your love makes everything better—even the pain of pinching and pulling, the blades of the pruning shears, and the prescribed burns of our lives. Though we may have scars from the parts of our flesh that must be removed, we trust that You will bring us to a place of fruitful abundance. In Jesus' name we pray. Amen.

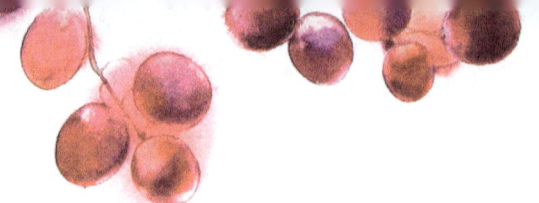

Day 4:
THE TECHNIQUE

When a vine is under-pruned (too many buds remain), it produces many small clusters of tiny grapes that may fail to ripen properly. If the vine is over-pruned (too few buds remain), the yield is low and the vegetative growth excessive. Even if pruning is done each year, it can adversely affect the health of the vines if done incorrectly. Improper pruning will always result in a vine that is out of balance and more susceptible to environmental stressors and disease. That's why the technique of our pruning matters. It's one thing to know when to prune and what to use while doing it, but if you don't understand how to prune, everything else is of little consequence.

So, how does The Vinedresser employ the timing and tools of pruning to remove what hinders our growth?

Because He is the Master Gardener, He knows the exact methods to shape us into His likeness. Today, we will study some biblical examples of the different ways—or techniques—the Lord has used to prune His people. Most importantly, we will pay special attention to the outcome of their pruning experience. Did they receive it and ultimately flourish, or did they resist it and suffer the consequences of disobedience?

THE SPIRIT SPEAKS

Turn to Genesis 4:1-16. After reading the text, answer the following questions:

What did Cain offer to the Lord? (v 3)

What did Abel offer to the Lord? (v 4)

Why do you think the Lord favored Abel's offering over Cain's? (vv 4-5)

What was Cain's initial response to the Lord favoring Abel's offering? (v 5)

What does the Lord say to Cain? (vv 6-7)

What does Cain eventually do? (v 8)

What was the outcome of Cain's decision? (vv 11-14)

In the face of Cain's anger, the Lord reminded him that He'd accept his offering if he did well. If Cain had listened to the Lord, he might've received the corrective pruning of his flesh and not been overtaken by sin. Likewise, we must be receptive to the nudges of the Holy Spirit when He speaks.

Have you ever experienced the corrective stirring of the Holy Spirit? Describe it:

Now turn to John 16:7-11. What does the Holy Spirit do?

Can you describe a time when you've felt the conviction of the Holy Spirit as a pruning technique?

In 1 Kings 19:11-12, the Lord reveals Himself to the worn-out prophet, Elijah. Elijah had just witnessed the miraculous power and might of God (read 1 Kings 18 and 19 for the full story), and now in his retreat to save his own life, he's exhausted and in need of respite. The Lord tells Elijah, "Go out and stand before me on the mountain." Then the Scripture reveals:

> *The Lord passed by, and a mighty windstorm hit the mountain. It was such a terrible blast that the rocks were torn loose, but the Lord was not in the wind. After the wind there was an earthquake, but the Lord was not in the earthquake. And after the earthquake there was a fire, but the Lord was not in the fire. And after the fire there was the sound of a gentle whisper. (ESV)*

Sometimes the Lord doesn't reveal Himself in an earth-shattering message that descends from the clouds. Sometimes we receive correction, direction, and counsel through His still-small voice.

How does the Holy Spirit speak to you (i.e., through dreams, through Scripture, etc.)?

I believe the Holy Spirit is gentle in His initial approach; however, if we ignore or resist His promptings, then He uses other techniques to command our attention. In Session 3, Day 2, we discussed the Holy Spirit as the *Paraklētos*—our comforter, advocate, intercessor, counselor, strengthener, and standby.[14] John 14:26b further reveals this about the Holy Spirit: "He will teach you all things. And He will help you remember everything that I have told you" (AMP). Sometimes the Holy Spirit works through someone else to help prune us and remind us of His teachings, as we see in 2 Samuel.

SOMEONE IS SENT

Turn to 2 Samuel 11. ANSWER the following questions about the passage:

What were David's sins? (vv 2-4)

What was the outcome of the sin? (v 5)

What did David try to do to cover his sin? (vv 6-13)

When his cover story failed, what did David strategically do next? (vv 14-16)

What was the outcome of this coverup? (v 17)

What was the Lord's response to David's actions? (v 27)

Now turn to 2 Samuel 12. READ the passage, and ANSWER the following questions:

What did the Lord do? (v 1)

What was David's response to the story he was told? (vv 5-6)

What did the prophet, Nathan, tell David? (vv 7-9)

What was the outcome of David's sin? (vv 10-12, 14)

What was David's response? (v 13)

David received the Lord's corrective pruning technique, and he repented. However, his actions were not without consequence. From the moment his sin was exposed, the prophet Nathan told David that his family would live by the sword and that the son born out of his transgressions would die. Ultimately, the fruit of David's branch was affected by his sin.

Turn to Psalm 51, which is often considered David's confession of sin following Nathan's confrontation. What portions of this restoration prayer speak to YOU most?

David lived to be very old (1 Kings 1:1), and the rest of his life was not without more pruning (2 Samuel 24; 2 Chronicles 22). However, David was consistent in his repentance. Though he fell short (as we all do), he continually surrendered to the repeated pruning of the Lord. Throughout his lifetime, David's fruit ultimately flourished under the counsel and provision of the Lord—in fact, Jesus Christ, the incarnate Son of God, arose from David's lineage (Matthew 1:1-17).

Have you ever experienced someone being divinely sent to prune *you*? If so, explain:

Have *you* ever been the one "sent" to speak loving correction into someone else's life? If so, how did it go?

Twenty years ago, I had a conversation with my friend Angie that I'll never forget. She had no idea that the Lord would use her corrective words to drastically shake me out of my sin. Her delivery was gentle but truthful. She saw me headed down a destructive path and, lovingly, told me that I was better than my behavior. Though her words stung at first, I went home and truly thought about the perspective *she* had about *my* life. I remember studying my reflection in the mirror the morning following that conversation. I said out loud to the face staring back at me, "Who are you? What have you become?"

Later that night, I wrote the following poem:

"My Rescue"

I am withered and dying and tired of lies.
I am stuck in this pit, and I want to die.
Where did I go? Who am I now?
I look in the mirror, and I'm terrified of how
I've changed and become something I'm not.
I'm not of this world, so, please...

Rescue me.
Rescue me from my hopeless despair.
My heart longs to feel that You are still there.
Rescue me from my shame and my fear.
My soul longs to know that You are still near.

I'm living a life that's one big disguise.
I'm not whom I say—one lie after lie.
Help me, Lord!
You're the only one who can hear.
Please listen now, wipe away my tears.

I hold on and try not to fall.
I keep my eyes upon You.
You're the bearer of all
The burdens that weigh me down.
You smile upon me.
Break the chains that have me bound.

I'm lost and confused, unsure of myself.
I've turned my back and put You on a shelf.
I'm broken and torn and don't feel like me.
I look in the mirror and dislike what I see.
Shattered dreams and many promises broken.
Get me out of this nightmare; I need to be woken.

Please...rescue me.
Rescue me from my hopeless despair.
My heart longs to feel that You are still there.
Rescue me from my shame and my fear.
My soul longs to know that you are still near.

It was as though the fog had lifted, and I could clearly see again. I prayed and asked the Lord to forgive me and help adjust my behavior. That prayer of repentance led to a complete rededication of my life to the Lord. I am so very thankful that He used my friend to keep me from a path of ruin and even more regret.

But what would have happened if I *hadn't* heeded the warning?

What do you think would've happened to David if he had he ignored the words of Nathan?

I imagine his story would have been completely different.

Now let's turn our focus to a technique that is used as a direct result of our refusal to accept the earlier pruning techniques applied by The Vinedresser.

SAY "SAYONARA"

In this last lesson, let's discuss one of Jesus' disciples who walked with Him as one of the chosen 12 disciples—Judas Iscariot. Judas <u>ignored all opportunities</u> to heed the corrective warnings of God and ultimately paid the price with his life.

Read John 6:60-71.

Now answer the following questions by either CIRCLING your response or <u>FILLING IN</u> the blank.

1. **Jesus told His disciples that there were some among Him who didn't believe He was the Son of God. TRUE or FALSE**
2. **Many of Jesus' disciples deserted Him. TRUE or FALSE**
3. **Jesus called Judas Iscariot _____ . (v 70)**

Now turn to John 12 and answer the following questions:

Who challenged the seemingly "wasteful" use of expensive perfume? (v 4)

What was ironic about his protest? (v 6)

What secret sin had this same man been committing? (v 6)

What was Jesus' response to the protest? (v 7)

This passage is the first mention of Judas' pattern of sinning. Though he judged Mary's actions as wasteful and used the excuse that the valuable perfume could have been used for the poor, this passage reveals the truth that he didn't actually care for the poor. Though he was one of Christ's closest, chosen followers (someone in His inner circle), Judas was still overtaken by sin. He was a fraud, a liar, and a thief.

Now turn to Luke 22, and answer the following questions.

Under whose influence did Judas act? (v 3)

What did Judas do? (v 4-6)

What did Jesus say? (vv 21-22)

What intimate form of betrayal did Judas use? (v 48)

For roughly three years, Judas had spent day and night with Jesus. He had walked closely with the Messiah and had been in His physical presence, yet Satan was STILL able to enter into him. If Judas, who walked intimately with the Lord, could be overtaken, how much more on guard must you and I be? The reality is, Judas did not truly believe. Even though he called Jesus "master" and "rabbi," he did not really believe that Jesus was the Messiah. He was *associated* with Jesus but had no true *connection* with Him.

Now turn to Matthew 27:1-5 and use the word bank below to complete the sentences.

Judas felt_____after realizing that Jesus was condemned to death. (v 3)

Judas realized he had_____. (v 4)

Judas_____himself. (v 5)

HANGED   REMORSE   SINNED

The Bible doesn't give us any detail about Judas' initial call to become one of Jesus' first disciples, but I imagine that he did not commit his life to ministry thinking he'd betray The One who had called him. Judas had a gradual decline into the pit of sin that ended with the ultimate kiss of betrayal.

Judas' slow fade ended with the price of his life. After the realization of what he had done, Judas believed his only option was suicide. Peter told fellow believers of Judas' gruesome death by saying he began as "one of our number and shared in this ministry," yet in the end, "He fell headfirst, his body burst open and his intestines spilled out" (Acts 1:18, CSB).

Like Judas, we don't wake up one day and decide to fall headfirst into ruin. We start to get bold in our sin, thinking we haven't been caught just yet, so we continue with it—but there is always a price to be paid for sin.

Jesus did not desire Judas' demise. In fact, Jesus said, "And this is the will of God, that I should not lose even one of all those he has given me, but that I should raise them up at the last day" (John 6:39, NLT). On the very night of His betrayal, Jesus even washed Judas' feet, knowing full well that he would be the disciple to betray him (John 13:2-5; 10-12). Judas thought 30 pieces of silver was a high price; little did he know that Jesus would pay the highest price conceivable by sacrificing His life so none of us would have to die in our own sin and shame.

All three of the men we discussed today (Cain, David, and Judas) were given warnings. Each of these men had intimate relationships with the Lord, but only David recognized the pruning techniques and repented. The lesson for us is that we must be vigilant because sin is always crouching at our door (Genesis 4:7). Like a wild beast, sin is incessantly lying in wait, ready to devour us. Though it will never be easy, we cannot fight the pruning techniques in our lives. We must endure the life-giving, fruit-bearing pruning process because the alternative is a dried, barren, and dead branch that will be chopped off and thrown into the fire (Matthew 3:10). I pray that we recognize the pruning techniques in (and on) our lives before it's too late—long before it is time to say, *sayonara*.

Day 5:
THE TRAINING

One afternoon, my basketball teammates and I were on the gym floor, stretching, girl-gabbing, and waiting for the start of practice. I remember our coach rounding the corner while holding a box filled with strange-looking goggles. She set them down and told each of us to put on a pair. As a fashion-conscious middle schooler, I remember thinking how silly we all looked and, more importantly, how little I could see!

Since many of my teammates (myself included) were new to the sport, our coach used these goggles as a training device to help with our coordination and dribbling skills. She wanted us to learn to dribble by relying on spatial awareness and muscle memory rather than having to look down at our hands to bounce the ball. In a nutshell, these goggles restricted our downward vision, which forced us to look straight ahead and learn to dribble by feel. My coach understood that, with the right training, we could hone our skill. Though I haven't played competitive basketball in over 15 years, to this day, I can still dribble a ball without looking at it.

When we're just starting out—in life, ministry, careers, or any new skill—we need guidance and the necessary training to grow and develop.

Can you think of anything else that can be improved with the right training method?

Today, as we finish studying the pruning of the grapevine and its fruit-bearing branches, we will discover how expert cuts are critical in training the vine.

Most vine training requires between three and four years to produce any quality fruit. In the first year of planting, the vinedresser focuses on establishing a strong, straight trunk and a solid root foundation. In the second and third years, the vinedresser's attention turns to cordon (or branch) establishment. Most vinedressers remove all fruit from the vines during trunk and cordon initiation because it competes with root and shoot formation. When the cordons have become fully established, the grapevine is considered mature. Once maturity is reached, double pruning is initiated (a second pruning during the dormant season).[15]

Why do you think the vine has to be mature to handle the double pruning?

We can compare this process to our spiritual development. If new believers endured drastic pruning before their roots were established, they might forfeit their development as their foundation wouldn't be strong enough to withstand extreme pruning techniques.

Two of my favorite funny ladies, Kathy and Ruth, put on an annual comedy skit for a women's ministry retreat. The premise of one performance involved a certain "Sister Super Christian" being appalled at the behaviors of a brand-new Christian. She kept trying to get the new believer to act, think, and understand the ways of God like a mature Christian should. This hilarious duo expertly portrayed the concept that, although a new Christian instantly receives all the gifts and fruit of the Spirit and their sin is washed white as snow (Isaiah 1:18), maturation must take place over time. Like a newly established grapevine, "baby believers" in Christ have to mature over time and cannot be expected to have an instant revelation of the entire Bible. In fact, NO ONE alive today has a total comprehension of the Christian faith!

What might happen if a new believer is pruned too harshly in the first few years of being a Christian?

That's why training and the process of our development are vital. For grapevines, different training methods are used to bring about a harvest because different varieties of rootstock produce their best fruit if trained in specific ways. I have found this concept to be true for us, too. The ways that God chooses to prune and train *me* might be completely different from how He chooses to prune and train *you*.

Each of us is uniquely designed; therefore, our pruning and training experiences are distinct as well. Where I am planted may differ from where someone else is planted. Our surroundings, environment, and native predators may be utterly different. Like grapevines, we are trained based on our unique circumstances, needs, level of growth, and maturity.

How might spiritual pruning and training vary for people?
Can you think of any examples?

Dig Deeper

Cane pruning is used in cooler regions. By limiting the vine's growth to the trunk, the vine is less vulnerable to frost and better protected. In contrast, spur pruning is common in warmer growing regions.[16]

cane pruning

spur pruning

©Kazakova Maryia /Adobe Stock

Once upon a time, I used curse words in everyday conversation—until I heard someone say that cursing was a crutch for an unimaginative mind and showed a lack of self-control. Instantly, I was convicted and knew this behavior needed to stop. Still, it took training for my mind to stop using those choice words; I had to be trained to catch myself before letting a bad word slip out. For months, I wore a rubber band on my wrist with "Matthew 12:34" written on it as a reminder that "Out of the heart the mouth speaks." Whenever I used profanity, I snapped the rubber band against my skin.

Ultimately, the key to successful, effective training is yielding to the process. In other words, training requires submission.

Turn to James 3:8. Explain this verse in your own words.

To "nip something in the bud" is an idiom that means to stop or suppress it at a very early stage. The metaphor references snipping a bud before it has the opportunity to bloom.[17]

Now turn to James 4:7. What three things are outlined in this single verse?
1.

2.

3.

Now look ahead one verse to James 4:8. What is the conditional statement?

If we_____, He will_____.

The negative reinforcement of smacking myself with a rubber band was a painful, yet effective training tool. However, I required more than just a physical training method to correct my behavior. I needed a <u>submitted heart</u>, and this would be achieved only by <u>drawing near to Him</u>. As I grew in my relationship with the Lord, my heart was changed in the process. As Matthew 12:34 says, out of the overflow of my transformed heart, my language was transformed.

Where has the Lord used His pruning cuts to train you? What former thoughts or behaviors have been pruned from you?

Turn to John 15:3. Write it here:

Most translations use the word "clean" or "cleansed." The New Living Translation writes it this way: "You have already been pruned and purified by the message I have given you." This word "clean" in Greek is *katharos* (kä-thä-ro's), and we get our word "cathartic" from this same root word, which means "to cleanse, purge" or "the process of releasing, and thereby providing relief from, strong or repressed emotions."[18]Jesus used it metaphorically in reference to the cleansing of the vine by pruning so that it could bear fruit (John 15:2). Can you picture a gnarled, weedy vine that, once the superfluous or dead branches are cut back, actually looks clean? Can you imagine how the cleansing cuts of the pruning tools can actually be cathartic?

In John 15:3, what did Jesus say we have been cleansed by?

What do you think He meant by this?

In this next section, we are going to capture the meaning of the cleansing cuts that train us. In John 17, we read Jesus' longest prayer captured in Scripture. He begins with first praying for Himself (vv 1-5), then for His disciples (vv 6-19), and lastly for all believers (vv 20-26).

Turn to John 17:17. Write the verse here:

Now turn to Ephesians 5:25-27. How did Christ sanctify (make holy and clean)the church?

Read Titus 3:1-8 and list the key points in each verse:

    Verse 1:

    Verse 2:

    Verse 3:

    Verse 4:

    Verse 5:

    Verse 6:

    Verse 7:

    Verse 8:

Titus 3:1 in *The Amplified Bible* says, "Be prepared and willing to do any upright and honorable work." We are told to first submit, then prepare, and finally do the work. Sometimes we are placed in a job, situation, or season for a preparatory purpose. We must recognize that, in each phase, we are being trained and prepared for a bountiful harvest. Many people want the harvest, but not all are willing to train for it.

Is the Lord currently training you in a specific area? How are you submitting to the process?

Titus 3:3-8 continues to discuss all that we have been saved from and saved for. In Session 3 of this study, we discussed sanctification (being separated from our sin and set apart for God as holy). This process is not something we can manufacture or produce through our own works. Thus, we are cleansed, pruned, and purified through The Word and renewed by the Holy Spirit. And as a result of true faith, we inevitably express our salvation by producing good works—or bearing fruit (Titus 3:8). From the moment of salvation, we are justified—made right—by His grace. Then, we begin the journey of being "trained on the trellis," but we cannot rush the process.

Dig Deeper

The symbolic act of baptism does not save us, but it serves as a profound symbol of the work of God who cleanses one from the corruption of sin at the time of salvation.[19]

Have you experienced wanting something right away? Have you ever wanted to bypass the training process to get to the end result? If so, explain:

Think about it this way. Would you want someone operating on you on his or her first day of medical school? While I am all for students getting hands-on learning, I'll pass on being someone's surgical "guinea pig." Give me the practitioner with a proven record and a career built on years of training!

I can't think of any field where experts became proficient without training. Can you?

The reality is that training requires discipline, and discipline requires a mind set on continual growth.

Discipline requires the mental, emotional, and spiritual fortitude to recognize that the end result is completely worth the temporary discomfort. The pruning cuts that shape us are never enjoyable, but they are necessary for our growth and fruit production.

Turn to Hebrews 12 and answer the following questions:

What two things does verse 1 tell us to DO?

    1.

    2.

How do you think this relates to the pruning/training process?

In Hebrews 12:3-4, whom are we to fix our eyes upon?

How does His example help us endure?

In verses 5-6, who does the Lord discipline?

In verses 10-11, we discover:

God's discipline is _____ for us. (v 10)

This kind of discipline is enjoyable while it's happening: (v 11) _____.

This is the end result of Godly training and discipline: (v 11) _____.

TRAINING REQUIRES ENDURANCE

I know some of you enjoy running, but the very thought of running makes me cringe. Years ago, I decided it'd be a great idea to run a half-marathon. I followed the training schedule, and on the day of the race, after 13.1 miles, I actually crossed the finish line. However, I was promptly escorted to the medic tent because I'd passed out. So I understand why Paul used the metaphor of running a race when he wrote about endurance and the strenuous training we would withstand in order to live this fruit-bearing life.

Turn to 1 Peter 3:14-15. Summarize each verse here:

Verse 14:

Verse 15:

Again, we see that our hearts and minds have to be sanctified. We have been grafted into and connected to The Vine. As Christians, we have been freed from the impurity of our sin (washed through pruning) and have been united to God by our faith. That's why Peter tells us to always "Be ready." In Greek, this word is *hetoimos* (he'-toi-mos) and comes from the root word for "fitness" or to "be fit."[20] This is the same concept we read about earlier in Titus 3:1—to be ready, be prepared, and "be fit" to work.

Unfortunately, when it comes to fitness, we don't get to stop once we've "arrived" at our goal. If you've ever engaged in any type of exercise or fitness regime, you know that once you stop you lose all your physical gains. We have to keep going because training is continual until we finish the race (2 Timothy 4:7). Remember that endurance is defined as "*the ability to keep doing something difficult, unpleasant, or painful for a long time.*"[21]

Following Christ is not easy; that's why we weren't meant to do it alone.

TRAINING REQUIRES TEAMMATES, COACHES, TEACHERS, and MENTORS.

<u>Mentorship</u> allows us to learn from one another.

We need the advice and counsel of mature believers to help guide us. In turn, we need to be mentoring others as well. When we are able to pour into others, they can pour into someone else. If something (or someone) is continually poured into, it (he or she) will eventually overflow. God uses us to create that overflow. When we come alongside and pour into others, we are making a choice to teach others about God, build them up, and make an eternal difference.

Investing in people matters. It has everlasting significance and can change the trajectory of someone's story. While you may not see immediately how your presence, words, or prayers impact others, the investment is important. When you see the potential in someone and invest well, both you and the other person open up to a deep and meaningful relationship that could last for years.

Let's look at a biblical example of mentorship in action. Turn to Exodus 17:9-10.

Whom does Moses command to fight the Amalekites?

Now turn to Exodus 24:13. What had this same man become?

Read Deuteronomy 34:9. What was Joshua full of (or filled with) and why?

Turn to Joshua 1:1-9. In your own words, summarize what happened.

After Moses' ministry was established, he enlisted Joshua as his apprentice. Joshua spent over 40 years with Moses, learning to be under—and in—authority. Due to his training and the mentorship he had received, Joshua was able to step into his new role and eventually lead the Israelites in their conquest of the Promised Land.

Don't waste the short time you have on earth trying to do everything on your own. Take advantage of the vast wealth of knowledge and experience of mature believers. God's plan for your life depends on it.

Do you have a spiritual mentor? If so, who?

If not, whom can you look to as a spiritual mentor?
(Mentors don't necessarily have to be older than you—just a bit further along in their spiritual journey.)

Dig Deeper

Before Moses shepherded the people of Israel, he first had to learn to be a shepherd under his father-in-law, Jethro. For 40 years, he lived as a foreigner in the land of Midian and tended sheep in the wilderness before he was commissioned to free the Israelites. (Exodus 3:1; Acts 7:30)

I challenge you to reach out. Ask someone to meet for coffee, tea, or lunch and start the conversation. The other side of mentorship is that it requires us to invest, too. When we fulfill the call of discipling others, we are given the awesome privilege of pouring into the empty spaces that God has allowed us to help fill. Don't let a lifetime of knowledge and experience die with you. Take advantage of the energy and ambition of the next generation to carry on God's plan for both of your lives.

Are you mentoring anyone now? If so, who?

If not, whom are you being challenged to help train?
(a new believer, teens, little ones, etc.)

We need one another to survive the pruning of our lives. Pursuing a life dedicated to the Lord is not without trial and suffering, but the reward is worth all the pruning, training, difficulty, and pain we may endure.

I'd like to use *The Message's* paraphrase of 2 Timothy 3:16-17 to end this week in prayer:

Father, there's nothing like the written Word of God for showing [us] the way to salvation through faith in [You]. Every part of Scripture is God-breathed and useful one way or another—showing us the truth, exposing our rebellion, correcting our mistakes, training us to live [Your] way. Through the Word, we are put together and shaped up for the tasks [You have] for us.

Thank You for loving us enough to correct, train, and discipline us. Help us receive the correction as a reminder of Your love. We thank You for the pruning cuts that purify us and wash clean—perfectly equipping us to produce a bountiful, overflowing harvest. In Jesus' name we pray. Amen.

HOW IS IT PRUNED?
from generation to generation...

BE *fruitful*

Here are this week's ways to DIVE DEEPER by yourself, with family, or with friends.

DISCUSS

This week, we discussed how fruit is pruned. Using the prompts below, start a discussion to solidify the learning.

- Why does God prune those He loves?
- Do you think an area of excess in your life needs pruning? Where do YOU need order?
- Discuss the different pruning techniques.
- Retell the story of Cain and Abel, David and Nathan, and Judas Iscariot.
- How have you been trained? Are you being trained?
- Do you have a mentor?
- Whom are you mentoring?

DISCOVER

FOR THE KIDS

- Search for the following *Superbook* episodes on YouTube or by visiting https://us-en.superbook.cbn.com/:
  - "Baptized!"
  - "The Road to Damascus"
  - "Let My People Go!"
  - "Caleb and Joshua"

DESIGN

Using the prompts below, start creating your own masterpieces.

- If you have a garden or any living plants, get out your pruning tools and start removing unwanted parts.
- Visit the Warrior Raiser Pinterest board for activities about this week's lesson.

DIG IN

READ

For children, here are a few books my kids have loved:

- *The Secret Garden* by Frances Hodgson Burnett
- *We Are Growing!* by Laurie Keller

REVIEW

- "Goad": a slender piece of timber, blunt on one end and pointed on the other; the pointed end was used to urge oxen to move.
- "Kick against the goads": an idiom for a futile and pointless exercise.
- *Dema*: "to weep, tears." A metaphor for the juice from olives/grapes that, when cut into or crushed, "weep" tears/juice.
- "Nip it in the bud": an idiom meaning to stop or suppress something at a very early stage, like nipping a bud before it has the opportunity to bloom.
- *Katharos*: "to cleanse, purge" or "the process of releasing, and thereby providing relief from, strong or repressed emotions."
- Endurance: the ability to keep doing something difficult, unpleasant, or painful for a long time.

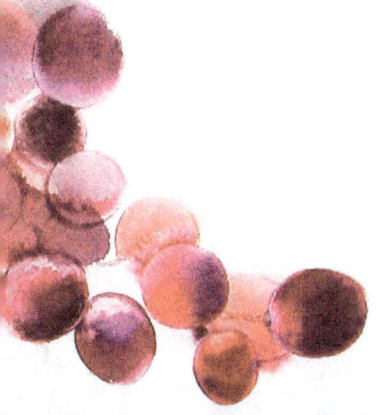

HOW IS IT PRUNED?
from harvest to table...

BE *fruitful*

Whether you're cooking for one or having a potluck, enjoy the process of artfully putting the ingredients together to make a delicious masterpiece. Be encouraged to consider the elements of your week-long study that apply to the recipe you are preparing.

DELICIOUS DELIGHTS

FIG FLATBREAD

Serves 4

INGREDIENTS

- 1 cup arugula, loosely packed
- 6 figs, thinly sliced crosswise, divided
- 1 red onion, small, thinly sliced
- ¼ cup balsamic vinegar
- ½ tsp black pepper
- ½ tsp kosher salt
- 14 oz pizza dough, store-bought
- 1 Tbsp olive oil
- 8 oz goat cheese, crumbled (optional)

INSTRUCTIONS

- Preheat the oven to 450°F. Heat the oil in a saucepan over medium heat. Add the red onion and ¼ teaspoon each of kosher salt and pepper. Cook, stirring, until tender, 2 minutes.
- Roll the pizza dough into a ¼-inch-thick, 17 x 11-inch rectangle. Place on a large baking sheet lined with parchment paper. Sprinkle with the remaining ¼ teaspoon of each salt and pepper. Top evenly with cooked onions, one-third of the fig slices, and cheese. Bake until the crust is lightly browned and done, 15 to 20 minutes.
- Meanwhile, cook the balsamic vinegar in a small saucepan over medium-high until it has been reduced by half, about 5 minutes.
- Top the flatbread with the remaining figs, the arugula, and the balsamic reduction.

KALE & GRAPE SALAD

Serves 4

SALAD INGREDIENTS

- 1 lb chicken breast, grilled with salt & pepper (optional)
- 1 apple, diced
- 2 -3 celery ribs, roughly chopped
- 1 cup grapes, halved
- 1 bunch of red kale, stems removed and torn into small pieces
- 1 cup walnuts (optional for candied walnuts)

DRESSING INGREDIENTS:

- Zest of 1 lemon
- 2 Tbsp honey
- 2 Tbsp lemon juice
- ¾ cup mayonnaise
- ¼ tsp pepper, freshly ground
- ¼ cup olive oil
- 2 Tbsp white balsamic vinegar (substitute apple cider vinegar in a pinch)

INSTRUCTIONS

- In a small bowl, mix the dressing ingredients until smooth.
- In a large bowl, toss the torn kale with the salad dressing. Top with sliced chicken breast, candied walnuts, celery, grapes, and apples. If making ahead, store the prepared salad without dressing the kale.
- Dress the salad right before serving.

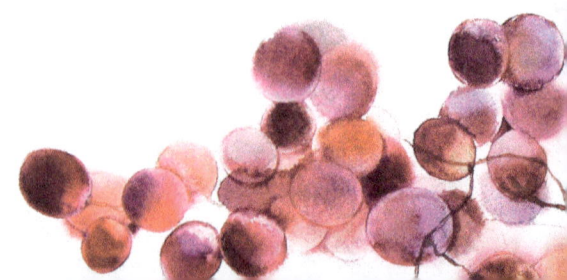

Session 7

HOW IS IT HARVESTED?

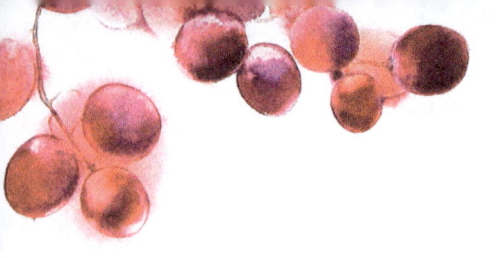

VIDEO TEACHING

KEY VERSE

"When you produce much fruit, you are my true disciples. This brings great glory to my Father" (John 15:8, NLT).

THE BIG IDEA

When we're full of good fruit, it's time to be harvested. The fruit of the harvest is the lasting fruit that remains.

- _____ provides _____.

- _____ gives _____.

- _____ helps us _____ respond.

Regardless of the preservation process of our good fruit, before it can _____ it has to be _____.

If fruit isn't_____it turns BITTER. And after that, it _____.

Harvest is the culmination of all our _____ , _____ , and _____.

Video sessions available at warriorraiser.com/fruitful   #FruitfulBibleStudy
Answers: *Context/clarity; Clarity/comprehension; Comprehension/carefully; remain/reaped; reaped/rots; sowing/tending/reaping*

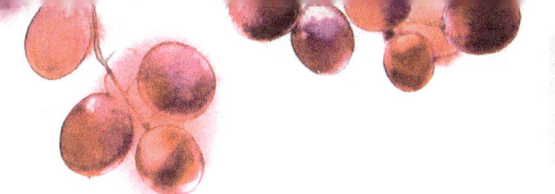

Discuss

Have you ever jumped to a conclusion or filled in the gaps of a story with your own narrative because you didn't have the full context of the situation?

Thinking about the examples of fruit that turns bitter, do you have an example of your own fruit that's stayed on the vine too long?

WHO or WHAT is your fruit that remains and is lasting?

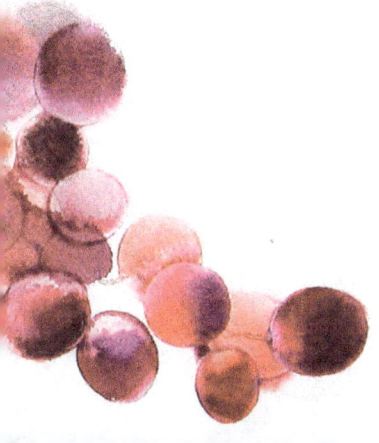

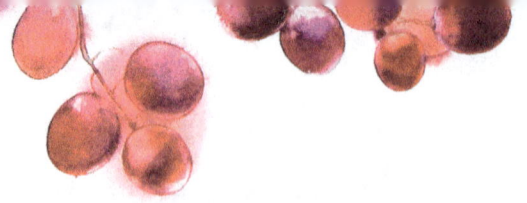

Day 1:
THE SIGNS

One beautiful fall morning, I drove 45 minutes outside of the city center and found myself in the green, lush, and rolling hillsides of Ohio. As I drove past fields of corn and soybeans, I reflected on the beauty of the landscape. Alone in my car, I had the rare moment to drive with no noise to distract me. I took the opportunity to pray and thank God for the majesty of His handiwork. Looking out my window, I couldn't help but swell with appreciation for all the beauty of the countryside, knowing that farmers would soon be harvesting their crops.

Harvest. That's exactly where I was headed that particular crisp, autumn morning. I was on my way to volunteer at a local vineyard and help with their harvest.

After a few hours of working in the vineyard, my shoulders began to ache as I made my way down each row, snipping off the full clusters of Petite Pearl grapes from the mature vines. Dodging bees and fruit flies, I gave my best effort to fill the baskets positioned under the ripe, hanging fruit. As I harvested, I dove into conversation with the other workers, including the two owners, Valerie and her husband, Robin.

It was a wonderful, hands-on experience. I learned so much in the vineyard that day, including how they knew when it was time to harvest: chemistry and intuition.

Robin shared that harvest is within sight when the grapes begin to change color. Once the deep purple or red color has set in, he walks through the vineyard and samples grapes to determine, by taste, if they are ready. The other giveaway is the pesky fruit flies and buzzing bees. Their mere presence indicates the fruit has matured. With this intel, he then applies science. Using a refractometer (a special scale), he determines the sugar content (in degrees brix) of the grapes. The higher the sugar, the riper the grapes. He then chooses to either let the grapes hang a little longer or harvest them.

Making this decision is somewhat of a gamble. If he leaves them to continue maturing, they may be subject to predation by all those pesky critters that love ripe fruit. On the other hand, if he pulls them too early, they may not be sweet enough, and grapes aren't like bananas—they don't continue to ripen once they've been cut from the vine.

Clearly, even a seasoned vinedresser can make costly mistakes. That's why I am so thankful that our Heavenly Father is an *infallible*, expert Vinedresser.

Turn to Isaiah 55:11. Rewrite the verse in your own words:

Now turn to Hebrews 13:8 and write it here:

Although we may not understand God's ways, we know that they are flawless. While trusting in His perfect timing and plan is not always easy, He will always bring forth a return on His investment.

Ebbs and flows. Dips and dives. Highs and lows. That's what this adventure of life is. Like the zig-zag line of a stock market, the only thing predictable about this fruit-bearing journey is that it is unpredictable. When the climate changes and the world around us drastically shifts, we often experience worry, fear, or anxiety. But we can be reassured that God is <u>constant</u> and <u>never-changing</u>.

Regardless of fluctuations in market trends, seasons of famine or drought, or cultural unrest, The Vinedresser knows the exact moment our fruit is fully prepared. He knows when it's time to harvest the fruit we bear. Our challenge is to recognize the signs of readiness. Sometimes they are obvious, while at other times, they are more subtle.

Let's circle back to the very beginning of our study. Do you remember the six definitions of fruit? (Turn back to Session 1, Day 1 if you need a refresher.) We've reached the point in our study where we'll discover how we harvest *our* fruit.

If you recall, the Greek word for fruit is *karpos*. Today, we will dig into the word *karpophoreo* (kar-pof-or-eh'-o), which means *"to be fertile; to bear or bring forth fruit."*[1] Harvest is the time to BRING FORTH our collective fruit: the fruit of our womb, the fruit of our finances, the fruit of our lips, the fruit of our witness, the fruit of our good works, and our internal fruit (the Fruit of the Spirit).[2]

As we read earlier, in nature, some signs of the grape's readiness include its color, character of taste, and the presence of critters. Today we'll draw connections between these indicators and the readiness of our spiritual harvest.

Without tasting fruit, how do you know when it is ripe?

Luke 8:14 says, "And that which fell among the thorns, these are they that have heard, and as they go on their way they are choked with cares and riches and pleasures of this life, and bring no fruit to perfection" (ASV).

<u>UNDERLINE</u> the last part of this verse.

Here the word "perfection" is translated from the Greek *telesphoreō*, which means "to bring fruit to maturity."[3] The etymology of this word is a compound of two words: *telos* (a finality, a completed purpose, the end) and *pherō* (to carry, to bear, to bring forth, to produce). Jesus used it here to explain that we are to bear our fruit to its <u>perfection</u> and completion. Like a pregnant woman, we are to bring forth—or birth—<u>fully developed</u> and mature fruit.

During the first trimester of most pregnancies, an expectant mother may not appear to be pregnant to others. But the woman who is carrying new life KNOWS it and FEELS it. She experiences the internal signs and symptoms of physical and emotional change. However, the outward evidence of that change isn't apparent to anyone else until about four to six months have passed. If you are pregnant, have ever been pregnant, or know anyone who's been pregnant, you recognize signs that determine the readiness for delivery of the baby.

How does a mother know she is ready to deliver her baby? What are the physical signs?

Like a baby who is ready to be born, our fruit shows signs of maturity.

Now turn to Hebrews 5:12-14. What metaphor conveys the author's frustration with the lack of spiritual maturity?

I remember wanting my babies to first roll over, then sit up, and then crawl. When they finally started to walk, things really got interesting! As we witness in young children, our physical development is a journey from total dependence to eventual independence. Our spiritual maturation, however, is the complete antithesis. Born into sin, we begin this life separated and apart from God (Psalm 51:5). During the process of true spiritual maturity, we begin to recognize our complete dependence on God and begin to fully rely on Him. As we grow and mature in our relationship with Him, we realize that we effectively cannot live without Him.

Clearly, following Jesus isn't just a one-time decision; it's a daily process of abiding and growing. This growth is also a biblical imperative. <u>The expectation isn't that we grow old in our faith or physically mature by default because we age</u>. Instead, we are challenged to mature in our faith—to develop and change spiritually. A person's spiritual maturity is based on their willingness to pursue spiritual wisdom and understanding (Philippians 1:9-11; Colossians 1:9). This is why we can be spiritually mature even when we are physically young.

Turn to Hebrews 6:1-8. Using this passage, answer the following questions:

What are we challenged to do? (v 1)

What is said of ground that bears a good crop for the farmer? (v 7)

What is said of ground that bears thistles and thorns? (v 8)

What does spiritual maturity LOOK like to YOU?

When we think of ripe fruit on the vine, we can see the evidence of its maturity by certain signs. As believers in Christ, we should see some of our spiritual fruit fully ripen and be ready for harvest in this lifetime.

Have you already had any of your fruit harvested? If so, what was it and how did you know it was time for it to come off the vine?

If you can't think of any previously harvested fruit, do you have any that is still maturing on the vine? (For example, have you started talking to your neighbor about the Lord? Did you recently join a local church ministry or group?)

For some of our fruit, we may never see the outcome of its harvest until we get to Heaven. Think about the course of your life. Are you the <u>fruit of someone's witness</u>? Have you been influenced by <u>the fruit of someone else's good work</u> or <u>financial gift</u>? Perhaps they'll never know, but maybe it was the <u>fruit of their lips</u>—through a song they sang or a book they wrote—that profoundly influenced you.

Let me give you a personal example. The fruit of a woman named Christy Fay has impacted my life. She's a pastor, author, and speaker whom I have never met or even seen in person. I participated in a group Bible study that worked through her book *Reclaimed: Uncovering Your Worth* and watched her video teachings. At the culmination of the study, I was compelled to action; I felt a burning desire to teach the Word and begin writing. Christy has no idea that her fruit affected me in such a profound way.

Honestly, it wasn't even the content of her study that motivated me. It was seeing her: a young woman, in the midst of her mothering journey, allowing God to use her to advance the Kingdom. I thought, "If she can do it, Lord, so can I." To be clear, it wasn't a competitive drive, but rather a, "Lord, use me too" type of motivation.

Can you recall any influencers on your life whether they knew it or not? Explain how they've impacted you and/or challenged you to grow spiritually:

In nature, red grapes gradually turn from green to red as they ripen. This is known as véraison (verr-ray-zohn), which is French for "change of color of the grape berries."[4]

From the first sign of fruit, experienced vinedressers know that it takes weeks for the sugar to fully set and for ripeness to occur. Unlike grapes, our spiritual véraison takes much more time.

THE CHARACTER OF TASTE

Have you ever eaten a green, unripe grape? If so, how did it taste?

The unfermented juice from green, unripe grapes is called *verjus* (vair-ZHOO), which comes from the French words for green (vert) and juice (jus). The flavor of green, unripe grapes is sour because they have higher acidity due to their lack of maturity.[6]

Dig Deeper

Veraison (verr-ray-zohn) is arguably the most important moment in a grape's annual lifecycle. It is when grapes turn from green to red and begin to sweeten naturally.[5]

Do you recall our discussion about the Sodbuster's commitment in Session 3? Sometimes, when we are tired and weary, we want to say, "Okay, I'm done. That's good enough."

Turn to Galatians 6:9. Write it here:

A few years ago, I was really struggling in my leadership and felt unqualified, frustrated, and ready to give up. I was not enduring well and was having to deal with difficult things—those pesky critters that show up as soon as the fruit ripens. I wanted to walk away. Then the Lord highlighted Leviticus 19:23-25 to me during a time of study:

> When you enter the land and plant fruit trees, leave the fruit unharvested for the first three years and consider it forbidden. Do not eat it. In the fourth year the entire crop must be consecrated to the LORD as a celebration of praise. Finally, in the fifth year you may eat the fruit. If you follow this pattern, your harvest will increase. I am the LORD your God (NLT).

It was the fifth anniversary of the ministry I led. If I had left prematurely (when the fruit was still sour and green), I might have missed the ripe harvest that would eventually become a celebration of praise. We don't have to get caught up in running to the "next best thing" because, sometimes, the best thing is to remain—to be still, watch our fruit mature, and propagate the next generation.

Delayed satisfaction is difficult for most of us, especially if we can immediately satiate our desire for it. I could have quit. I could have walked away, but I might have missed out on the reward: to eat of the fruit and see the harvest increase. In today's modern world, most of us can obtain anything with the push of a button, swipe of a card, or type of a text. In most residential or urban areas, food can be delivered to our doors in 30 minutes or less, we can stream any show we choose, and we can use social media to learn what every one of our friends is doing.

Instant (or immediate) gratification is a term that refers to "*the temptation, and resulting tendency, to forego a future benefit in order to obtain a less rewarding but more immediate benefit.*"[7] It's only human to want instantaneous gratification; we are driven by the desire to experience pleasure. Yet when allowing our fruit to mature—changing from sour and green to sweet and red—we have to give it time. If we pursue instantaneous gratification, if we try to harvest too soon or birth a baby prematurely, there may be no viability of life. To bring forth fully mature fruit, we must allow the necessary time for it to develop.

Now turn to Hebrews 12:12-13. What do these verses encourage us to do?

When it comes to harvest, we want our fruit to be fully matured, but we can't give up before our fruit is ready to be harvested. Otherwise, the only thing it'll be good for is verjus, a sour salad dressing.

Now, I'd like you to think of a ripe, plump grape. Imagine the crunch of the first bite and then the juices that flow from it.

What does it TASTE like?

In viticulture (the cultivation of grapevines), that flavor you just described is referred to as *terroir* (*tear-wah*), which originates from the French word "terre" and is loosely translated as "land" or "earth." It is believed that both the terrain and the training of the vinedresser impart a unique quality to the flavor and character of the harvest. There are even differences in the same variety of grapes from different regions, vineyards, or even different sections of the same vineyard because the unique aspects of a vineyard influence the flavor of the harvest.[8]

Companion crops (like hyssop, geraniums, and clover) also affect the terroir of the harvest. This is the deliberate art of planting different plants in close proximity to each other to benefit one or both. In the case of hyssop, bees love the flowers while the rest of the plant deters pests and improves the grape's flavor. And clover is a wonderful cover crop that increases soil fertility.[9]

All the things we've discussed in this fruit-bearing journey (the soil, seasons, surroundings, canopy, climate, pruning techniques, training methods, companion crops, and so on) become part of the terroir. They all influence the character of the flavor.

Using the concept of terroir, who and what are influencing the TASTE of YOUR fruit?

THE CRITTERS

At the beginning of today's lesson, I mentioned having to carefully avoid the bees and fruit flies as I snipped off the ripe grape clusters. These critters are a clear sign that the fruit is nearing harvest. If the sugar content of the grapes has peaked to a level that attracts birds, bees, fruit flies, and all the other creatures that love ripe fruit, then we know our fruit is ready. In the same way, we know the enemy wants our fruit. He wants to destroy it.

Robin mentioned that, before they harvest, they have to remove the bird netting from the vines. He informed me that the birds don't want to eat the grapes necessarily, but that they peck holes in the skin to get the seeds. Once they have created a wound on the surface of the grape, it becomes an entry point for disease and insect infestation (specifically fruit flies). Ah, those destructive birds and tormenting flies are a symbolic representation of the enemy—Satan! The birds come after the seed—the promise and the presence. The flies infiltrate what we've produced, causing total destruction and complete ruin.

Fruit flies can be a problem year-round, but they are especially common during late summer/fall because they are attracted to ripe grapes. Naturally, as grapes mature on the vine, the amount of sugar and yeast increases—and fruit flies feed on this sugar and yeast. To digest it, their gut bacteria break down the sugars into compounds they need. One of those is *acetobacteria*, which converts alcohol into acetic acid, the primary chemical component of *vinegar*.[10]

How would you describe the smell and taste of vinegar?

Turn to Numbers 20:1-13. After reading the passage, answer the following questions:

1. What was the problem? (v 2)

2. What did the Israelites do and say? (vv 3-5)

3. What were Moses and Aaron instructed to do? (v 8)

4. What did Moses actually end up doing? (vv 9-11)

5. What was Moses' punishment? (v 12)

Part of me doesn't blame the guy. He'd been dealing with the incessant complaints of the Israelites for 40 years as they wandered in the wilderness. Still, he allowed his bitterness toward the people to affect his obedience.

6. What was this place named? (v 13)

The name of this place is translated as "strife" or "contention."[11]   Psalm 106:32-33 says this of Moses' striking the rock: "They angered God again at Meribah Springs; this time Moses got mixed up in their evil; Because they defied God yet again, Moses exploded and lost his temper" (MSG).

We have to recognize the signs of the harvest so our fruit doesn't turn pungent, acidic, and bitter. When we don't harvest our fruit in time, we run the risk of becoming infected, infested, and full of contention. We have to recognize when it is time to harvest the fruit we bear because once we bring forth the harvest of a particular vintage (grapes produced in a specific season), we set our sights on beginning again.

At the end of the day I spent gathering the grapes, Robin said this of the harvest:

> *This is the culmination when you figure out what all of your hard work has produced. We know how much of it we've produced, and we know how good it is. And by the way, this is not the end; now the work to turn it into something else begins.*

That's a perfect synopsis of this fruit-bearing journey. Once we bring forth a harvest, it is not the end. It is the beginning of a new celebration of praise.

To end the day, let's pray.

Father, help us recognize the signs of our harvest. Though we may never know the full impact of the fruit we produce throughout our lives, there will be times when we will be fully aware of the harvest season. Lord, we ask You to give us discernment to know when it is time to snip off the ripe clusters of our fruit so they don't hang too long, risking bitterness and destruction. We trust that You are the Expert Vinedresser, knowing the exact time to bring forth the fruit of our lives. Please use all of it as a celebration of praise to You. We pray that You be honored with it all. In Jesus' name we pray. Amen.

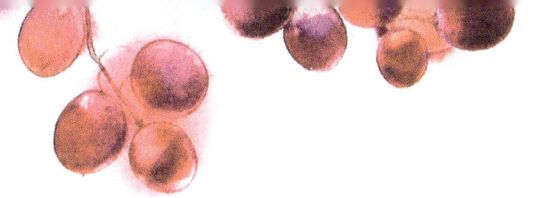

Day 2:
THE SICKLE

Today we will study how we reap our harvest.

Once we know the signs of readiness and maturity, it's time for the full, ripe clusters of fruit to be removed from the branches. At the end of our growing season, it's finally time to cut off and gather what we've labored to produce.

When we know our fruit is ripe for harvest, it's time to apply the sickle to carefully remove it from the branches. With its semicircular blade, this hooked vine knife is used to make swift cuts to the stem of the grape clusters, which relieves the branch of the weight of its delectable yield. Today, sickles are made of metal and wood, but historically, they were often made using individual pieces of flint (or other stone) attached to a "blade body" of carved wood or animal bone, such as a shoulder blade or mandible. Note that a sickle is not used for pruning but rather as a <u>reaping</u> tool and a <u>weapon</u>.

Let's begin by discussing its use as a reaping tool.

REAPING

2 Corinthians 9:6 says, "The person who sows sparingly will also reap sparingly, and the person who sows generously will also reap generously" (CSB).

What does it mean to "sow sparingly"?

What does it mean to "sow generously"?

2 Corinthians 9:7 goes on to say, "Each person should do as he has decided in his heart—not reluctantly or out of compulsion, since God loves a cheerful giver" (CSB).

What did Paul mean by needing to "decide" in our heart before we give?

Dig Deeper

The sickle is one of the most ancient harvesting tools, consisting of a metal blade, usually curved, attached to a short wooden handle. The short handle forces the user to harvest in a stooped or squatting position.[12]

©Berdsigns /Adobe Stock

What does it mean to be a "cheerful giver"?

2 Corinthians 9:8 ends with, "God is able to make every grace overflow to you, so that in every way, always having everything you need, you may excel in every good work" (CSB).

What is the promise for a cheerful, generous giver?

Match the following verses with their promises:

Proverbs 11:24	Give freely and become more wealthy; be stingy and lose everything.
	It is more blessed to give than to receive.
Proverbs 11:25	
	Give, and you will receive. Your gift will return to you in full—pressed down, shaken together to make room for more, running over, and poured into your lap. The amount you give will determine the amount you get back.
Luke 6:38	
Acts 20:35	The generous will prosper; those who refresh others will themselves be refreshed.

What can <u>YOU</u> give cheerfully and generously?

Whether it is the fruit of our womb, finances, lips, witness, good works, or internal fruit (the fruit of the Spirit), when we give generously and cheerfully, we reap the blessings. When we give, we get—it's just like the "less is more" principle. We have a heavenly promise, and we will reap the reward.

To put it another way, we cannot hoard what we've been given.

If you have ever struggled with hoarding or have been affected by it, you may understand that hoarding is a disorder in which one has a skewed perception of the value of material possessions.[13]

Hoarding possessions will never bring true joy. I know this all too well because there are hoarders on both sides of my family, and I have felt the pain of this disorder and the dysfunction it causes. For my grandmother, we saw it happen slowly over time. When my mother and aunt helped her move from her home in Florida, they had to wade through the massive amounts of sewing material, knick-knacks, kitchen supplies, *TIME* magazines, *National Geographic* magazines, and a lifetime of "stuff she needed." By the time they got to the garage and unearthed food in her deep freezer from the late 80s, they were ready to give up. Maybe she couldn't part with her possessions because she'd lived through The Great Depression or was a first-generation immigrant who'd lived in poverty.

When we hoard what we've been given and hide it away in secret, we rob ourselves of a visible, abundant harvest. God calls us to spread the seed of our gifts—talents, resources, and skills that we've been gifted with—because the amount of our harvest is directly proportional to the amount of our sowing. Remember, <u>we always reap what we sow</u> (Galatians 6:7).

What have you been "hoarding" that you need to give away?
(Your testimony? Your time? Your expert skill set? Your finances?)

What does this world need that only YOU have to offer?

GLEANING

In the following section, I'd like you to look up the passages and answer the questions.

Verses	What crops are harvested?	What instruction is given?
Leviticus 19:9-10		
Deuteronomy 24:19-20		

Merriam-Webster defines "to glean" as "to gather grain or other produce left by reapers; to gather information or material bit by bit."[15]

The commandment of gleaning reflects God's desire for people with abundance to provide for the poor and marginalized. When crops were ready for harvest, some of the yield was allowed to fall to the ground so that the poor could gather what they needed. Israelite law required that the corners, or margins, of the fields not be harvested. The purpose of the law was to feed the poor, orphans, widows, and foreigners. It served as a safeguard for those who had no capacity to care for themselves.

Dig Deeper

A hoard is a stock or store of money or valued objects, typically one that is secret or carefully guarded.[14]

Turn to Deuteronomy 10:18-19.

To whom does the Lord give justice and show love?

Why did the Israelites need to be reminded of their time in Egypt? (v 19)

Let's revisit our earlier discussion from 2 Corinthians 9. We previously studied that when (not if) we give (materially and spiritually), God will generously provide all that we need, and there will always be plenty of leftovers to share (v 8).

Turn to 2 Corinthians 9:9 and write it here:

Now read 2 Corinthians 9:10-13 and answer the following questions:

Who supplies all that we need?

Who supplies every opportunity for us to do good?

Who produces a harvest of generosity (or righteousness) in us?

What two things happen when we give generously? (v 12)
1.

2.

Whom do we glorify when we give generously?

Dig Deeper

A margin is the edge or border of something. The "marginalized" are those who are socially disadvantaged and relegated to the metaphorical margins of society.[16]

God's character is evident in His concern for the most vulnerable and oppressed. When our fruit is harvested, nothing is wasted because God has a contingency plan for it all. In fact, gleaning is not just a process that benefits only those without physical food. When we "gather information bit by bit" by studying The Word, the revelatory knowledge we receive becomes spiritual nourishment to us—body, mind, and soul (Matthew 13:11, Galatians 1:12). We have the capacity to be completely filled with the fullness of life and the power that comes from gleaning the Word of God. Through this enriching power, we can accomplish infinitely more than we could ever dare to ask or hope for (Ephesians 3:19-20) and produce even more abundant, ripe fruit for the harvest.

GATHERING

When the sickle is applied to the vine and the ripe fruit is removed, it's finally time to gather our harvest. Once gathered, it must be judged. Remember that not every branch on the vine bears the same type, quality, or quantity of fruit.

How does the Vinedresser determine whether He keeps the fruit or discards it?

In the next section, look up the following passages and fill in the chart.

Dig Deeper

Passages	What TWO things are being compared?
Matthew 13:24-30, 36-43	
Matthew 13:47-50	

In Judges 15:15-16, Samson used the jawbone of a donkey as a weapon. The jawbone tool became not only the toothed sickle as well as the serrated saw, but also—and most conspicuously—a fearful weapon.[17]

Jesus' lessons were simple stories infused with the mysteries of God. He used comparisons rooted in familiar, everyday life, but they always led to a deeper understanding.

In these two parables, what was Jesus' overarching message?

There will come a day when the sickle will be applied to the fruit-bearing branches. This tool of final judgment will separate the good from the bad, the wheat from the weeds, and the good fish from the bad.

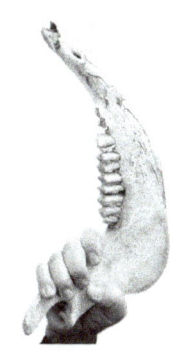

In the next section, let's see how the sickle is used as a tool of judgment. Look up the following passages and fill in the chart.

Passages	What is cut down?	What happens to what's been cut down?
Matthew 3:10		
Matthew 7:17-20		
John 15:5-6		

How do we know if our fruit is actually good? Let's turn to the Scripture to determine the biblical definitions of "good fruit."

The Greek word used to describe the type of fruit we are to bear is *kalos* (kä-lo's), which means, "*beautiful, handsome, excellent, eminent, choice, surpassing, precious, useful, suitable, commendable, admirable.*"[18]

Look up the following Scriptures, fill in the blanks, and answer the questions:

Matthew 5:16, NLT
"Let your _____deeds shine out for all to see, so that everyone will _____your heavenly Father."

Based on this passage, how will we know if we truly produce *good* fruit?

Titus 3:14, NLT
"Our people must learn to do _____ by meeting the
_____ needs of others; then they will not be _____."

The Good News Translation says it this way: "Our people must learn to spend their time doing good, in order to provide for real needs; they should not live useless lives."

Dig Deeper

The Grim Reaper is death personified. The scythe-wielding reaper of souls for the afterlife was used heavily during the medieval period.[19]

Can we produce good works and still be useless and unfruitful? Can you think of an example of this?

Jeremiah 12:13, NLT

"My people have _____ wheat but are _____ thorns. They have worn themselves out, but it has done them _____ good. They will harvest a crop of_____ because of the fierce anger of the LORD."

Ultimately, the fruit we produce can discredit or reinforce the message of the Gospel. If the motivation of our heart is for us to receive glory through our "good" deeds, then it is utter fruitlessness. I don't want to wear myself out and waste time developing useless fruit that is not God-honoring. I want others to see Jesus when they see me. I want my good deeds to glorify Him. I want my life to reinforce the Gospel message when they see the fruit produced in—and through—me.

As we end this day, I want you to think about the fruit that's been harvested from your life. Has it been *good*? Or have you been busy being useless and worn out? While we live out our days on Earth, we produce a harvest that will be reaped, gleaned, gathered, judged, and finally stored. I pray that it is good fruit that brings God glory.

As we close today, I'd like to end with a prayer adapted from Psalm 1.

Father, help me walk rightly with You; please guard my path. Lord, as I glean understanding from Your Word, I am filled with spiritual nourishment. As I meditate on Your Word, You continue to reveal Your will for my life. I want to be like a strong tree, deeply rooted by streams of water, yielding abundantly good fruit. I don't want my works to be useless and wither away, only to be blown like chaff in the wind. Help my fruit to be reaped for an eternal harvest, bringing You glory with all I do. In Jesus' name I pray. Amen.

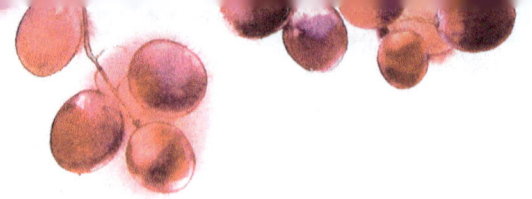

Day 5:
THE SYMBOL

"Mommy! Mommy! Mommy! Can I pleeeease have a penny and 50 cents?"

"Why, Elias?"

"I want a squished penny."

"What?"

Confused, I look in the direction of his tiny, pointed finger. My eyes settle on one of those ubiquitous coin machines that draws in visitors at tourist destinations. Nodding my head, I reluctantly give in to his request to create an overpriced memento from our trip that will, inevitably, be lost in the abyss of my minivan. But I do not begrudge his asking. It doesn't take much to please Elias, and I find delight in the brief moment of happiness he experiences as he cranks the handle on the Penny Press Machine. At the end of one full turn, an elongated coin emerges, imprinted with a custom image to commemorate our visit.

Smiling and satisfied with his new treasure, he places it carefully in his pocket, tapping it a few times to secure it. He now has a keepsake that will forever remind him of this excursion—that is, until he loses it. I appreciate the illustration this opportunity provides. The intricate embossing of the machine imprints an image onto a simple coin that forever changes its design and worth. Before it passed through the machine, it was worth only one cent. After it endured over 5,000 pounds of pressure, it came out the other side with its value increased fiftyfold. Every time Elias looks at his "squished penny," he will be reminded of this place.

THE SYMBOL

I'd like you to look around and take in your surroundings. Do you see specific objects and instantly recognize a brand or a logo? Perhaps you looked over at a candle flickering on the table, tapped your cell phone to check a message, or sipped from your barista-poured coffee.

How do you know where these items have come from? Who manufactured, created, or produced them? What is the physical SYMBOL that indicates their origin?

Read the following passages and answer the questions:

Genesis 17:10-14

>   **What was the physical sign of belonging to God? (vv 10-12)**

What would happen to those without this sign? (v 14)

Deuteronomy 30:6

How did the sign of belonging to God change?

Dig Deeper

Brit milah (breet mee-LAH) in Hebrew literally means "covenant of circumcision" (also known as a bris) and is used to describe the Jewish circumcision ceremony for an eight-day-old boy, marking the covenant between God and the Jews.[20]

There has always been an intimate way of determining who belonged to God. I realize this subject may make some readers shift in their seats. Is it because it's such a personal topic? Does it feel uncomfortable to allow our thoughts to go to such a private matter (no pun intended)? Some of you may be thinking, "This was an Old Testament covenant, so it no longer applies." Fair enough.

Turn to Ephesians 2:11-14.

What used to separate Jews and Gentiles? (v 11)

What allowed BOTH groups to have the covenant promises of God? (v 13)

God has always desired for His people to *want* to love, know, and follow Him. Before Jesus paid the ultimate sacrifice and gave us the Holy Spirit, there had to be a *physical* sign of His covenant—one that would be painful and costly. Over time, the people of Israel strayed from the foundation of their faith and relied solely upon the fact that they were Jewish by birth. They thought their heritage alone bought them a free pass to receive the blessings of Heaven. This is why God required more—a circumcision of not only the flesh but also the heart.

Now turn to Romans 2:28-29. Summarize these verses in your own words.

God wants more from His people than mere conformity to a set of rules and regulations. This is why the world has confused religion with relationship. It's not about serving an esoteric deity who will punish us if we fail to satisfy Him. Mere outward compliance to covenant standards does not please God. His intent has always been that outward signs reflect the inward reality of a transformed heart.

So let's talk about those outward SYMBOLS.

In the following section, have some fun matching companies with their famous slogans or logos. Try to do it without looking them up!

Slogan/Logo	Company/Organization
"Where's the beef?"[21]	
"I'm Lovin' It"[22]	
"Have it your way"[23]	
"Eat Mor Chikin!"[24]	
"Melts in your mouth, not in your hands"[25]	
"Breakfast of Champions"[26]	
"The Quicker Picker Upper"[27]	

Without seeing the companies or the products, you could probably tell right away what most, if not all, of these slogans or logos represent.

Why do products have labels?

What do you think organizations consider when they create a label?

What attracts you to a product? For instance, when you are shopping, why do you look over certain products but stop and pick others up?

At first, these answers may seem obvious, but great precision, thought, and design goes into the creation of a brand, label, logo, tagline, slogan—*all* of it.

I once took Graphic Design 101 in college, and it was one of the courses that I found fascinating. In fact, much of what I learned has stuck with me, even from a consumer point of view. I learned that when it comes to marketing, the most important function of design labeling is to help consumers identify the brand. Now think about the transformative process of how God's people have been identified as belonging to Him.

How do we identify true Christ followers today? What is our tell-tale brand? What are our signature SYMBOLS?

Dig Deeper
The ichthys was the secret symbol for recognizing other believers. It referenced the miracle of Jesus' multiplication of the loaves and fish (Matthew 14:19; Luke 19:16). ΙΧΘΥΣ is an acronym for "Iēsous Christos, Theou Yios, Sōtēr"; it's translated into English as "Jesus Christ, Son of God, [Our] Savior."[28]

What makes Christians attractive to the world around us?
(This is more than physical attributes.)

THE SEAL

Now turn to Ephesians 1:13-14.

When we received the message of salvation, what did God do to us? (v 13)

In verse 14, the *Christian Standard Bible* says it this way: "The Holy Spirit is the down payment of our inheritance, until the redemption of the possession, to the praise of his glory."

Let's dissect this verse. What does the first part mean?

What does "to the praise of his glory" mean?

Once we hear and believe the truth, we are marked with the defining SEAL of the Holy Spirit. The Greek word for seal in this passage is *sphragizō* (sfrä-ge'-zo), which means "*to prove, confirm, authenticate, or place beyond a doubt.*"[29] Paul used this word as a reference to an official mark placed on an important item. The seal was usually made from hot wax and impressed with a signet ring. This seal was unique. When someone looked at the mark, it identified the item with the authority of the person to whom the signet belonged.

When the world looks at YOU, can they identify that you belong to Jesus? If so, how?

It has to be more than a fish decal on our car, a cross necklace around our neck, or a biblical insignia tattooed on our body. Ultimately, the presence of the Holy Spirit in—and on—our lives should *prove, confirm, authenticate, and place beyond a doubt* that we belong to God.

Dig Deeper

The signet ring, traditionally seen as a symbol of family heritage, was used to officially mark documents. The name comes from the Latin *signum*, which means "sign."[30]

In addition, our ripe harvest brings benefits to us and the world around us. It is meant to be used and enjoyed, and ultimately it is to the praise of His glory! The good fruit of our lives should burst forth from us as an expression of love for The One to whom we belong.

What's interesting is that grapes, whether they will be eaten fresh as table grapes, used for grape juice, or used for making wine, jam, jelly, grape seed extract, raisins, vinegar, or grape seed oil, <u>MUST</u> first be sealed before they can ever be sent out.

So let's talk about the sealing process.

Why do we SEAL products?

What happens when products are sealed INCORRECTLY?

What are INDICATIONS that a product has NOT been sealed correctly?

If you've ever canned fruit or vegetables, you know there is a scientific process that must be implemented for the safe preservation of your harvest. Though home canning can be an excellent way to preserve our produce and share it with family and friends, it can also be risky—or even deadly—if not done correctly and safely. If done *incorrectly*, you could seal in deadly toxins and permanently taint your produce.

Clostridium botulinum, a microorganism found in soil, can survive, grow, and produce a toxin in certain conditions, such as when food is improperly canned. The toxin can affect your nervous system, paralyzing or killing you. You cannot see, smell, or taste botulinum toxin, but even a small taste of food containing this toxin can be deadly. That's why most produce can be safely sealed only with an appropriate amount of pressure and heat.[31]

Turn to 2 Timothy 2:19-24.

In this passage, Paul uses this same word *sphragizō* in his second letter to his apprentice, Timothy.

To truly bear the inscription (or seal) of the Lord, what must we do? (v 19)

Dig Deeper

In 2015, one of the largest botulism outbreaks occurred at a church potluck in Ohio. Sadly, one woman died and 23 others were hospitalized. It was traced back to a potato salad made with home-canned potatoes.[32]

To be used as a vessel of honor that bears good fruit, we have to rid ourselves of impurity and also do *this*. (vv 22-24)

To be marked and sealed as belonging to God means to turn away from—or purposefully remove—the toxins in our lives. Like the pounds of pressure needed to imprint and elongate a coin or to safely seal a vessel set apart for canned goods, we go through the pressure and heat of suffering and trials to remove the impurity and, ultimately, seal in the goodness.

What happens when a product has been sealed for TOO LONG?

Sometimes the sealing process isn't the problem, but rather, the preserved product has exceeded its shelf-life. Our senses allow us to recognize if something looks funny or smells off.

The Message says it this way: "Everywhere we go, people breathe in the exquisite fragrance. Because of Christ, we give off a sweet scent rising to God, which is recognized by those on the way of salvation—an aroma redolent with life" (2 Corinthians 2:14-15a).

UNDERLINE the portions of the above Scripture that relate to our signature scent.

Our actions and our aroma will give us away—for g<u>ood</u> and <u>bad</u>.

This past year, I walked into an AC Hotel by Marriott. The moment the automatic doors opened, I was greeted by their signature scent. It's called "Between the Woods," and the creators have tapped into the science of how scents elicit memories. Earthy and inviting notes of cut grass, roots, fig leaves and stem, gum resins, amber elements, and fir balsam are diffused into the hotel's open spaces, creating warm and comforting impressions of the hotel's identity. The creator of the signature scent, Frederick Bouchardy, said of the unique fragrance, "It's a return-to-home element of the scent that will link all the hotel properties around the world together. They will always smell the same—the scent is the first thing when you walk in, and the last thing when you leave."[33]

As Christians, do we have a "signature scent" that invites warmth and comfort? Is there a "return-to-home element" that links us all together? Do we emit pleasing aromas that are similar to one another? Will our fragrance make us recognizable? Does our scent make people stop and ask, "What are you wearing?" Do we give off a sweet scent, an aroma that evokes life and reminds others that we belong to Christ? Do our actions point people toward Jesus or are they tainted and toxic, like a bad botulism outbreak, causing people to be turned away, leading them to death?

What's ONE THING that you will commit to do TODAY to be a sweet aroma to the world around you? How will you share your signature scent with your coworkers, neighbors, friends, family, etc? (If you're unsure, ask God to give you opportunities to be a pleasing fragrance to others.)

When we've been sealed by the Holy Spirit, we undergo a <u>transformative preservation process</u>. God's seal is not like the insignia impressed upon a "squished penny" from a Penny Press Machine. God's seal is His Holy Spirit, who is God Himself present with His people. This seal identifies us and provides a guarantee that we belong to Him. The seal is an indication that the impurities have been removed and the harvest preserved safely.

In John 15:10, the Bible reveals, "If you keep my commands you will remain in my love, just as I have kept my Father's commands and remain in his love" (CSB). The words "keep" and "have kept" are both from the root word *téreó* (tay-reh'-o), which means "*to keep, guard, observe, or watch over.*"[34]It's a metaphor for preserving the Father's will. Proper sealing preserves and guards with a guarantee from the manufacturer. Sealing verifies that our produce is ready. Eventually, the seal will be broken for the fruit of our harvest to be enjoyed.

In the end, Scripture says we reap <u>WHAT</u> we sow, not <u>WHERE</u> we sow (Gal 6:7). Grapes grown in California can end up on a table across the country in Ohio. A vintage produced in Italy can be shipped across the world to Argentina. A jam jarred in France can end up on toast in Australia. (You get the picture.) At the culmination of Jesus' lesson on bearing fruit, He challenges us to keep and preserve the Father's will, and John 15 ends with His commanding us to "Love one another as I have loved you" (vv 12, 17). Jesus appointed His disciples—*you* and *me*—to "go and produce fruit and that your fruit should remain" (John 15:16, CSB).

As we finish our study tomorrow, we will identify the next steps to practically go out into the world and produce good, healthy fruit that <u>remains forever</u>.

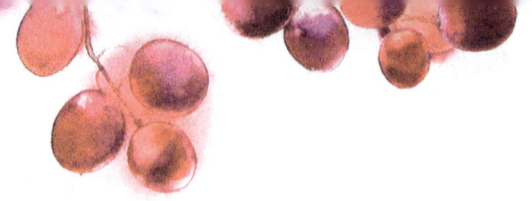

Day 4:
THE SEND-OFF

When I wasn't playing basketball in high school, I was running track. I appreciated the fundamental differences between the two sports—outdoor vs. indoor, training styles, uniforms, shoes, skills, competition style, etc. For example, track and field requires a entirely different mindset. Unlike basketball, track is an individual sport with a team component, and teammates don't all compete in the same way—some run sprints, others run distance, and some participate in field events. I was a sprinter and a long-jumper.

What I loved most about track were the meets. I remember the thrill and rush of my heart before the start of each race. All the athletes would convene near the starting blocks. Laces tied, cleats checked, warm-ups completed, we'd wait, each of us pulsing with adrenaline, for the familiar words from the race official: "Runners, take your mark."

With eagerness, I'd place my right foot in the rear kick-off position on the starting block and methodically situate my left foot on the front pedal. I'd splay my thumbs and index fingers out, slowly putting each hand directly behind the starting line. Propping my weight on my hands, I'd raise my hips in a ready-set stance, preparing my body to thrust forward. I'd lift my head and inhale deeply, allowing the air to fill my lungs, and then slowly exhale. I'd strain my ears to drown out the surrounding noise, intensely listening for the pop of the starting gun. With my mind clear, I'd fix my gaze ahead, my eyes never wavering from the finish line.

What does every athlete in every race hope for?

Turn to 1 Corinthians 9:24-27. Answer the following:

    In a race, who runs?

    Who gets the prize?

    What prize are we running for?

Now turn to Philippians 3:12-14. Answer the following questions:

    Can perfection be achieved?

    What does Paul encourage us to focus our energy on?

    Write verse 14 in your own words:

Turn to 2 Timothy 4:6-8. As you read Paul's final words to Timothy, what stands out most?

Even if you have zero competitiveness flowing through your blood, you probably understand that the purpose of every race is to cross the finish line. But before we can finish, we must start.

Today is about YOUR start.

Turn to Psalm 37:3. Write it here:

God has everything under control. When we follow the conditions of His Word, we reap a satiating harvest that lasts forever.

Now turn to Philippians 1:6 and write it here:

Let today be the day your good work begins because He will be faithful to complete it.

Now write Philippians 4:13 here:

For every single thing God has called you to do, He will infuse you with His strength to accomplish it. Every fruit that has ever been produced has an origin story. The formula is simple:

1. **TRUST** God and **DO** good.
2. **BEGIN** a good work because God is faithful to complete it.
3. **DO ALL THINGS** through Christ's strength **WITHIN** you.

I pray that this study isn't one you finish and think, "Well, that was nice." I want this to be a book you pick up repeatedly. I pray that all your training helps you steady your gaze and fix your thoughts on what lies ahead. When you feel unsure about what to do or how to move forward, I want you to be able to review all the excellent work you've done in this study so that it will propel you to action.

Do you remember my question at the beginning of this study?

I asked if you, Dear Friend, were ready.

Will you join me on the starting line?

Will you put all your training into action?

As we end our time together, I want to provide a synopsis of all the pieces of your fruit-bearing journey. It's a CliffsNotes version of all that we've worked through.

- **Why should you start?** (John 15:1-8; Matthew 5:16, 7:20; Colossians 1:10)

- **What motivates you to start?** (What do you ENJOY doing? What do you LOVE to do with your TIME? What are you PASSIONATE about? What do you DREAM about doing?)

- **WHERE should you start? What is your METRON?** (Where do you have a physical presence and spiritual stewardship right now? This could be your neighborhood, workplace, school, gym, social club, online network, church, small group, etc.)

- **To whom are you drawn to help? What breaks your heart?** (This could be the poor, widows, orphans, victims, children, teens, young adults, mothers, families, couples, etc. Remember that not every need is your calling. Many things may stir you, but what specifically breaks your heart to move you to action? Consider broken families, Christians not living like Christians, poverty, sex-trafficking, shut-ins, terminal illness, domestic violence, substance abuse, etc.)

- **What do you have to start with?** (Your spiritual gifts, passions, desires, talents, time, finances)

- **What do you do well? What are your strengths?**

- **What's your area of expertise?**

- **What do you already have?**

- **Who is your wise counsel? Who are your teammates?** (Who can pray with you and be a healthy sounding board for your thoughts and ideas?)

- **How will you start? What's your small beginning? What's ONE thing you will commit to doing TODAY to move forward in being fruitful?** (Zechariah 4:10)

Together, we've "studied, divided, and examined" The Word of Truth, so we can "show ourselves approved and worthy of our calling" (2 Tim 2:15). As we journeyed through discovering what our specific fruit is—how we plant, produce, protect, prune, and harvest it—I hope you were strengthened in your knowledge.

I pray that our time together has motivated, encouraged, and prepared you for action. Now I trust that the presence of God will move you forward so your life can be used mightily for the Kingdom of Heaven.

At the end of this life, I want us to be like Paul and confidently say, "My life has already been poured out as an offering to God...I have fought the good fight, I have finished the race, and I have remained faithful" (2 Timothy 4:6-7, NLT).

Let's end our final time together with a prayer from Philippians 1:9, 11.

I pray that your love for each other will overflow more and more, and that you will keep on growing in your knowledge and understanding. May you always be filled with the fruit of your salvation—those good things produced in your life by Jesus Christ—for this will bring much glory and praise to God. In Jesus' name, I pray. Amen!

It is time.

Runners, take your mark.

   Ready.

      Set.

         <u>GO</u> <u>BE</u> <u>FRUITFUL</u>!

HOW IS IT HARVESTED?
from generation to generation...

BE *fruitful*

Here are this week's ways to DIVE DEEPER by yourself, with family, or with friends.

DISCUSS

This week, we discussed how fruit is harvested. Using the prompts below, start a discussion to solidify the learning.

- What have you been "hoarding" that you need to give away? What does this world need that only YOU have to offer?
- Review the symbols on Day 3. Can you think of any other symbols—or brands—you see regularly?
- What's ONE thing you will commit to doing TODAY to move forward in bearing fruit?

DIG IN

READ

For children, here are a few books my kids have loved:

- *It's Harvest Time!* by Jean McElroy
- *We Gather Together: Celebrating the Harvest Season* by Wendy Pfeffer
- *Apples and Pumpkins* by Anne Rockwell

REVIEW

- Veraison: When the grapes turn from green to red and naturally begin to sweeten
- *Karpophoreo*: To be fertile; to bear or bring forth fruit
- *Telesphoreō*: to bring fruit to maturity
- "Verjus": The unfermented juice from green, unripe grapes
- "Terroir": The "land" or "earth" that gives grapes their unique flavor
- "Hoard": A stock or store of money or valued objects, typically one that is secret or carefully guarded
- "Glean": To gather grain or other produce left by reapers; to gather information or material bit by bit
- ΙΧΘΥΣ (ichthys) An acronym translated into English as "Jesus Christ, Son of God, [Our] Savior"

DESIGN

Using the prompts below, start creating your masterpieces!

- Visit the Warrior Raiser Pinterest board for activities about this week's lesson.
  - Create your own mulling spice
  - Harvest crafts
  - Make your own dehydrated wreath
  - Make your own grape juice
  - Make your own jam
  - Make your own vinegar
- Visit a local farmer's market
- Visit a local fruit farm and go picking
- Visit a local vineyard and volunteer to help with the harvest
- Harvest and preserve fresh herbs
- Visit a local Candle Lab and create your own signature scent
- Visit a local perfumery and make your own signature scent, or order a kit online
- Take time to have communion. It doesn't have to be elaborate. It's the heart behind the act of worship and remembrance that matters most. Grab some grape juice and crackers and read 1 Corinthians 11:23-27.

DISCOVER

Check out fruit harvest videos on YouTube

FOR THE KIDS:

- Samson and the Philistines- https://www.youtube.com/watch?v=WHOp8rqAb7Q
- Aesop's Fables "The Fox and Sour Grapes"-https://youtu.be/wfgAaMiCwPs
- The Fox and Sour Grapes (1941)- https://youtu.be/Op6_4e0mMN0

HOW IS IT HARVESTED?
from harvest to table...

BE *fruitful*

Whether you're cooking for one or having a potluck, enjoy the process of artfully putting the ingredients together to make a delicious masterpiece. Be encouraged to consider the elements of your week-long study that apply to the recipe you are preparing.

DELICIOUS DELIGHTS

CHARMING CHARCUTERIE

Serves 8-12

INGREDIENTS:

- 8 oz Italian dry salami
- 6 oz smoked prosciutto
- 4 oz prosciutto
- 1 bunch Champagne grapes
- 1 bunch Concord grapes
- 6 oz fresh blackberries
- 6 oz fresh raspberries
- 6 oz fresh strawberries
- 6 figs, fresh
- 2 Granny Smith apples
- 2 Honey crisp apples
- 5 oz pecans, sweet and spicy
- 5 oz cashews
- 4 oz smoked almonds
- 4 oz pumpkin spice pumpkin seeds
- 10 oz wheat crackers, stone ground
- 8 oz gouda cheese
- 8 oz cheddar cheese, sharp
- 8 oz french brie, traditional
- 4 oz pepper jack cheese
- 11 oz fig butter or spicy fruit jam

INSTRUCTIONS

- Start with a large board or platter.
- Place small bowls on first, then fill with fruit spread and nuts. Add cheese, then add larger crackers.
- Add the larger items (brie, strawberries, and figs).
- Add a section of medium-size items (sliced cheese and smaller crackers).
- Add the meats. Roll to form meat fans, or fold into quarters
- Fill open areas with blackberries and raspberries
- Serve immediately

HARVEST SALAD WITH APPLE CIDER VINAIGRETTE

Serves 6

DRESSING INGREDIENTS

- ¼ cup extra virgin olive oil
- ¼ cup apple cider vinegar
- 2 Tbsp maple syrup (substitute honey)
- 1 Tbsp Dijon mustard
- ¼ tsp kosher salt
- ¼ tsp ground black pepper

SALAD INGREDIENTS

- 8 cups crisp romaine or green leaf lettuce, chopped (approximately 1 head of lettuce)
- 2 medium tart red apples, cored and diced (do not peel) (recommended: Fuji or Honeycrisp)
- 1 cup dried cranberries
- 1 cup chopped pecans, toasted
- 4 oz feta cheese
- 8 slices of bacon, cooked and crumbled (optional)

INSTRUCTIONS:

- Add all the dressing ingredients to a jar with a lid. Seal and shake.
- Add all the salad ingredients to a large bowl, lightly drizzle the dressing over the top, and toss.

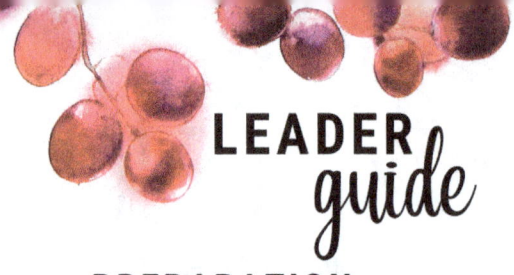

LEADER *guide*

PREPARATION

THANK YOU for answering the call to lead! Facilitating a Bible study is vital in advancing the Gospel message, and your leadership will help set the group study's tone, pace, and success.

As you ready your heart and mind to begin each session, be encouraged to spend time in prayer. Ask the Holy Spirit to direct the conversation and permit Him to move within the group. Pray for each participant and the relationships that will blossom from your time together.

- **Determine** meeting location, day, and time. Decide what you'll offer participants (e.g., refreshments, childcare).
- **Use the communication pieces** available on www.warriorraiser.com to promote the study.
- **Be prepared.** This seems like a no-brainer, but group members will be able to sense your investment by your preparation. Preview the session videos and have questions ready. Get to the meeting early and set up the room in advance (e.g., audio/video, tables, chairs, refreshments).
- **Remember** that participants will join at various stages of spiritual maturity. **Accept** them as they are, but **establish expectations** that encourage ongoing commitment.
  Other things to consider:
  - You don't need to have all the answers to lead well.
  - Awkward silence is okay. You don't need to fill the void with your voice.
  - If you're vulnerable, they will be, too; you may have to share first.

- **Connect with your members** throughout the study time. Establishing a group communication platform will keep participants engaged throughout the week. Send personal notes, texts, and social media posts to let them know you're praying for them. When people feel valued, they remain engaged.
- **Respect the time parameters** of the group while still allowing God to move. As the leader, you have the authority to get the conversation going and keep it on track. Leave time at the end of each session for directed conversation, personal celebrations, and prayer.

SESSION 1

Meet the participants in the study. Use a creative icebreaker or a simple method to introduce the group members. Ask what drew them to participate in this study. Share *your* expectations for your time together and determine what each participant desires to gain from this study.

1. WELCOME
Discuss the logistics of your meeting: dates, times, and breaks for special occasions. Discuss the flow of your group:
Watch Video→Discuss Video→Review Daily Study→"Be Fruitful" application→Prayer.
2. WATCH
Session 1 video *From Creation to Revelation*.
3. DISCUSS
After watching the video teaching, lead the discussion questions (p 14).
4. NEXT STEPS
Remind the group to complete their personal study for *Session 2* throughout the week (pp 18-48).
5. CLOSE IN PRAYER

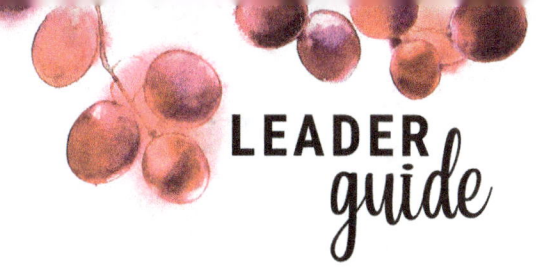

SESSION 2

1.WELCOME

Welcome the participants to *Session 2*. *Suggestion: Have a bowl of grapes (or a fruit medley) to represent the uniqueness of our spiritual fruit.*

2. WATCH

Session 2 video *What Is Fruit?*.

3. DISCUSS

After watching the video teaching, lead the discussion questions (p 17).

4. REVIEW

Session 2 answers and personal responses to daily reflection (pp 18-48). *Have 2-3 questions ready to discuss.*

5. NEXT STEPS

Remind the group to complete their personal study for *Session 3* throughout the week (pp 54-93).

6. CLOSE IN PRAYER

Pray for discernment and that the Lord would provide direction and clarity for each person. Ask God to reveal His will for their lives.

SESSION 3

1.WELCOME

Welcome the participants to *Session 3*. *Suggestion: Have different seeds available to represent the small beginnings of each fruit.*

2. WATCH

Session 3 video *How Is It Planted?*.

3. DISCUSS

After watching the video teaching, lead the discussion questions (p 53).

4. REVIEW

Session 3 answers and personal responses to daily reflection (pp 54-93). *Have 2-3 questions ready to discuss.*

5. NEXT STEPS

Remind the group to complete their personal study for *Session 4* throughout the week (pp 99-139).

6. CLOSE IN PRAYER

Pray that each participant would be sensitive to the value and importance of her small beginnings. Pray that they recognize they don't have to do grand things to make a difference.

SESSION 4

1.WELCOME

Welcome the participants to *Session 4*.

2. WATCH

Session 4 video *How Is It Produced?*.

3. DISCUSS

After watching the video teaching, lead the discussion questions (p 98).

4. REVIEW

Session 4 answers and personal responses to daily reflection (pp 99-139). *Have 2-3 questions ready to discuss.* *Pay special attention to page 102 and ask if anyone had a personal response to the prayer of salvation.*

5. NEXT STEPS

Remind the group to complete their personal study for *Session 5* throughout the week (pp 145-186).

6. CLOSE IN PRAYER

Feel free to use the final, written prayer on Day 5, p 139.

SESSION 5

1.WELCOME

Welcome the participants to *Session 5*.

2. WATCH

Session 5 video *How Is It Protected?*.

3. DISCUSS

After watching the video teaching, lead the discussion questions (p 144).

4. REVIEW

Session 5 answers and personal responses to daily reflection (pp 145-186). *Have 2-3 questions ready to discuss.*

5. NEXT STEPS

Remind the group to complete their personal study for *Session 6* throughout the week (pp 192-230).

6. CLOSE IN PRAYER

Feel free to use the closing prayer from p 177 to end the meeting.

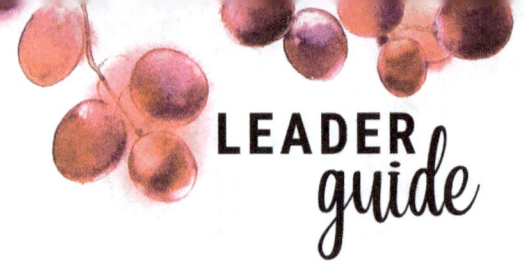

LEADER *guide*

SESSION 6

1. WELCOME

Welcome the participants to *Session 6*. *Suggestion: Bring pruning tools as a visual; you can even bring a branch to demonstrate the cutting methods.*

2. WATCH

Session 6 video *How Is It Pruned?*.

3. DISCUSS

After watching the video teaching, lead the discussion questions (p 191).

4. REVIEW

Session 6 answers and personal responses to daily reflection (pp 192-230). *Have 2-3 questions ready to discuss.*

5. NEXT STEPS

Remind the group to complete their final, personal study for *Session 7* throughout the week (pp 236-265).

6. CLOSE IN PRAYER

Feel free to use the final, written prayer on Day 5, p 230.

SESSION 7

1. WELCOME

Welcome the participants to the final session, *Session 7. Suggestion: After watching the video, take communion together.*

2. WATCH

Session 7 video *How Is It Harvested?*.

3. DISCUSS

After watching the video teaching, lead the discussion questions (p 235).

4. REVIEW:

Session 7 answers and personal responses to daily reflection (pp 236-263). *Have 2-3 questions ready to discuss.*

5. NEXT STEPS

You can choose to end the study time at this point or meet one additional time to have a wrap-up and celebration.

6. CLOSE IN PRAYER

WRAP-UP & CELEBRATION

God is a fan of celebrations. Just look at all the feasts in the Bible! So for this last gathering, be encouraged to celebrate and feast together! Invite the participants to bring one of the recipe selections from the weekly "Be Fruitful." You may also want to choose one of the crafts or activities provided in the "Be Fruitful" sections and have that available for your meeting time. Have some fun with this last meeting time, and make a plan for your future!

1. WELCOME

Welcome the participants to your Wrap-Up & Celebration.

3. DISCUSS

Review what they wrote on page 14 of the study. Have them share their biggest takeaways. Celebrate what's been revealed and reflect on what God has done throughout the seven sessions together.

5. NEXT STEPS

Plan for your future study. Be encouraged to check out www.warriorraiser.com for additional resources and material.

6. CLOSE IN PRAYER

Lord, we thank you for the clarity and confidence to boldly move forward in fulfilling all that we have been appointed and empowered to do. Even if we're afraid, we are comforted with the knowledge that You have equipped us to bear fruit for our good and Your glory! In Your precious and Holy name, we pray, Amen!

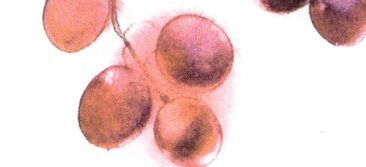

Endnotes

SESSION 1

1. "*Abad*." Strong's: 5647. Accessed online at biblehub.com.
2. "*Shamar*." Strong's: 8104. Accessed online at biblehub.com.

SESSION 2

1. "Botany English Definition and Meaning." Lexico Dictionaries | English. Lexico Dictionaries. Accessed online at https://www.lexico.com/en/definition/botany.
2. "Plant." Definition in the *Cambridge English Dictionary*. Accessed online at https://dictionary.cambridge.org/us/dictionary/english/plant.
3. "*Karpos*." Strong's: 2590. Accessed online at blueletterbible.org.
4. "*Sha'al*." Strong's:7592. Accessed online at biblehub.com.
5. "*Dudaim*." Genesis 30:14 commentaries. Accessed online at https://biblehub.com/commentaries/genesis/30-14.htm.
6. Sorge, Bob. *Exploring Worship: A Practical Guide to Praise & Worship*, 78. Kansas City, MO: Oasis House, 2011.
7. Wherry, Edgar T. "Apparent Sun-Crack Structures and Ringing-Rock Phenomena in the Triassic Diabase of Eastern Pennsylvania." *Proceedings of the Academy of Natural Sciences of Philadelphia*. 64 (1912): 169–72. https://doi.org/https://www.jstor.org/stable/4063462.
8. "*Euaggelistés*." Strong's: 2099. Accessed online at biblehub.com.
9. Aesop and B. E. Perry. Aesopica. New York: Arno Press, 1980.
10. Rydelnik, Michael, and Michael G. Vanlaningham. *The Moody Bible Commentary*, 371. Chicago: Moody Publishers, 2014.
11. "*Métron*." Strong's: 3358. Accessed online at biblehub.com.
12. Zepp, Ira G. *A Muslim Primer: Beginner's Guide to Islam*, 5. Fayetteville: University of Arkansas Press, 2000.
13. Patty, Sandi. *Masterpiece. Sandi Patti and the Friendship Company*. A & M Records, n.d.
14. "Official Obituary." Billy Graham Memorial, February 26, 2018. https://memorial.billygraham.org/official-obituary/.
15. "*Selah*." Strong's: 5542. Accessed online at blueletterbible.org.
16. Addington, Thomas, and Stephen Graves. *A Case for Calling: Fulfilling God's Purpose in Your Life at Work*. Nashville, TN: Broadman & Holman Publishers, 1998.
17. Roosevelt, Theodore, and Hermann Hagedorn. *Theodore Roosevelt, an Autobiography*, 337. New York, NY: Scribner, 1926.

SESSION 3

1. "Sodbuster Definition & Meaning." Dictionary.com. Dictionary.com. Accessed online at https://www.dictionary.com/browse/sodbuster.
2. Luciani, Joseph. "Why 80 Percent of New Year's Resolutions Fail." US News Health. Accessed online at https://health.usnews.com/health-news/blogs/eat-run/articles/2015-12-29/why-80-percent-of-new-years-resolutions-fail.
3. Howard, David M. "Judges 11:39." Commentary. In *ESV: Study Bible: English Standard Version*, 515. Wheaton, IL: Crossway Bibles, 2016.
4. "Mondegreen Definition & Meaning." Merriam-Webster. Merriam-Webster. Accessed online at https://www.merriam-webster.com/dictionary/mondegreen.
5. "Plumb Line Definition & Meaning." Merriam-Webster. Merriam-Webster. Accessed online at https://www.merriam-webster.com/dictionary/plumb%20line.
6. "*Synergeō*." Strong's: 4903. Accessed online at blueletterbible.org.
7. "*Paraklétos*." Strong's: 3875. Accessed online at blueletterbible.org.
8. "*Mashach*." Strong's: 4886. Accessed online at blueletterbible.org.
9. "*Chrisma*." Strong's: 5545. Accessed online at blueletterbible.org.
10. "*Gethsémani*." Strong's: 1068. Accessed online at blueletterbible.org.
11. "*Qidron*." Strong's: 6939. Accessed online at biblehub.com.
12. "*Christos*." Strong's: 5547. Accessed online at biblehub.com.
13. "Red, White & Boom!: Ohio's Largest Fireworks Display." Accessed online at https://redwhiteandboom.org/.
14. Spurgeon, Charles H. "Rightly Dividing The Word of Truth." *The Metropolitan Tabernacle Pulpit: Sermons Preached and Revised 21*, 21:87. London: Passmore Alabaster, 1875.
15. TerKeurst, Lysa. *Uninvited: Living Loved When You Feel Less than, Left out, and Lonely*, 207. Nashville, TN: Nelson Books, an imprint of Thomas Nelson, 2016.
16. The Byrds. "*Turn! Turn! Turn!*." Genius. Accessed online at https://genius.com/The-byrds-turn-turn-turn-to-everything-there-is-a-season-lyrics.
17. "Generation." Definition in the *Oxford Advanced Learners' Dictionary*. Oxford University Press. Accessed online at https://www.oxfordlearnersdictionaries.com/definition/english/generation?q=Generation
18. Ibid., Spurgeon, 89.
19. Ibid., Spurgeon, 90.
20. "Dormancy (n.)." Etymology. Accessed online at https://www.etymonline.com/word/dormancy#etymonline_v_31797.
21. "Pesach: Passover." Judaism 101 (JewFAQ). Accessed online at https://www.jewfaq.org/holiday.htm.
22. Ibid., TerKeurst,112.
23. "Allopathy." Farlex Partner Medical Dictionary. Accessed online at https://medical-dictionary.thefreedictionary.com/allopathy

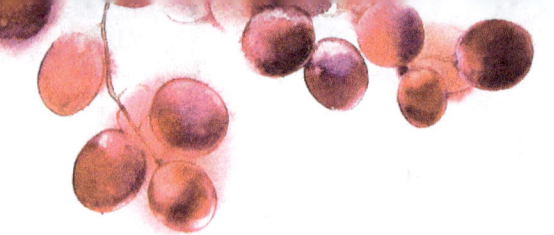

SESSION 4

1. Powers, Tom. *In The Organic Backyard Vineyard: A Step-by-Step Guide to Growing Your Own Grapes*, 9. Portland, OR.: Timber Press, 2012.
2. Ibid., Powers, 67.
3. "*Chaba.*" Strong's: 2244. Accessed online at biblehub.com.
4. "*Charis.*" Strong's: 5485. Accessed online at blueletterbible.org.
5. "*Kaluptó.*" Strong's: 2572. Accessed online at biblehub.com.
6. Ibid., Powers, 19.
7. "Boiling Frog Syndrome." The Free Dictionary. Farlex. Accessed online at https://idioms.thefreedictionary.com/boiling+frog+syndrome.
8. Vine, W. E. "Lukewarm." *Vine's Expository Dictionary of New Testament Words*. Westwood, NJ: Barbour & Co., 1985.
9. "Torpor Definition & Meaning." Dictionary.com. Accessed online at https://www.dictionary.com/browse/torpor.
10. "Fervor Definition & Meaning." Dictionary.com. Accessed online at https://www.dictionary.com/browse/fervor.
11. "Relativism." Oxford Languages and Google. Accessed online at https://languages.oup.com/google-dictionary-en/.
12. Platt, David. *Counter Culture: a Compassionate Call to Counter Culture in a World of Poverty, Same-Sex Marriage, Racism, Sex Slavery, Immigration, Persecution, Abortion, Orphans, Pornography*, 19. Carol Stream, IL: Tyndale House Publishers, Inc., 2015.
13. Ibid.
14. Caine, Christine. *20/20: Seen, Chosen, Sent*, 170. Nashville, TN: LifeWay Press, 2019.
15. Graham, Billy. "Billy Graham: In the World, but Not of It." Decision Magazine, Accessed online at https://billygraham.org/decision-magazine/february-2016/a-classic-billy-graham-message-in-the-world-but-not-of-it/.
16. Fernandez-Armesto, Felipe. *Pathfinders: A Global History of Exploration*, 194. New York, NY: W. W. Norton & Company. 2006.
17. Sproul, R.C. "What Does 'Coram Deo' Mean?" Ligonier Ministries. Accessed online at https://www.ligonier.org/learn/articles/what-does-coram-deo-mean.
18. "*Sham.*" Strong's: 8033. Accessed online at biblehub.com.
19. "*Thygatēr.*" Strong's: 2364. Accessed online at blueletterbible.org.
20. "*Kraspedon.*" Strong's: 2899. Accessed online at blueletterbible.org.
21. "*Menó.*" Strong's: 3306. Accessed online at biblehub.com.
22. "*Egkentrizō.*" Strong's: G1461. Accessed online at blueletterbible.org. https://www.blueletterbible.org/lexicon/g1461/niv/mgnt/0-1/.
23. Stafne, Eric. "Grafting Grape Vines." Grapes, June 20, 2019. https://grapes.extension.org/grafting-grape-vines.
24. Kumar, G.N.M. *Propagation of Plants by Grafting and Budding*,3-5. Pacific Northwest Extension, September 2011.
25. Fruit Salad Trees. "Different Fruit on the Same Tree." Fruit Salad Trees. Accessed online at https://www.fruitsaladtrees.com/.
26. Mallory, J.P, and D.Q Adams. *The Oxford Introduction to Proto-Indo-European and the Proto-Indo-European World*, 434. Oxford: Oxford University Press, 2009.
27. "Panic." The Free Dictionary. Farlex. Accessed online at https://www.thefreedictionary.com/panic.
28. Ibid.
29. Baessler, Liz. "How Does Vivipary Work: Why Are Seeds Germinating Prematurely." Gardening Know How. Accessed online at https://www.gardeningknowhow.com/garden-how-to/propagation/seeds/what-is-vivipary.htm.
30. "Viviparous." Merriam-Webster.com Dictionary. Accessed online at https://www.merriam-webster.com/dictionary/viviparous.
31. "Did God Abandon Jesus on the Cross? Billy Graham Answers." Billy Graham Evangelistic Association, March 24, 2016. https://billygraham.org/story/did-god-abandon-jesus-on-the-cross-billy-graham-answers/.
32. Britannica, T. Editors of Encyclopaedia. "seaweed." *Encyclopedia Britannica*, February 14, 2021. https://www.britannica.com/science/seaweed.
33. "*Shalom.*" Strong's: 7965. Accessed online at biblehub.com.
34. Savageau, Julie Metzger. 2014. "I felt anxious leading up to today…" Facebook, June 4, 2014.

SESSION 5

1. Wargo, Eric. "How Many Seconds to a First Impression?" Association for Psychological Science, July 1, 2006. https://www.psychologicalscience.org/observer/how-many-seconds-to-a-first-impression.
2. "*Methodeía.*" Strong's: 3180. Accessed online at blueletterbible.org.
3. "*Kardia.*" Strong's: 2588. Accessed online at blueletterbible.org.
4. *Resolving Everyday Conflict: Biblical Answers for a Common Problem*. Spokane Valley, WA: Peacemaker Ministries, 2012.
5. Bishop, M. C. and Coulston, J.C.N. *Roman Military Equipment from the Punic Wars to the Fall of Rome*, Second Edition, 61. United Kingdom: Oxbow Books, 2006.
6. Adkins, Lesley, Adkins, Roy A. *Handbook to Life in Ancient Rome*, 85. United Kingdom: OUP USA, 1998.
7. Balfour, John Hutton. *The Plants of the Bible, Trees and Shrubs*,21-21. United Kingdom: n.p., 1857.
8. Modzelevich, Martha. Flora of Israel: Salvadora Persica, 2005. http://www.flowersinisrael.com/Salvadorapersica_page.htm.
9. "*Machaira.*" Strong's: 3162. Accessed online at blueletterbible.org.
10. Spurgeon, C. "The Sword of the Spirit by C. H. Spurgeon." Blue Letter Bible. Last Modified 18 Apr, 2001. https://www.blueletterbible.org/Comm/spurgeon_charles/sermons/2201.cfm
11. *PANDORA Ads - The Unique Connection. YouTube.* YouTube, 2015. https://www.youtube.com/watch?v=4lfGufM67BA.
12. Marino, Lori, and Debra Merskin. "Intelligence, Complexity, and Individuality in Sheep." Animal Sentience 4, no. 25, 2019. https://doi.org/10.51291/2377-7478.1374.

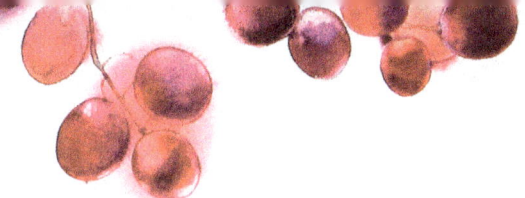

13. Shirer, Priscilla Evans. *The Armor of God, 27*. Nashville, TN: Lifeway Press, 2015.
14. Lucado, Max. *God Will Carry You Through, 9*. Nashville, TN: Countryman, a division of Thomas Nelson Publishers, 2013.
15. Campbell, Christopher. *Phylloxera: How Wine Was Saved for the World*, 129–30. London: HarperCollins, 2004.
16. Riley, Charles V. "The Grape Phylloxera." The Popular Science Monthly 5, May, 1874. https://doi.org/https://en.wikisource.org/wiki/Popular_Science_Monthly/Volume_5/May_1874/The_Grape_Phylloxera.
17. "Differential Diagnosis English Definition and Meaning." Lexico Dictionaries | English. Lexico Dictionaries. Accessed online at https://www.lexico.com/en/definition/differential_diagnosis.
18. "Banned & Challenged Classics." Advocacy, Legislation & Issues, April 23, 2021. https://www.ala.org/advocacy/bbooks/frequentlychallengedbooks/classics.
19. "Houseflies." World Health Organization, Retrieved September 25, 2017. https://www.who.int/water_sanitation_health/resources/vector302to323.pdf
20. "Beelzebub." JewishEncyclopedia.com. Accessed online at https://jewishencyclopedia.com/articles/2732-beelzebub.
21. Keller, W. Phillip. *A Shepherd Looks at Psalm 23*, 138–39. Grand Rapids, MI: Zondervan, 2007.
22. Ibid., Keller, 140.
23. "Treatment Plan Definition." NHI Dictionaries. National Institutes of Health. Accessed online at https://www.cancer.gov/publications/dictionaries/cancer-terms/def/treatment-plan.
24. "*Rapha*." Strong's: 7495. Accessed online at blueletterbible.org.
25. "*Sōzō*." Strong's: 4982. Accessed online at blueletterbible.org.
26. Sproul, R.C. "Jesus, the Great Physician: Reformed Bible Studies & Devotionals at Ligonier.org: Reformed Bible Studies & Devotionals at Ligonier.org." Ligonier Ministries. Accessed online at https://www.ligonier.org/learn/devotionals/jesus-great-physician.
27. Spurgeon, Charles Haddon. *The Metropolitan Tabernacle Pulpit: Sermons Preached and Revised*, 39. United Kingdom: Passmore & Alabaster, 1856.
28. "*Bēthesda*." Strong's: 964. Accessed online at blueletterbible.org.
29. Dickinson D, Wilkie P and Harris M. "Taking medicines: Concordance Is Not Compliance." BMJ. Retrieved June 17,2022.1999;319(7212):787. https://www.bmj.com/content/319/7212/787.1
30. "Kintsugi." Wikipedia. Wikimedia Foundation, Accessed online at https://en.wikipedia.org/wiki/Kintsugi.

SESSION 6

1. "*Airō*." Strong's: 142. Accessed online at blueletterbible.org.
2. Doyle, Charles Clay, Wolfgang Mieder, and Fred R. Shapiro. *The Dictionary of Modern Proverbs*. New Haven: Yale University Press, 2012.
3. Maxwell, John C. *Failing Forward: Turning Mistakes into Stepping Stones for Success*. Nashville, TN: Nelson, 2000.
4. "Goad." Oxford Languages and Google. Accessed online at https://languages.oup.com/google-dictionary-en/.
5. Martindale, Wayne, Jerry Root, and Linda M. Washington. *The Soul of C.S. Lewis: A Meditative Journey through Twenty-Six of His Best-Loved Writings*, 233. Carol Stream, IL: Tyndale House Publishers, 2010.
6. Coonin, Arnold Victor. *From Marble to Flesh: The Biography of Michelangelo's David*. Italy: Florentine Press, 2014.
7. Poe, Harry Lee. *The Fruit of Christ's Presence*, 22. Nashville, TN: Broadman Press, 1990.
8. "U.S. Forest Service." Fig Wasps. Accessed online at https://www.fs.fed.us/wildflowers/pollinators/pollinator-of-the-month/fig_wasp.shtml.
9. "Dimah." Strong's: 1832. Accessed online at biblehub.com.
10. "*Dema*." Strong's: 1831. Accessed online at biblehub.com.
11. Chisholm, Hugh. "Lacrymatory." *Encyclopedia Britannica* 16, 11th ed., 16:55. Cambridge University Press, 1911.
12. "Prescribed Fire in the South - Southern Group of State Foresters." Southern Foresters. Accessed online at https://southernforests.org/fire/prescribed-fire-in-the-south.
13. "How Trees Survive and Thrive after a Fire." National Forest Foundation. Accessed online at https://www.nationalforests.org/our-forests/your-national-forests-magazine/how-trees-survive-and-thrive-after-a-fire.
14. "*Paraklētos*." Strong's: 3875. Accessed online at blueletterbible.org.
15. Dohrn-Simpson, Robin. "Pruning Techniques and Tools." The Grapevine Magazine, April 12, 2019. Accessed online at https://thegrapevinemagazine.net/2019/04/pruning-techniques-and-tools/.
16. Puckette, Madeline. "Illustrated Grape Vine Training Methods." Wine Folly. Accessed online at https://winefolly.com/deep-dive/grape-vine-training-methods-illustration/.
17. "Nip (something) in the bud." McGraw-Hill Dictionary of American Idioms and Phrasal Verbs. Accessed online at https://idioms.thefreedictionary.com/nip+(something)+in+the+bud
18. "*Katharos*." Strong's: 2513. Accessed online at blueletterbible.org.
19. Rydelnik, Michael, John Hart, John Jelinek, John M. Koessler, Walter McCord, John McMath, William H. Marty, et al. *The Moody Bible Commentary*, 1783. S.I.: Moody Publishers, 2014.
20. "*Hetoimos*." Strong's: 2092. Accessed online at blueletterbible.org.
21. "Endurance." Cambridge English Dictionary. Accessed online at https://dictionary.cambridge.org/us/dictionary/english/endurance.

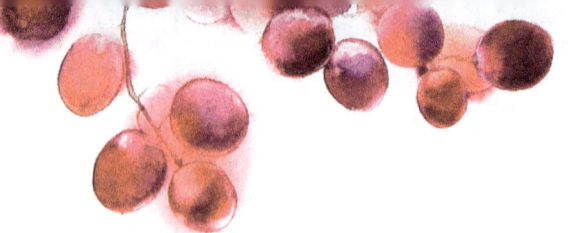

SESSION 7

1. "*Karpophoreó*." Strong's: 2592. Accessed online at biblehub.com.
2. Ibid.
3. "*Telesphoreó*." Strong's: 5052. Accessed online at biblehub.com.
4. "Veraison." Wikipedia. Wikimedia Foundation, April 15, 2022. https://en.wikipedia.org/wiki/Veraison.
5. Cox, Jeff. *From Vines to Wines: The Complete Guide to Growing Grapes and Making Your Own Wine*, 97–106. North Adams, MA: Storey Publishing, 2015.
6. "Verjus." American Heritage Dictionary of the English Language, Fifth Edition. Accessed online at https://www.thefreedictionary.com/Verjus.
7. "APA Dictionary of Psychology." American Psychological Association. American Psychological Association. Accessed online at https://dictionary.apa.org/immediate-gratification.
8. "Terroir Definition & Meaning." Dictionary.com. Dictionary.com. Accessed online at https://www.dictionary.com/browse/terroir.
9. "Companion crop." Merriam-Webster.com Dictionary. Accessed online at https://www.merriam-webster.com/dictionary/companion%20crop.
10. McGraw-Hill Dictionary of Scientific & Technical Terms, 6E. S.v. "Acetobacteria." Accessed online at https://encyclopedia2.thefreedictionary.com/Acetobacteria
11. "*Meribah*." Strong's: 4809. Accessed online at biblehub.com.
12. "Sickle." Merriam-Webster.com Dictionary. Accessed online at https://www.merriam-webster.com/dictionary/sickle.
13. "Hoarding Disorder." Mayo Clinic. Mayo Foundation for Medical Education and Research, February 3, 2018. https://www.mayoclinic.org/diseases-conditions/hoarding-disorder/symptoms-causes/syc-20356056.
14. "Hoard." Oxford Languages and google. Accessed online at https://languages.oup.com/google-dictionary-en/.
15. "Glean Definition & Meaning." Merriam-Webster. Merriam-Webster. Accessed online at https://www.merriam-webster.com/dictionary/glean.
16. "Margin." Oxford Languages and google. Accessed online at https://languages.oup.com/google-dictionary-en/.
17. Carus, Dr Paul. *The Story of Samson and Its Place in the Religious Development of Mankind*, 97. Chicago, IL: Open Court Publishing Co., 1907.
18. "*Kalos*." Strong's: 2570. Accessed online at biblehub.com.
19. McKenna, A.. "Where Does the Concept of a 'Grim Reaper' Come From?." Encyclopedia Britannica, Accessed online at https://www.britannica.com/story/where-does-the-concept-of-a-grim-reaper-come-from.
20. "Circumcision." JewishEncyclopedia.com. Accessed online at https://jewishencyclopedia.com/articles/4391-circumcision.
21. Wendy's. "Where's the Beef?" Television advertisement. The Wendy's Company, directed by Joe Sedelmaier, 1984.
22. McDonald's. "I'm Lovin' It." Television advertisement. McDonald's Corporation, directed by Paul Hunter, 2003.
23. Burger King. "Have it Your Way." Television advertisement. Burger King Corporation, Batten, Burton, Durstine and Osborne, 1974.
24. Chick-fil-A. "Eat Mor Chikin." CFA Properties, Inc. The Richards Group, 1995.
25. M&M's."Melts in your mouth, not in your hands." Mars Incorporated. Forrest Mars, 1954.
26. Wheaties. "The Breakfast of Champions." General Mills Inc. Knox Reeves, 1936.
27. Bounty. "The Quicker Picker Upper." Procter & Gamble Co, 1965.
28. "Ichthus English Definition and Meaning." Lexico Dictionaries | English. Lexico Dictionaries. Accessed online at https://www.lexico.com/en/definition/ichthus.
29. "*Sphragizō*." Strong's: 4972. Accessed online at blueletterbible.org.
30. "Signet." Oxford Languages and google. Accessed online at https://languages.oup.com/google-dictionary-en/.
31. "Botulism." MedlinePlus. U.S. National Library of Medicine. Accessed July 30, 2022. https://medlineplus.gov/botulism.html.
32. McCarty, Carolyn L., Kristina Angelo, Karlyn D. Beer, Katie Cibulskas-White, Kim Quinn, Sietske de Fijter, Rick Bokanyi, et al. "Large Outbreak of Botulism Associated with a Church Potluck Meal — Ohio, 2015." MMWR. Morbidity and Mortality Weekly Report 64, no. 29 (2015): 802–3. https://doi.org/10.15585/mmwr.mm6429a6.
33. AC_Hotels. "The Scent of Sanctuary." Medium, May 2, 2018. https://medium.com/@AC_Hotels/the-scent-of-sanctuary-95ea6fed1302.
34. "*Tēreō*." Strong's: 5803. Accessed online at blueletterbible.org.

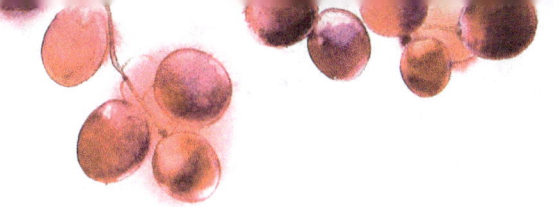

Stay in Touch

WARRIOR RAISER

with Angela Johnson

Life is challenging, but we don't have to do it alone. Warrior Raiser helps women understand their divine calling to be warriors who raise future warriors for the Kingdom of Heaven.

WWW.WARRIORRAISER.COM

SOCIAL

Stay connected with Angela on social media.

 @warriorraiser

 Warrior Raiser

BLOG & PODCAST

Stay connected with Angela's teaching online and through her Warrior Raiser podcast.

 www.warriorraiser.com/blog

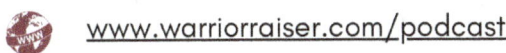 www.warriorraiser.com/podcast

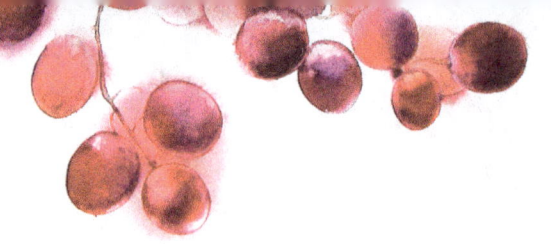

VIDEO ACCESS

To stream *Fruitful* Bible study video teaching sessions, scan the QR Code below:

VIDEO LICENSE
Because you've purchased a physical copy of the Bible study, you now have access to stream the teaching content with an individual-use video license.

This video access entitles you to one non-transferable, single-seat license to view all seven Bible study sessions. Please do not share your access with others. All videos are subject to expiration at the discretion of Warrior Raiser, LLC.

Do not post any part of the study sessions to YouTube, Vimeo, any social media outlet, or any other online service for any purpose. Any unauthorized posting is considered copyright infringement, is prohibited by the terms of use, and can negatively impact your YouTube or other service accounts.

LEADING A GROUP?
Each participant will need their own copy of the *Fruitful* Bible study book, which includes video access (see above license content). Because each participant has access to video content, you can decide to watch together using a smart TV (with YouTube viewing capability) or invite them to watch the videos on their own.

If you have any questions regarding access to these video sessions, please contact info@warriorraiser.com.

WWW.WARRIORRAISER.COM

www.ingramcontent.com/pod-product-compliance
Lightning Source LLC
Chambersburg PA
CBHW082144120626
46553CB00010B/2755